THE IRISH PEOPLE

Open-air mission, Co. Donegal, c. 1860.

FOR CIARA

THE IRISH PEOPLE

An Illustrated History

KENNETH NEILL

GILL AND MACMILLAN

First published 1979 by
Gill and Macmillan Ltd
15/17 Eden Quay
Dublin 1
with associated companies in
London, New York, Delhi, Hong Kong,
Johannesburg, Lagos, Melbourne,
Singapore, Tokyo

7171 0915 1

Layout and Design: Jan de Fouw, Dublin.
Typeset by Keyspools Ltd, Golborne, Lancashire.
Printed in Great Britain by Fletcher and Son Ltd, Norwich.

CONTENTS

Preface

Any general history which proposes to treat of a nation's development over several millenia must begin with an apology. It is impossible to write a book with as broad a scope as this one without making some omissions and without making complex issues seem simpler than in fact they are.

This brief illustrated volume, therefore, is not the last word on its subject. Nevertheless, it is hoped that *The Irish People* provides fresh insights for those already familiar with the country and its people as well as a useful introduction for those who know very little about either.

It would take several pages to list the names of all those who have helped to make this book a reality. I should, however, like to mention the assistance given to me by Hubert Mahony and Fergal Tobin, who have not only made it all possible, but whose professional advice and support have helped make *The Irish People* many times better than it might otherwise have been.

Border between Republic of Ireland and Northern Ireland

County Boundaries

0   75 km

ULSTER

DONEGAL
Letterkenny
Donegal
DERRY
Derry
Ballymena
ANTRIM
Belfast
Omagh
TYRONE
DOWN
Downpatrick
Armagh
ARMAGH
Newry
Sligo
FERMANAGH
Enniskillen
R.Erne
MONAGHAN
Monaghan
Dundalk
MAYO
SLIGO
LEITRIM
Leitrim
Cavan
CAVAN
LOUTH
Castlebar
ROSCOMMON
Longford
LONGFORD
Navan
MEATH
Roscommon
CONNAUGHT
Mullingar
WESTMEATH
R.Boyne
DUBLIN
Athlone
KILDARE
Dublin
Ballinasloe
R.Shannon
Galway
Tullamore
OFFALY
Kildare
R.Liffey
R.Barrow
Port Laois
LEINSTER
Wicklow
GALWAY
LAOIS
WICKLOW
CLARE
Nenagh
Ennis
Carlow
CARLOW
R.Nore
Kilkenny
R.Slaney
Limerick
Thurles
TIPPERARY
KILKENNY
LIMERICK
WEXFORD
MUNSTER
R.Suir
Clonmel
KERRY
Tralee
CORK
Wexford
Killarney
Mallow
WATERFORD
Waterford
R.Blackwater
Cork
R.Lee

7

Introduction

A prominent geographer once described Ireland as 'a wall-flower at the gathering of west-European nations'.[1] While his characterisation is perhaps a bit extreme, it remains a fairly accurate depiction of the island's international position. Ireland has never been a wealthy country. Nor has it ever been a strong military power. Small in size (not much larger than the American state of West Virginia) and sadly lacking in natural resources, Ireland has rarely counted for much at gatherings of European and world diplomats. Even compulsive conquerors like Napoleon and Hitler hardly gave a thought to this remote island on the European fringe.

Nature has not dealt Ireland a strong hand. Nevertheless, its people can point to some considerable achievements. The island has had a rich and varied history, and at times the Irish have wielded a cultural influence out of all proportion to their numbers. Today Ireland is perhaps the best-known 'small' country in the world. Not without reason; after all, what other island nation of five million people has produced three winners of the Nobel Prize for Literature over the past half-century?

The Irish influence has been considerable for another reason, one which ironically has been a direct result of the island's economic poverty. Since 1845 over seven million people have left Ireland to seek their fortunes in other parts of the world. Today there are eight times as many people of Irish descent outside Ireland as there are in it. Many of these would share the sentiments expressed by the late John F. Kennedy when he addressed Dail Eireann, the lower house of the Irish parliament, in the summer of 1963:

I am proud to be the first American President to visit Ireland during his term of office, proud to be addressing this distinguished assembly, and proud of the welcome you have given me. My presence and your welcome, however, only symbolise the many and the enduring links which have bound the Irish and the Americans from the earliest days. . . . No people ever believed more deeply in the cause of Irish freedom than the people of the United States. And no country contributed more to building my own than your sons and daughters.[2]

The progress of Irish history has of course been deeply affected by the fact that the country is surrounded by water. But unlike most island peoples, the Irish have never been seafarers. The bodies of water which encircle the country have been viewed by most Irishmen as obstacles rather than avenues to commerce with the rest of the world. Even today, the Irish fishing fleet remains miniscule in size, despite the country's 2,000 miles of coastline.

Why have the Irish done so little with the sea that surrounds them? A generally inhospitable coastline is part of the answer. But much more important is the fact that until the nineteenth century, the rich farmlands of the country were able to support most inhabitants with a minimal standard of comfort. It is not without reason that green is the national colour. Thanks to its moderate year-round temperatures and its consistently heavy rainfall (too heavy at times, it might be added, for the comfort of the inhabitants), Ireland possesses some of the most fertile land in Europe. The climate has always favoured pastoral agriculture over tillage. Today, the rich green fields of the east and south fatten many of the cattle consumed by Europeans from Brest to Brindisi.

Not all Ireland is so well-endowed, however. Thanks to that consistent rainfall, large areas of peat bog have formed wherever the underlying rock structure is non-porous. Such bad land often coexists with the good; for example, the Bog of Allen, one of the largest in the world, lies in the middle of the country's most productive agricultural region. But generally speaking, the proportion of poor land to good increases as one moves west across the island, and across the country's largest river, the Shannon. Traditionally, those areas west of the Shannon have been considerably poorer than those to the east.

Then there are the mountains. By international standards, Ireland's are not impressive; the tallest peak, Carrantohill, rises only 3,414 feet above sea level. But the Irish mountains make up in quantity for what they lack in quality. Virtually the entire coastline is ringed with rugged highlands, from the Mourne Mountains in the north east to Macgillycuddy's Reeks in the far south west.

Ireland has often been compared to a saucer. Inside the coastal ring of mountains lies a central basin that contains few major geographical obstacles aside from some fairly small rivers. This saucer-like arrangement has been very advantageous in one sense: throughout the island's history it has promoted a high degree of cultural unity. While travel in the more mountainous coastal regions has often been difficult, it has always been relatively easy for people – and ideas – to move across the central part of the country.

The coastal mountains have dictated the pattern of development in one other way. Easy access from the interior to the sea is available at only one point: the relatively flat expanse between Dublin and Dundalk. Not surprisingly, this has always been one of the most highly developed regions in the country. For centuries most of Ireland's international trade has moved through this eastern corridor. The first sophisticated civilisation developed in this area in prehistoric times. Today the 'eastern corridor' remains the focal point of the Irish economy.

The atlas, however, does not yield all of Ireland's geographical secrets so easily. While on a map the terrain of the north-eastern province of Ulster appears only somewhat rougher than usual, the medium-high region shown on the map actually consists of a compact series of steep hills known as drumlins. Today these seem little more than scenic variations of the terrain from the motor car window. In earlier times, however, these drumlins presented a formidable barrier. For the weary traveller on horse or foot, entering Ulster was like entering a maze; as each steep hillock was painfully traversed, it was followed by another, and another, and another.

Geography, therefore, stood in the way of Ulster's full participation in the affairs of the island. Ulster developed its own particular variation of Irish culture; even today, Ulster speech patterns are radically different from those of the rest of the country. Not surprisingly, the north-east was the last province conquered by the British during the sixteenth century. When the province was colonised by Scottish immigrants during the next century, geography contributed to the antipathy and hatreds which

developed between these people and the rest of the Irish population.

Examination of the singular position of Ulster leads naturally to consideration of another decisive geographical influence. While Ireland exists on the European fringe, it is not entirely without neighbours. The course of Irish history has been deeply influenced by people from her sister-island, Great Britain. Relations between Great Britain and Ireland, however, could hardly be described as neighbourly, especially during the last thousand years.

Unfortunately, Ireland and Britain could never really compete on equal terms. Great Britain has always been the larger, more populous and richer of the two British Isles. In view of these advantages, it was perhaps inevitable that British rulers would attempt to dictate the course of Irish affairs. With varying degrees of success, the British tried to mould the shape of Irish society. With varying degrees of intensity, the Irish for eight centuries resisted these attempts at political and cultural assimilation.

One last theme is worth bearing in mind while reading this book. As we have seen, the story of Ireland is very much the story of a nation far removed from the mainstream of European civilisation. In view of this isolation, it is not surprising that from ancient to modern times the Irish have been at heart a conservative people. There have been political revolutions, and there have been economic catastrophes, but dramatic social transformations have been few and far between. Witness how firmly the Irish adhered to Catholicism during the Reformation, in the face of considerable internal and external pressure. Witness the absence of real change in Ireland after independence in 1922.

This innate conservatism had yielded both negative and positive results. On the one hand, Ireland is a country, rich in tradition, which has often been a slave to its own past. On the other, the Irish are a people with as firm a sense of their own identity as any in the world.

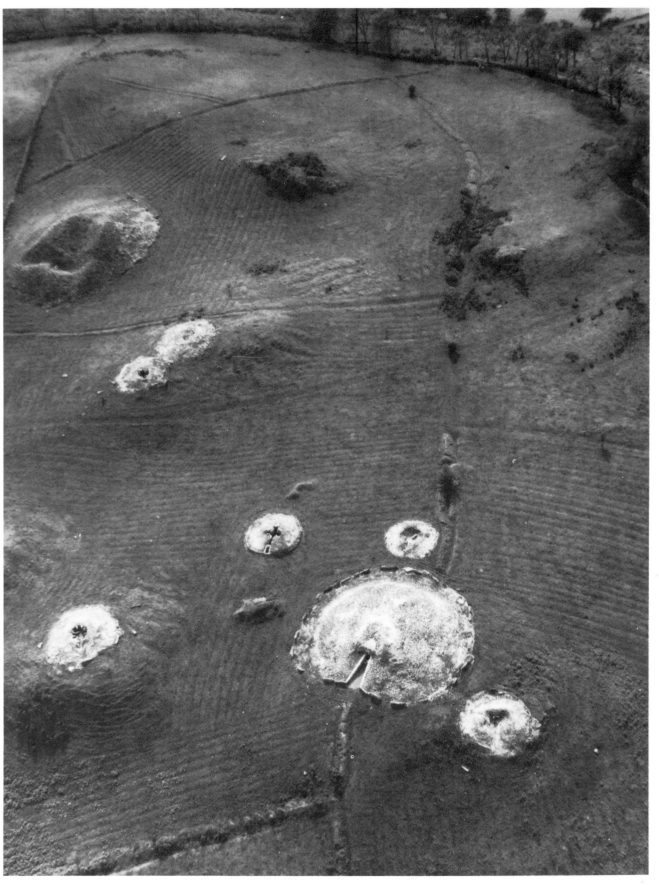

This aerial view of part of the passage-grave cemetery in the Boyne Valley reveals the cruciform shape of most of the burial mounds. Only the Knowth tumulus has more than a single entrance.

1 — The First Irishmen

*A land of fog and gloom . . . beyond it is the Sea of Death, where
Hell begins.*

Homer, *The Iliad*.

Homer was referring to the whole north-western corner of Europe when he made this statement over twenty-five hundred years ago. Nevertheless, it seems a most appropriate beginning for a book about Ireland, since it expresses sentiments which most Europeans have shared about the country since the time of the ancient Greeks. For centuries, the island was a faraway place about which little was known and even less was understood. To the Romans Ireland was *Hibernia*, a name derived from the Latin word for winter. As far as the Mediterranean world was concerned, Hibernia was Europe's Winter Land.

The late date at which human beings came to Ireland is one measure of the island's isolation. While anthropologists have established that the species *homo sapiens* is at least a million years old, the oldest human remains found in Ireland go back only to 7000 B.C.

These first Irishmen were a Mesolithic (Middle Stone Age) race who came to the country by way of the North Channel from Scotland. They were a primitive people, who supported a rudimentary existence by hunting and fishing, and seem to have settled primarily in Ulster, the province closest to their entry route.

Around 3700 B.C., during the New Stone Age, a second group of settlers began crossing over from Scotland. These Neolithic people were the country's first farmers. They used polished stone tools, and kept herds of domesticated animals such as cattle and sheep. They did not displace the existing population overnight; no doubt there were many centuries of gradual integration before the new culture fully replaced the old. But the ability of the newcomers to plant and till crops gave them a considerable advantage over their Mesolithic predecessors, and made it possible for them to live reasonably settled lives, encouraging the first development of communities.

Recent archaeological discoveries have provided much information about these Irishmen of the New Stone Age. Pit dwellings have been excavated near Cookstown, Co. Tyrone, along with the foundations of an early wooden house. Similar house foundations have been uncovered near Ballycastle, Co. Mayo, while the boundaries of Neolithic tillage plots have been detected in nearby Belderrig. Radio-carbon techniques have been used to date all of these sites to the period 3700–3500 B.C.

These stone axeheads date from around 7000 B.C. Discovered near Kilcormac, Co. Offaly in 1976, they are among the few Mesolithic artifacts found outside Ulster.

These antlers of a giant Irish deer were found near Jamestown, Co. Tipperary. This animal, which had an antler span of over nine feet, lived around 9500 B.C.

*The 'court cairn' at Creevykeel, Co. Sligo dates from around 2000 B.C.
A large number of hut sites have been found around this burial area,
which seems to suggest that Creevykeel was the site of a Neolithic village.*

Until these recent discoveries, most of our information about the Neolithic inhabitants of Ireland had been derived from their stone tombs. Like most primitive peoples, they placed great importance upon proper burial of the dead. Over twelve hundred 'court-cairns', as their stone tombs are often called, can still be seen today. Most of these burial chambers are simple, rectangular stone chambers designed for one or two corpses. They are found in all parts of the country, although there is a heavy concentration of burial sites in the Boyne River valley in Co. Meath. The hilly north bank of this river was obviously an area of special religious significance, for it is here that one finds the three huge tombs of Dowth, Knowth and Newgrange, which are among the most spectacular Neolithic artefacts in the world.

All three of these enormous tombs are roughly similar in size and design. Each contains a central burial chamber which is covered by large, overlapping boulders; these are used to form mounds over forty-five feet in height and 280 feet in diameter. Since each mound contains over 200,000 tons of stone, it is clear that their construction was the work of an organised and settled people.

Of the three tombs, Newgrange has been most carefully studied and restored. Built in approximately 3200 B.C., it contains a 65-foot long passage which leads to a 20-foot high burial chamber near the centre of the mound. Perhaps the most intriguing features of the tumulus are the spiral decorations which are carved onto the walls of the passage, and on the large kerb-stones which ring the mound. While the exact purpose of these magical or religious symbols will probably never be known, they do represent the first evidence of a spiral motif which was to remain an integral feature of Irish art for the next four millenia.

*The large stone which stands before the entrance of the tumulus at
Newgrange. Its enigmatic decorations reveal how important the spiral
motif was to these Neolithic artists.*

The dolmen was another type of Neolithic burial marker, consisting of three or more standing stones supporting a large capstone. The capstone at this particular dolmen at Proleek, Co. Louth, weighs several tons.

One aspect of the Newgrange tumulus that has long fascinated archaeologists is the roof-box which was installed to allow light to enter the passage-grave itself. While this admits sunlight into the passageway, its angle of construction is such that direct sunlight enters the central burial chamber for only twenty minutes each year: on 21 December, the date of the winter solstice. Since this fact can hardly have mattered to the permanent residents of the tomb, one can only presume that the central chamber served some ritual function for its Neolithic builders. Whatever the use of Newgrange and the other passage-graves, their design and construction indicate that a well-advanced civilisation flourished in Ireland three thousand years before the birth of Christ.

The next milestone of human development came, as elsewhere, with the adoption of advanced metal-working techniques. Bronze Age skills probably came to Ireland directly from the continent sometime between 2000 and 1700 B.C. The native inhabitants were soon producing metal brooches, rings, cauldrons, shields and collars equal to any in northern Europe. Gold seems to have been a popular and plentiful raw material. Mined

THE IRISH PEOPLE

in the Wicklow Mountains, this appears to have been the catalyst of the island's first foreign trade. Baltic amber and Egyptian faience beads have been found in sites dating from this period; these were no doubt imported in exchange for Irish gold.

The metalwork of Bronze Age Ireland reveals a society growing gradually more sophisticated, whose craftsmen produced a wide range of ornamental and practical goods. One particularly Irish form was the lunula, a crescent-shaped ornament designed to be worn around the neck: while nearly fifty lunulae have been discovered in Ireland, only a handful have been found elsewhere in Europe.

A collection of Bronze Age domestic implements discovered near Bishopsisland, Co. Kildare. Weapons are rarely found at household sites dating from both this and the Celtic period, indicating that warfare was largely confined to the aristocracy.

Irish Bronze Age craftsmen had special fondness for this type of flat gold collar, which is called a lunula because of its resemblance to the crescent of the moon. This particular lunula was found near Ross, Co. Westmeath and was produced around 1700 B.C.

A large bronze cauldron produced around 700 B.C. and uncovered near Castlederg, Co. Tyrone.

It is interesting to note the complete absence of human or animal representation in early Irish art. The emphasis is completely on decorative devices. At a time when European art, due largely to Greek influence, was becoming increasingly representational, Irish craftsmen continued to work with spirals, curves, and complex geometric designs. There are no human faces, no birds or horses. This avoidance of representational form became a permanent feature of Irish art. Over the next two millenia, it would serve as but one indication of how far Ireland was removed from the mainstream of European civilisation.

The year 1000 B.C. is usually accepted as the beginning of the Iron Age in Europe. Knowledge of how to mine and work this strong, durable metal did not cross the Irish Sea until much later, perhaps not until 500 B.C. When the Iron Age did finally come to Ireland it was brought by a new and most influential group of settlers: the Celts.

The Celts were originally an eastern European people. By the time they arrived in Ireland, however, they were distributed throughout the continent from modern Poland to Spain. Most anthropologists agree that two distinct groups of Celts settled in Ireland, one of these coming into the country from Britain by way of the traditional north-eastern route, the other arriving in the south-west directly from the continent, perhaps from the Iberian Peninsula. It took centuries for these two groups to integrate fully with the existing population and with each other, so that it is not until the dawn of the Christian era that we can truly speak of a 'Celtic Ireland'.

When this new civilisation was established, it represented a considerable advance on anything which the island had previously known. We are fortunate to have many sources for information about Celtic society. The archaeological remains are truly extensive; for example, the countryside is still dotted with over 30,000 Celtic ring forts or homestead sites. We also have Roman descriptions of contemporary Gaul and Britain, which are especially useful since the archaeological evidence indicates close similarities between these Celtic cultures and that of Ireland. Most importantly, we have the annals, law tracts, and sagas of early Irish literature.

While none of these works were transcribed before the seventh century A.D., oral transmission of knowledge was an important feature of Celtic scholarship, and accurate recitation was demanded. While allowance must be made for errors, the law tracts do give a fairly clear picture of society as it existed around A.D. 200. Even the sagas which describe characters and events that are certainly mythological shed light upon the social structures of Celtic Ireland, and provide us with what one historian has called 'a window on the Iron Age'.[1]

A beaten-bronze shield found near Lough Gur, Co. Limerick and dating from the eighth century B.C.

As this artist's reconstruction shows, a crannog was a Celtic residence built upon a natural or artificial island, where the inhabitants were given a large measure of protection from sudden attack. Crannogs were especially common in the thickly-forested midlands, where lakes and rivers are abundant.

A typical Celtic rath, at Lismore, Co. Louth. Because Irish agriculture has been traditionally pastoral, thousands of similar 'ring-forts' have been preserved.

The Irish Celts of two thousand years ago were a pagan people who spoke a language similar to their fellow-Celts on the continent. They lived in a completely rural environment. Since much of the country was still heavily forested, and since the wet Irish climate has never really favoured tillage, cattle-rearing was the chief occupation of the people. Most lived in isolated farm homesteads, the raths or ring-forts which even today can be seen in all parts of the countryside. The only settlements faintly resembling towns in Celtic Ireland were the clusters of wooden huts one might find around the slightly larger homes of kings or important nobles.

Most primitive cultures have fairly rigid social gradations, and Celtic Ireland was no exception. The ancient law tracts distinguished between no less than twenty-seven distinct classes of freemen! Rank depended on wealth as well as birth, however, and it was possible to rise or fall in status depending upon one's talents.

Below the various free classes were the slaves. While we have no way of knowing exactly what percentage of the population was unfree, it is clear that slavery was an important institution, as can be judged by the fact that the *cumal*, the price of a female slave, was one of the basic units of value in the simple barter economy of the time.

We do know that the land-owning farming class was the foundation of Celtic society. The yeoman farmer of this period was called a *bóaire*; he was literally, a 'cattle man'. It is impossible to improve upon this description of the possessions of one specific grade of *bóaire*, taken directly from the law tracts:

> He has the land of twenty-seven *cumals*. He is the *bóaire gensa*, with all the equipment of his house in their proper places: a cauldron with its spit and handles, a vat in which a measure of ale can be brewed, a cauldron for ordinary use, smaller vessels, including iron cups and kneading-troughs and mugs, so that he has not to borrow them, a washing-trough and a washing vessel; tubs, candlesticks, knives for cutting rushes, ropes, an adze, an auger, a saw, a pair of shears, an axe; the tools for every season, every implement unborrowed; a whetstone, a bill-hook, a hatchet, spears for killing cattle; a fire always alight, a candle on the candlestick without fail, a complete plough with all its outfit....
>
> There are two buckets in his house always; a bucket of milk and a bucket of ale .... He is a man who has three sacks in his house every season: a sack of malt, a sack of salt for the cutting up of joints of his cattle, a sack of charcoal for irons. He has seven houses, a kiln, a barn, a share in a mill, a house of twenty-seven feet, a pigsty, a calf-fold, a sheep-fold; twenty cows, two bulls, six oxen, twenty pigs, twenty sheep, four boars, two brood-sows, a saddle-horse, an enamelled bridle....
>
> He has a bronze cauldron into which a hog fits. He has pasture in which there are always sheep, without need to change ground. He and his wife have four changes of clothes.[2]

Obviously, it would be impossible for every *bóaire* to match this incredibly intricate description. Indeed, the precision of this extract perhaps reveals as much about the legal system as it does about agriculture.

This magnification of a small section of the Tara Brooch makes it possible to appreciate the amazing intricacy that was such an important feature of Celtic art. This section is, in reality, barely one inch long.

The main passageway in the prehistoric tumulus at Newgrange, Co. Meath, constructed over four thousand years ago.

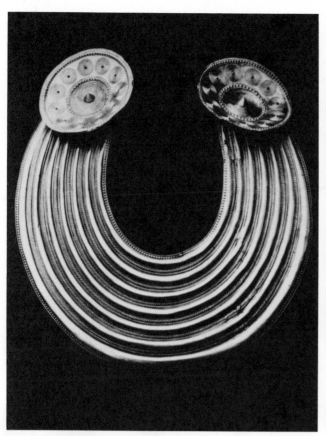

This ornate lunula from Gleninsheen, Co. Clare was produced around 650 B.C. (right)

An aerial view of what once was a large Celtic settlement at Rath-croghan, Co. Roscommon. Rathcroghan is mentioned in the Táin Bó Cúailgne *as the royal residence of Queen Mevb of Connaught.*

Within Celtic society, those who resolved legal problems held perhaps the highest position. These lawyers, called *brehons*, did not easily come by their exalted positions. It took years for the aspiring *brehon* to commit to memory the reams of legal detail which today fill dozens of volumes.

The Celtic legal tradition was very specific. It provided exact compensations for virtually every crime and laid out elaborate procedures to be followed in cases of inheritance. No one was above the law; in the saga literature, even kings defer to the judgements of *brehons*. Whatever it may have lacked, Celtic Ireland possessed one of the most highly-developed legal systems in the ancient world.

The *brehons* were part of an intellectual aristocracy known as the *aes dana*. The most important of the other 'learned ones' were the *druids*, the priests of the pagan Celts. They administered the rituals of the great festivals which marked the changes of the seasons, which were the primary religious events of each year. They also functioned as prophets and soothsayers.

Poetry and music also played an important part in aristocratic Celtic life. Numerous grades of poets, bards and harpists are mentioned in the law tracts. Most esteemed were the *filí*, the poets who specialised in praising nobles and warriors in verse. Like all other members of the *aes dana*, the *filí* went through long years of training. During this apprenticeship, poets memo-rised the sagas, and composed verses of their own, always while lying down in the dark.

Each *file* was usually attached to a particular king or lord, although he was free to travel and be entertained by other nobles in return for his poems. In addition to reciting songs of praise and tales from the sagas, the poet was expected to be an expert on genealogies: thanks to the imaginative powers of their *filí*, most Celtic aristocrats could trace their family roots back to the Flood.

One measure of the high place of the *filí* in Celtic society can be found in the law tract which states that a master poet was entitled to travel with a retinue of twenty-four attendants. None dared to trifle with these powerful men; their satires could expose even the mightiest king to public ridicule. Note how this disgruntled *file* dealt with a patron he considered miserly:

> *Ro cúala*
> *ní tabair eochu ar dúana:*
> *do-beir aní as dúthaig dó,*
> *bó.*
> I have heard
> he does not give horses for poems:
> he gives what fits his kind,
> a cow.[3]

In addition to composing poems and genealogies, the *filí* were also the custodians of Celtic mythology. They committed hundreds of tales and legends to memory, many of which have survived. Of these, perhaps the most interesting are the stories which deal with the exploits of the Red Branch champions, the leading warriors of Ulster.

Unlike most Celtic saga literature, this group of tales has its roots in actual history. The wars between the warriors of Ulster and Connaught, which are described in these tales, probably reflect the real struggle which took place between those Celts who entered the country from the north and those who came into the south directly from the continent. The personalities in these stories, however, are anything but real. As in the saga literature of other European countries, heroes and heroines are given superhuman and supernatural powers.

The most famous of the Ulster sagas, the *Táin Bó Cuailgne*, the 'Cattle Raid of Cooley', is probably the closest thing there is to an Irish epic. The *Táin* tells the story of how the armies of Queen Mevb of Connaught tried to capture the Ulster king's proudest possession, the Brown Bull of Cooley. But the plot of the *Táin* serves mainly as a vehicle through which the exploits and prowess of Cuchulainn, the greatest Irish mythological hero, can be described.

This Irish Achilles is portrayed in remarkable fashion. With the sister of the King of Ulster for his mother and the Celtic god Lug as his father, the boy

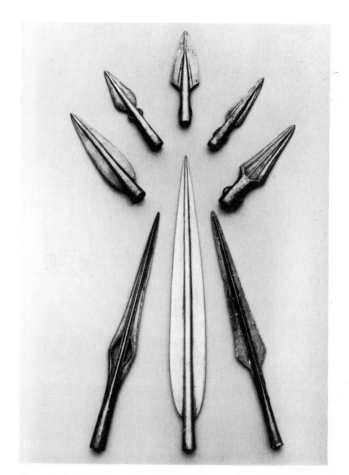

Spearheads dating from the late Bronze Age, 1000–500 B.C. These were no match for the iron weapons of the Celts, who began to come into the country towards the end of this period.

Dun Aengus, the 'fort of Angus', built on a cliff edge on the island of Inishmore in Galway Bay. There are several similar Celtic structures on this and the other Aran Islands.

Cúchulainn learns the arts of war from the goddess Scáthach, and is soon able to perform feats which no other man can do. The young warrior perfects the salmon leap and is able to step on a lance in flight and stand erect on its point! Cúchulainn's most dreaded attribute is his 'warp-spasm', a terrifying seizure which transforms him into a wild and monstrous warrior able to destroy his enemies by the score.

As the cattle raid begins in the *Táin*, the warriors of Ulster are struck down by a mysterious disease; only young Cúchulainn is spared its debilitating effects, and stands alone between the invading army of Queen Mevb and the precious Brown Bull of Cooley. For six months he holds back the enemy, slaying the best champions which Connaught can throw against him. The climax comes with his defeat of Ferdia, the greatest of the Connaught warriors, after a titanic struggle lasting four days. But this great victory is laced with sorrow, for Ferdia and Cúchulainn had been foster-brothers. Their struggle reveals much about a Celtic society where honour and social esteem were considered much more important than personal friendships. 'Think of my ill-fame and shame', says Ferdia to Cúchulainn before their combat, 'if we part now, though foster-brothers, without a fight.'[4]

Ogham stone, Co. Kerry. Ogham was a primitive form of script in which the different lines represented the characters of the alphabet.

After the defeat and death of Ferdia, the other Ulster warriors recover from their illnesses and after a great battle, the invading army is defeated. The warriors of Connaught find an easy explanation for their defeat; as one of Queen Mevb's generals wryly comments: 'We followed the rump of a misguiding woman. It is the usual thing for a herd led by a mare to be strayed and destroyed.'[5]

The *Táin* has suffered from the fact that no single comprehensive manuscript of the saga has been preserved. The work as we know it today is the combination of several incomplete versions, with the result that there is much repetition and tedium. Yet it remains a most intriguing story, filled with drama, vivid description, and a sexual openness rarely found in later Irish literature. Those sections of the saga written in verse have few equals in European heroic literature. One could hardly improve upon Cúchulainn's lament for his beloved Ferdia:

> It was all play, all sport
> until Ferdia came to the ford.
> A like learning we both had,
> the same rights, the same belongings,
> the same good foster-mother
> – her whose name is most honoured.
>
> All play, all sport
> until Ferdia came to the ford
> Misery! A pillar of gold
> I have levelled in the ford,
> the bull of the tribe-herd,
> braver than any man.
>
> All play, all sport
> until Ferdia came to the ford.
> I thought beloved Ferdia
> would live forever after me
> – yesterday, a mountain-side;
> – today, nothing but a shade.[6]

Thanks to its sagas, its bards and its legal system, Celtic Ireland possessed remarkable cultural unity. This was combined, however, with an equally remarkable degree of political decentralisation. Celtic Ireland was divided into over one hundred different states, called *tuatha*. Each of these states had its own ruler, who was known as either *rí* (king) or *taoiseach* (chief). While groups of *tuatha* were often dominated by one 'high king', there does not seem to have been any one King of Ireland until at least the fourth century A.D. Even then the office was largely ceremonial. For most of the Celtic period, therefore, each *tuath* – most of which were much smaller than modern counties – was master of its own affairs.

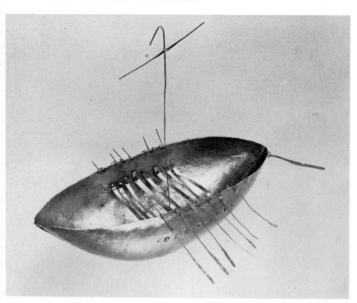

One of the most beautiful of Celtic artifacts, this model boat was discovered in a hoard of gold objects found at Broighter, Co. Derry, and dates from the first century B.C.

The so-called 'Petrie Crown', a small bronze object thought to have been part of the regal adornment of a Celtic king. The surviving section, only five inches wide, dates from the second century A.D.

What powers were wielded by the rulers of these statelets? In fact the *rí* had very little of the authority which we usually associate with the word 'king'. Although he occupied the highest social position within his state (no king, for example, was ever allowed to touch a menial tool like an axe or a spade), he had few real functions off the battlefield. Celtic rulers had no legislative powers; laws were promulgated and interpreted by *brehons*, not kings. Since the units of government were so small, rulers had no need for civil servants, although each king did retain a *brehon* of his own, to act as arbiter of disputes within his *tuath* and as his attorney in matters involving neighbouring states.

Perhaps the most powerful constraint upon the power of a Celtic *rí* was the fact that his position was not hereditary. Every king was merely a nobleman who had been selected for the position for his lifetime. Only his personal property could be passed on to his heirs; all royal trappings, including land, belonged in a primitive sense to the state.

Alone among the major peoples of Europe, the Celts did not practice primogeniture. The first-born was shown no preference in questions of either inheritance or succession. A king could be succeeded by any of his male relatives who shared the same great-grandfather. This rather large group included his brothers, nephews, and first and second cousins, in addition to members of his immediate family. At the death of a *rí*, a convention of the nobles of the *tuath* chose a new king from this extended 'royal family'. No records survive to tell us exactly who was eligible to be an elector in such an election, although it seems reasonable to assume that the general pattern was subject to local variations.

This complex system of succession was in keeping with the legalistic bent of Celtic society which we have already observed. Yet whatever delight it provided the *brehons*, it certainly proved difficult to operate. In the harsh tribal environment, almost every royal election must have been accompanied by civil war, as disgruntled factions expressed their dissatisfaction with the electoral result. The Celts themselves seem to have recognised this problem; since it became customary in many areas for an heir-apparent (*tánaiste*) to be designated during each king's lifetime. Yet this seems to have provided no real solution; in many cases election of a *tánaiste* only extended discord and faction-fighting throughout a king's reign.

In spite of these internal squabbles, the Celtic noble class as a whole possessed considerable powers. Most of these were the result of the economic control which they exerted over rural Celtic society, a society which possessed its own peculiar feudal system.

In Celtic Ireland, wealth was measured in terms of cattle rather than land. A noble would rent out his cattle with the understanding that they would become his client's property after a certain period of time. During this period, however, the client would be obliged to repay the lord in milk and calves; he would also be required to provide certain personal and military services. At first glance this system would seem to favour the clients, who would eventually have their own cattle and thus no further need of the nobles. But in the primitive Celtic world bovine (and human) mortality rates were usually high enough to maintain a crude equilibrium in this system.

This primitive stone figurehead was discovered at Boa Island, Co. Fermanagh, and dates from around 100 B.C. This two-faced figure, probably of a Celtic deity, is the earliest known example of human representation in Irish art.

Living off leases of great herds of cattle, the Celtic nobility was thus an idle class, which could afford to devote its energies to warfare, that time-honoured sport of aristocrats. Combat usually revolved around cattle raids, as each group of nobles tried to increase its supply of this most valuable resource. Leading such cattle raids seems to have been the major function of the ruler of each *tuath*. Here the king was in his element, as this extract from the *Táin Bó Cuailgne* so vividly shows:

> Seldom will you find a champion of better style and bearing than [Rochad Mac Faithemain]. . . . He wore a purple cloak wrapped around him, with an elaborate gold brooch on his white breast. He carried at his left a curved shield with a knob of silver, graven with all kinds of coloured animals. He held in his hand a long bleak-bladed javelin and a keen quick spear. A sword of gold with a gold hilt hung at his back. A red-embroidered, hooded tunic wrapped him round. He was half an army in himself, a barrier in battle, a ravening mastiff![7]

This brilliant gold collar was part of the hoard found at Broighter, Co. Derry, along with the model boat opposite.

These spiral designs on pieces of bone were probably done by apprentice Celtic metalworkers, or by master craftsmen perfecting their technique.

Despite its *brehons* and its *filí* Celtic Ireland was still a primitive society. People lived and died by the sword, in conditions of filth and grime which we would find intolerable. It was a rugged masculine world where women (despite the literary exceptions) were meant to be seen rather than heard, and where violent behaviour was both tolerated and expected.

In spite of the emphasis upon the martial arts and a political situation which seems only one step removed from anarchy, the Irish world of the pre-Christian era was remarkably stable. For over seven centuries life changed very little for the tiny population, probably never more than a quarter of a million. Why was this the case?

We have already looked at two factors which contributed to stability; the great respect that was accorded tradition, and the primacy of the legal system within this tradition. To these must be added the institution of the family. Family structure provided the cultural cement for Celtic Ireland. Most criminal law, for example, affirmed the responsibility of the family for the crimes of an individual; it centred upon compensations to be paid to the family of the victim by the family of the offender. As in most European societies of the period, the individual was of himself unimportant; his family ties and connections defined his position and place in daily life.

The paramount importance of the family is reflected in the unusual Celtic custom of 'fosterage'. It was customary for the son of a noble to spend his entire childhood living in the household of a distant relative or family friend. Indeed, the saga literature is replete with examples of the close ties between foster parents and their adopted children which this system was designed to produce. Perhaps this was an attempt to prevent social life from becoming too nuclear; fosterage may well have developed as an attempt to reproduce the closeness of family relationships on a larger scale. Whatever the origins of this custom, it clearly reflects the Celtic view that the family group was the major force for social motivation and individual control.

Thus there were factors at work in Celtic Ireland that helped to compensate for some of its anarchic tendencies. It would be a mistake, however, to concentrate exlusively upon these internal conditions. After all, Celtic cultural patterns proved anything but resilient on the continent. In less than a century, Gaul was transformed by the Romans from a Celtic society to a predominantly Latin one. Even Britain was heavily Romanised as a result of the minimal military presence of legions on that island.

Geographical isolation was probably the principal cause of social stability in Celtic Ireland. The system flourished because it was exposed to few external stresses. The greatest event of this period, the rise and fall of the Roman Empire, went almost completely unnoticed on Europe's westernmost island.

For six centuries Ireland was in a state of geographical quarantine. But this was a situation which could not and would not last forever. In the next chapter we shall look at the first European incursion; in succeeding chapters we shall see how subsequent invasions demonstrated the fragility of the Celtic way of life.

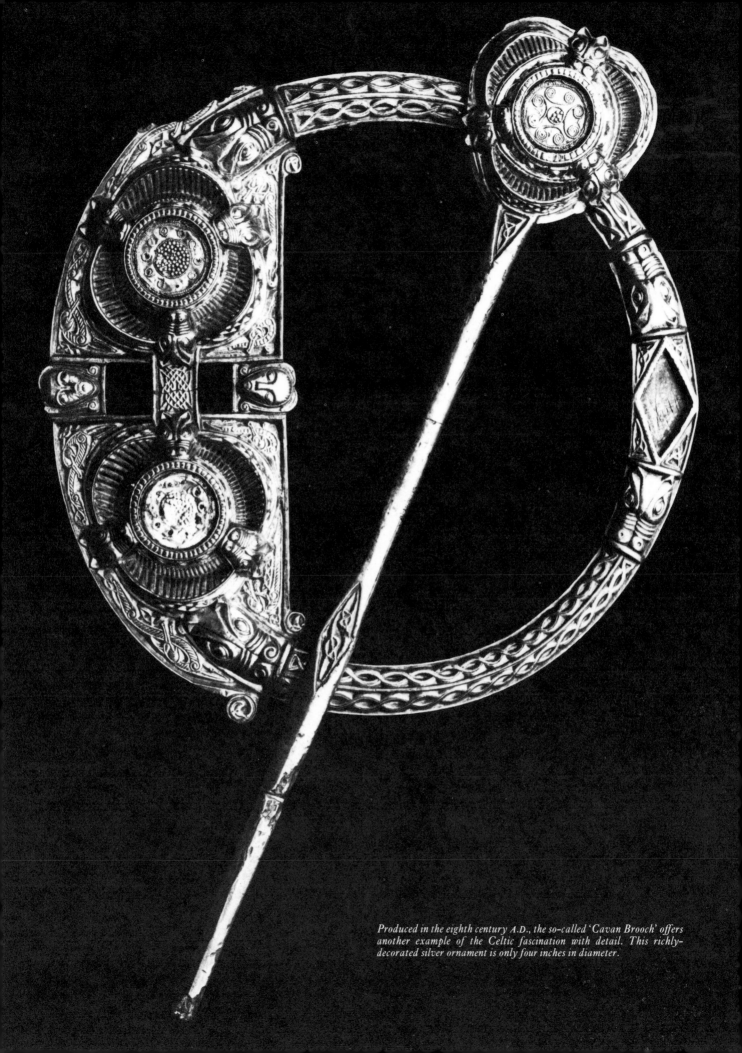

Produced in the eighth century A.D., the so-called 'Cavan Brooch' offers another example of the Celtic fascination with detail. This richly-decorated silver ornament is only four inches in diameter.

2—The Celtic Twilight

Wherefore, then, be astonished, ye great and little that fear God, and you men of letters on your estates; listen and pore over this. Who was it that roused me up, the fool that I am, from the midst of those who in the eyes of the world are wise, and powerful in word and in everything? Yes, He inspired me – me, the outcast of this world – before others to be the man who, with fear, reverence and without blame, should faithfully serve the people of this country to whom the love of Christ conveyed me.

St Patrick, *Confessio.*

Croagh Patrick, the Mayo mountain where Patrick is said to have spent six weeks in prayer and penance, emulating Christ's forty days in the desert.

These humble words were written in the fifth century by the most famous Irish personality of all time. But many who celebrate his feast day every 17 March are not aware that Saint Patrick was actually a Briton. Throughout his long missionary career he considered himself a foreigner in Ireland, a man whose roots lay on the other side of the Irish Sea.

Patrick the Briton was more than the founding-father of the Irish Catholic Church; he was also the first Irish historical figure who has left us an identifiable written record of his life. The son of a prosperous government official in Roman Britain, young Patrick was captured by a group of Irish raiders and sold into slavery in their country. He spent six years working as a shepherd in the west before he was able to escape and return to his native land. At home, however, he was unable to forget Ireland. In visions he heard voices telling him to return to the pagan Celts with the Message of God. After

training for the priesthood, he set off for Ireland with a group of followers sometime around A.D. 430.

The next thirty years of his life are shrouded in mystery; Patrick's own brief autobiography is virtually our only source for information about his career. He must have travelled extensively, however, since nearly every Irish county has its share of legends associated with his miracles and conversions. By the time of his death around A.D. 460, the Christian Church seems to have been reasonably well established, especially in the north. Patrick made his own headquarters at Armagh, the traditional residence of Ulster's most powerful kings. To the present day this small town has retained its ecclesiastical importance: the Archbishop of Armagh is still considered Ireland's leading churchman.

This statue of St Patrick stands at the foot of Croagh Patrick. The woman on the right is about to climb the mountain barefoot, a traditional penitential exercise. In this instance, she spent all night at the summit, where there is a church, before descending, again barefoot, the next morning.

We shall probably never know just how important a part Patrick played in the conversion of Ireland to Christianity. Later hagiographers were at pains to make him a national saint, so much so that the activities of an earlier missionary named Palladius are almost completely obscured. While the real Patrick may never have driven the snakes off the island, as the most famous legend claims, he must have been both a shrewd administrator and an awe-inspiring evangelist.

No matter how great the force of Patrick's personality, other factors must have played a part in the amazingly rapid conversion of the Irish. The fact that the indigenous religion was pantheistic and not tied to strict doctrine helped immeasurably; from the beginning the Celts seem to have been willing to accept Christ as just another divinity, thereby giving early missionaries a valuable foothold. Natural events also worked in their favour. A great plague struck Ireland during the 540s, killing up to half the population and probably convincing many of the survivors that the new religion offered their only hope for the future. The missionaries themselves seem to have been clever diplomats, willing to combine elements of druidic ritual with Christian practice. For example, the Irish Christian Church probably popularised the feast of All Saints, and arranged for this to be celebrated on 1 November, the same day as the great Celtic harvest festival of Samhain. Indeed the modern celebration of Hallowe'en seems to have derived from this linking of Celtic and Christian holidays.

Whatever the reasons, Ireland was a Christian country by A.D. 600. Unlike much of the rest of Europe, this conversion was achieved without bloodshed; early Christian Ireland produced dozens of saints, but not a single martyr. Patrick and his contemporaries were the successful architects of one of the greatest evangelising feats in history.

Maire and Liam de Paor have described the conversion of Ireland to Christianity as 'the last and strangest conquest of Imperial Rome'.[1] But after a thousand years of near-total isolation, tribal Celtic society bore little resemblance to that of Romanised Europe. Not surprisingly, the newly-founded Irish Church soon differed greatly from the European model.

From the beginning, Patrick had tried to establish the Roman ecclesiastical system of dioceses and bishops. But this arrangement made little sense in a Celtic world where there were no major population centres. Furthermore, each *tuath* received its own bishop, giving the island a most unwieldy total of over a hundred.

The Celts seem to have had more liking for a religious institution of the early Desert Fathers: the monastery. The idea of a 'family' of monks was easily assimilated by a society where kinship ties were of paramount importance. Over seventy monasteries were founded during the fifth and sixth centuries, and by A.D. 700 abbots had replaced bishops as the real leaders of the Irish Church.

These early Irish monasteries had little in common with the massive stone structures of later centuries. They were much simpler organisations, consisting of clusters of wooden huts used by individual monks, gathered around a few larger buildings used for community purposes. As a result of their impermanent construction, few traces of these complexes can be found today, except in isolated western areas where stone was more plentiful than wood.

The sixth- and seventh-century Irish Church placed great emphasis on asceticism. The monk followed a daily regimen of manual labour, prayer and discipline. This strict monastic ideal can be easily detected in some of the early Irish 'penitentials', lists of penances which were drawn up for the assistance of priest-confessors. The following excerpts from one sixth-century penitential give a clear indication of the ascetic bent of the early Irish Church:

3　If anyone intends fornication or murder he has already, by his intention, committed the sin in his heart which he did not complete by deed; but if he quickly does penance, he can be helped. His penance is this: half a year he shall do penance on an allowance of bread and water, and he shall abstain from wine and meat for a whole year.

22　If one has sworn a false oath, great is the crime; it can hardly, if at all, be expiated, but none the less it is better to do penance and not to despair: for great is the mercy of God. This is his penance: he must ... do penance for seven years and for the rest of his life do right, not taking oaths.

47.　If the child of anyone departs without baptism and was lost through negligence, great is the crime of occasioning the loss of a soul. But its expiation is possible, since there is no crime which cannot be expiated through penance so long as we are in this body; the parents shall do penance for an entire year with bread and water and not sleep in the same bed.[2]

Voluntary renunciation of one's native land was considered an excellent penance; exile was both an exercise of self-denial and emulation of Saint Patrick. Desire for this 'white martyrdom', as it was called, led hundreds of Irish monks to go abroad during the seventh and eighth centuries. Many felt compelled to bring Christianity to the still-heathen peoples of north-central Europe. Irish monasteries were founded throughout the continent during this period, and exerted tremendous influence over the development of medieval European Christianity. Irish monks, for example, were responsible for replacing the ancient system of public absolution with the custom of private confession which the Catholic Church uses to this day.

> The great settlement of Tara has died
> 　　with the loss of its princes;
> Great Armagh lives on
> 　　with its choirs of scholars.
> The fort of Emain Macha has melted away,
> 　　all but its stones;
> Thronged Glendalough is the sanctuary
> 　　of the western world.
> Old cities of the pagans are deserts,
> 　　without worship, like Lug's place
> The little monastic sites settled by twos and threes
> 　　are now thronged with hundreds, with thousands.[3]

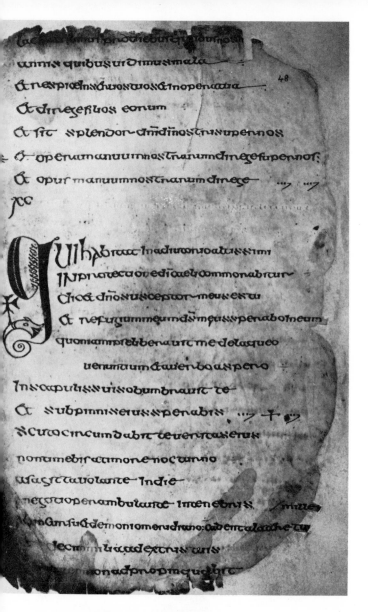

The Irish monk who wrote these stanzas at the end of the eighth century was obviously in a triumphant mood. He had good reason; the Irish Christian Church dominated not only his own society but much of northern Europe as well.

A page from the Cathach, *an Irish manuscript of the Psalms produced during the sixth century. Supposedly written by Columba (Columcille), the Irish missionary who converted the Picts of Scotland to Christianity, it is the oldest surviving Irish manuscript. Even at this early date however, the Irish had developed their own distinctive literary script, and were making tentative use of ornamental lettering. (left)*

Columbanus was perhaps the most influential missionary Ireland sent to Europe during the seventh century; he was largely responsible for revitalising the Church in central Europe, and for the tremendous growth in monasticism during this period. A scholar as well as a monk who devised his own strict monastic rule, Columbanus founded the great abbey at Luxeuil, where this likeness stands today. (below left)

Dating from the eighth century, this small stone church at Gallarus, Co. Kerry is one of the few buildings to survive intact from the early Christian period. The archaeological evidence indicates that this inverted boat design was quite common. (below)

The eighth-century Ardagh Chalice is a masterpiece of Celtic metalwork.

An artist's conception of a ninth-century Irish monastery community. Each monk had his own individual cell of wattle or straw, while the stone buildings were used for community purposes. Note the round tower in the background; these became increasingly common after the Viking raids began.

This eminence had been achieved at a price, however. The eighth century had seen a gradual drift away from the earlier spiritual fervour. Perhaps this was inevitable. Monastic control of the Irish Church brought abbots both power and wealth. Most monasteries founded after A.D. 600 were sited in the rich farmlands of the central part of the country, where they enjoyed the patronage of kings and nobles. Leading positions within each monastery became hereditary. Fewer monks remained celibate; even fewer took their vows as seriously as their predecessors.

Without this decline in monastic standards, however, the so-called 'Golden Age' of Irish artistic achievement might never have occurred. Early Christian Ireland, like ancient Sparta, left few traces of its austerity. Increased monastic wealth, on the other hand, produced a more sophisticated society and helped to produce the outstanding Irish art treasures of the eighth and ninth centuries.

This period saw something of a renaissance in Celtic metalwork. While new techniques were imported from the continent, monastic craftsmen continued to work within the established tradition. Brooches, crucifixes, chalices, and reliquary shrines produced during this period all show the same emphasis on intricate geometric decoration that originated in the Irish Bronze Age. Spiralism, the use of curves and circles to produce a swirling effect, remained the major theme of Celtic metalworkers. Indeed, this motif was carried to near-perfection in the design of the two most famous objects of this period, the Tara Brooch and the Ardagh Chalice.

Literature and scholarship had been an integral part of early Irish monasticism, and continued to be important in the eighth and ninth centuries. Along with religion, Christian missionaries had brought the concept of written language to the Irish Celts. As a result, the country witnessed something of an intellectual revolution, as the natives seized upon this novelty with a vengeance. Indeed, the almost magical attraction of the written word must have been a powerful factor in the conversion of the educated classes to the new religion.

By the early seventh century, the Latin alphabet was being used to give the Irish language a written form. As one might expect, the transcription of centuries of oral tradition became one of the major activities of the monasteries. The official religious language, however, was not ignored. Monastic scribes devoted much of their time and energies to copying Latin biblical texts.

In time many of the larger monasteries developed elaborate *scriptoria*, where the production of manuscripts became a specialised operation. By the end of the seventh century it had become customary for ornamental lettering to be used in these books. Many also contained hand-painted illustrations and designs. These 'illuminated manuscripts' are the outstanding artistic legacy of eighth- and ninth-century Ireland.

Bible texts were also illuminated on the continent during this period. However, those manuscripts produced in Ireland and in the Irish monasteries of northern Britain were representative of a completely different environment. The motifs used in Irish illumination were the same as those used in Celtic metalwork. There was the same emphasis upon

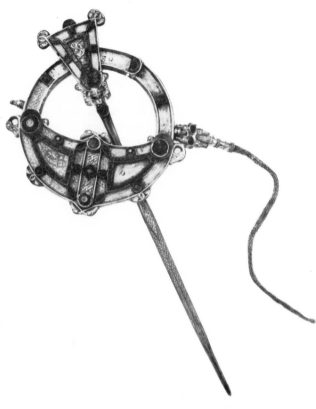

Little evidence remains of early monastic Ireland, but aerial photography has helped provide many new insights. This is a view of what was once one of the country's largest monasteries, at Ardpatrick, Co. Limerick. Only the outlines of the eighth-century settlement remain; the small church in the centre was not built before 1200. (above left)

Celtic metalworkers continued to produce high-quality objects during the early Christian period. They displayed their talent for minute design in objects like the Tara Brooch, produced in the early eighth century. This is an exact size reproduction. (above)

The 'shrine' of St Patrick's Bell, produced around A.D. 1100. Finely-decorated reliquary shrines like this were used when such relics were put on public display, as became customary during the eighth century. The objects were taken around the countryside, and public offerings on these occasions came to be important sources of monastic income.

geometric design and complex interlinear patterns. Unlike their European counterparts, Irish manuscript-artists were not very interested in depicting scenes from the texts they were illustrating. Those animal and human figures which do appear are contorted, imaginary figures whose reality becomes lost in a tangle of spirals and whirls.

There is little argument over which is the most beautiful Irish manuscript produced during this period. The Book of Kells was begun in the Irish monastery at Iona in Scotland, and completed at the sister-house at Kells, Co. Meath around A.D. 810. In it a wide range of

The Book of Kells, produced at Iona and Kells during the early ninth century.

As the ornamental letter from the Book of Kells shows, Celtic metalwork motifs and techniques were transplanted into the two-dimensional world of the illuminated manuscript by these monastic artists.

The Rock of Cashel in Co. Tipperary was the traditional seat of the kings of Munster. In 1101, however, the site was donated to the Church by Murtough O'Brien; the occasion was marked by a synod at which the foundations for twelfth-century reforms were laid. A Dominican Abbey was later built on the Rock.

*A full-page illustration of John the Evangelist from the Book of Kells.
Even when the human form is represented, it is placed in the midst of a
web of interlinear patterns which surround and envelop it.*

Dating from the eleventh century, the Clonmacnoise Crucifixion Plaque is a relatively rare depiction of human figures, a motif not common in Celtic art.

The round tower at Glendalough, Co. Wicklow, built during the tenth century.

Skellig Michael, off the coast of Kerry, The remains of a sixth-century monastery are still visible on this remote, rocky pinnacle.

Portrait of Christ, from the introductory section of the Book of Kells.

In 'carpet-pages' like this one from the Book of Kells, the illustrators let their imaginations run wild, producing a fabulous network of design.

The Christian missionaries, the first 'invaders' which Ireland had known for nearly a thousand years, came to the island with benevolent intentions. Not so the Vikings, the next group of outsiders to appear upon the Irish scene. Driven from their homelands on the Norwegian coast by population pressures, these warriors in their longships terrorised most of nothern Europe. From the Atlantic islands to the Seine Valley, Norse raiders struck wherever their boats could take them.

The first Viking attacks on Ireland occurred at the beginning of the ninth century, although the most intensive raiding took place between 830 and 850. In their search for booty they concentrated their assaults upon the wealthiest section of the Celtic community: the Church. Many of the larger monasteries were attacked ten or twelve times. It is no coincidence that the Book of Kells was the last great illuminated manuscript; even that work had to be finished at Kells because of a Viking attack on the monastery at Iona.

While plunder was their initial interest, the Norsemen had more permanent ambitions in Ireland. As they became more familiar with the country, many decided to stay permanently. Their sea-faring experience and numerous overseas connections made the Vikings natural traders, and their colonies quickly became the first Irish towns. Most modern Irish cities were founded by them: Limerick, Cork, Waterford, Wexford and, of course, Dublin. The future capital was founded on the River Liffey in 841 and became an important textile centre, forging strong trade links with the thriving British port of Bristol.

During the early part of the tenth century there was another period of Viking attacks by raiders from Norse settlements in Britain and the Isle of Man. By this time the descendants of the original invaders had mingled considerably with the native population. They began to intermarry: many Norse converted to Christianity. By the end of the tenth century the Viking settlements in Ireland were different from the other *tuatha* of the country only in their urban character. The 'kings' of Dublin and other Norse city-states behaved and were treated the same as native Celtic rulers.

Tenth-century coins depicting the famous Viking long ships, the scourge of north-western Europe.

colour is used to illustrate the Four Gospels of the text with a truly prodigous amount of ornament. The work of at least four major artists and perhaps a score of assistants, the Book of Kells contains numerous full-page designs, while nearly every page has its share of decorated initials and exotic animals. The quality of this decorative art has never been surpassed. Only since the invention of photographic enlargement has it been possible for the viewer to begin to appreciate the amazing intricacy of these illustrations.

Irish artists of the eighth and ninth centuries seem to have dwelt in a fabulous world all their own, a micro-universe of design within design within design. But their work was in keeping with the spirit of Celtic society. The minutiae of the legal tracts, the elaborate descriptions found in the saga literature, the complicated rhyming patterns of early poetry, all share this fascination with complexity.

As the first to intrude upon the compact world of Celtic Ireland, the Viking has long been the whipping-boy of nationalist historians. Many of the latter were anxious to prove that Norse depravity destroyed the fabric of Celtic society, weakening respect for law, church and king alike.

The difficulty with this interpretation was that it assumed a certain stability in Celtic society. But in reality, the values of the ancient law tracts and sagas were not the same as those of the ninth and tenth centuries. The behaviour of the Vikings was not very different from that of Celtic rulers during this period. For example, two dozen monasteries were sacked by native armies during the eighth century, long before the first Viking attack. Among this total were several depredations by Feidlimid Mac Crimthainn, a colourful king of Munster who also happened to be Bishop of Cashel!

Clearly, even eighth-century Ireland was not the 'Isle of Saints and Scholars' so famous in popular legend. More correctly, it was a fossilised, semi-Christian society on the verge of political collapse, long before the Viking (and Norman) threats materialised.

What had happened? For one thing, the Celtic concept of kingship had changed dramatically during the early Christian period. Prior to this, boundaries between individual states had been fixed by time-honoured custom. Neighbouring kings might steal each other's cattle, but rarely each other's thrones. Each *tuath* had its own particular ruling family; members of this family might struggle for power, but for an outsider to participate was almost unthinkable. When on rare occasions an interloper did gain control of a *tuath*, he was called a 'stranger in sovereignty' by the *brehons*.

A system of mutual respect such as this was essential if the anarchic tendencies of the Celtic political system were not to get completely out of hand. But this seems to be precisely what happened during the eighth and ninth centuries. Ambitious kings no longer respected the status quo. Individual rulers jockeyed for power, aiming at control of their provincial kingdoms, and ultimately aspiring to the hitherto symbolic kingship of all Ireland. Ruthless political behaviour became the order of the day; suddenly the countryside abounded with 'strangers in sovereignty'.

Of the few theories which have been advanced to explain this change, those arising from archaeological excavations are the most helpful. Archaeologists point to a dramatic change in land usage sometime around A.D. 500. The evidence indicates widespread clearance of forest at that time. Indeed, it appears that most of the low-lying areas of the country had been cleared of timber by A.D. 1000.

Perhaps the Irish population was growing fairly rapidly during this period, despite recurring plagues. What does seem certain is that there was increasing pressure for land during the period between the sixth and tenth centuries. Even spread over such a long period, these clearances point to a fundamental change in Celtic society: land began to replace cattle as the basic unit of agricultural value.

This may appear to be a fairly minor distinction, but the new importance of land may well have upset a delicate balance within Celtic society. The traditional arrangement between lord and *bóaire* concerned cattle; the number of cattle which each farmer took from his overlord seems to have depended both on his initiative and his ability to clear land. If the supply of land became

Although infamous as warriors, the Vikings were also traders and skilled craftsmen, as this group of tenth-century Norse tools indicates.

Recent excavations in central Dublin have uncovered many aspects of the city's Viking heritage. This covered wooden conduit dates from the eleventh century.

 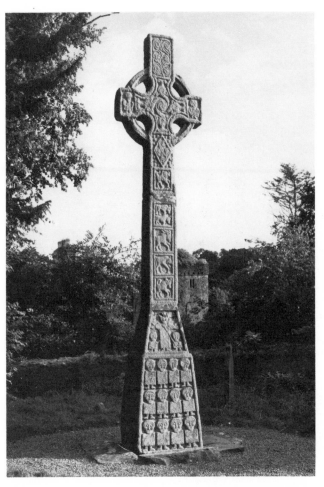

Stone crosses became prominent during the Viking period, perhaps because the political turbulence of that era discouraged metalwork and manuscript illumination. The south cross at Ahenny, Co. Tipperary (left) dates from the early eighth century; the cross and circle

arrangement became almost universal in later centuries. The ninth-century cross at Moone, Co. Kildare (right) was decorated with human and animal forms; note the Crucifixion and the Twelve Apostles on the base.

limited however, a system based solely upon the leasing of cattle no longer made sense. By the eighth century Celtic nobles may have found it both profitable and necessary to make tenancy arrangements with the farming class.

The development of rudimentary feudal patterns at the lower levels of society would have serious impact upon aristocratic behaviour. In the past, wars between neighbouring chieftains had nearly always consisted of a series of cattle raids. But after land replaced cattle as the basic unit of economic value, kings and rulers had ample reason for coveting and fighting to control the territory of other chieftains.

A closer look at the career of Brian Boru reveals just how drastic a change had taken place in Celtic politics. Brian began his career as the ruler of a small kingdom in what is now County Clare. In earlier times such a minor chieftain could never have hoped to become king of his own province, let alone ruler of the entire island. Yet in the anarchic conditions of the tenth century, Brian was

able to outmanoeuvre his rivals and rise to prominence. In 978, after defeating and killing his predecessor, he became king of Munster, ruling the province from the traditional royal site at Cashel.

Over the next twenty years, Brian gradually extended his power. Marching his army throughout the country, mixing caution with audacity, he was able to obtain the support of the leading rulers of Leinster and Connaught. Ultimate success came in 1002, when Brian received the submission of his most powerful rival, Mael Sechnaill, king of Tara and the dominant figure in the northern part of the country. For the first time in Irish history all the major rulers of the country recognised one overlord. With some justification, Brian took the title *Imperator Scottorum*, 'Emperor of the Irish'.

To many nationalist historians, the rise of Brian Boru to the high kingship was an indication that Celtic society had reached a new level of political maturity. In fact, Brian's success was a sign of weakness rather than strength. He had come to power in violation of nearly all the legal precepts upon which Celtic kingship was

based. His success confirmed the bankruptcy of the traditional political system. The law of the jungle had replaced that of the *brehons*.

Despite his considerable personal achievement, Brian Boru's career was an exercise in futility. His control of the country never went deeper than the strength of his army. There was no national civil service to administer this 'empire', which can only have had a marginal impact on everyday life in the country. After a brief reign Brian met a predictable end, dying in the Battle of Clontarf in 1014 while trying to subdue the rebellious king of Leinster and his Norse allies from Dublin. Since the high kingship was a new development without legal precedent, there was no mechanism to provide for an orderly succession after his death. The position was not made hereditary; in any event Brian's sons lacked the ability to hold together the frail structure which their father had created.

For the next century and a half anarchy prevailed, as the most powerful rulers in the country engaged in a constant struggle for the high kingship. Indeed, the very concept of a high kingship as understood in Brian's time was destroyed. With a few exceptions, most 'reigns' were brief, turbulent and brought to an end by violence.

During this period Celtic society came to bear a remarkable resemblance to that of Merovingian Gaul. Like sixth-century France, twelfth-century Ireland lacked both stability and direction. One contemporary poet captured the spirit of his age:

> Bad brotherhood within the *tuath*,
> Iniquitous law and great arrogance in kings,
> Unseasonable weather and wicked lords . . .
> Many judges without justice,
> Sovereignty destroyed by base kindreds,
> The portion of the hound by the cat,
> The big man's portion by the boy.[4]

One of the few wooden objects from this period to survive the ravages of time, this gaming board found in Ballinderry, Co. Westmeath was probably used for playing brandubh, *an Irish game similar to chess.*

Crannogs continued to be used as dwelling places of safety during this period. This modern reconstruction is in Co. Clare.

Ireland contributed scholars as well as monks to European society during this period. John Scotus Eriugena was the outstanding teacher and philosopher at the court of the Holy Roman Emperor in northern France. According to one source he was the victim of a rather unusual murder in 870; a group of students hacked him to death with their pens, because 'he tried to force them to think'.

The Cross of Cong, Co. Mayo was produced for a twelfth-century king of Connaught. By this date metalworking techniques were considerably less ornate than earlier.

3—Medieval and Early Modern Ireland

*The Irish had not so strictly offended God that it was His Will that
they should be entirely subjugated; nor were the deserts of the English
such as to entitle them to the sovereignty over and possible obedience of
the people they had partly conquered. . . . Therefore, perhaps it was the
will of God that both nations would be long engaged in mutual conflicts.*

Giraldus Cambrensis, *Expugnatio Hibernica*, 1189.

Today there is a tendency to take for granted the truth of Giraldus Cambrensis' twelfth-century prophecy. After all, Anglo-Irish hostility has been one of the major themes of European history for the past eight centuries. Before 1169, however, contacts between the two British Isles were remarkably limited. Christian missionaries may have entered Ireland from Britain, and there may have been a certain amount of trade between ports along the Irish Sea, but in terms of language, culture and politics, the two islands had developed along very different lines.

All this changed during the second half of the twelfth century, when the geographical proximity of Great Britain became a crucial factor in Irish affairs. Given the ruthlessness of Celtic politics during this period, British involvement was probably inevitable. It was only a matter of time before some ambitious chieftain looked across the Irish Sea for military assistance, and opened the Pandora's Box that was destined to bring so much sorrow to both countries for so many centuries.

For over thirty years during the mid-twelfth century, Dermot MacMurrough had been king of Leinster, one of the five large kingdoms of Celtic Ireland. In 1166, however, he was defeated in battle by the king of Connaught, and forced to surrender his throne. Although nearly sixty years old, Dermot was determined to regain his position. The traders of his south-eastern kingdom, which included the towns of Wexford and Waterford, had many fruitful contacts with western England and Wales, and it was natural for Dermot to turn to the rulers of these places for support in his hour of need.

Although less than eighty miles of water separate Wexford in southern Leinster from the town of Pembroke in south-west Wales, there was a world of difference between the two places. As we have seen, the Roman experience had left southern Britain with a distinctly European social system. Furthermore, the Anglo-Saxon invasions of the third and fourth centuries had introduced a Germanic element into the originally Celtic population. And in the eleventh century, the island experienced a political revolution which further distanced British society from that of Ireland.

Exactly one hundred years before Dermot MacMurrough was overthrown, William, duke of Normandy, sailed from northern France to England with a large army. After defeating a rival claimant to the throne at the Battle of Hastings, William the Conqueror became the first Norman king of England.

Descendants of the Norsemen who had settled in the Seine Valley several centuries earlier, the Normans were among the most sophisticated Europeans of the twelfth century, men with special talent for both warfare and efficient government. The Normans were the primary architects of the balanced system of overlords and vassals known to history as feudalism.

Dermot MacMurrough seems to have been familiar with Norman feudalism. Before enlisting allies in England, he first sought the permission of that country's supreme overlord, Henry II, count of Anjou, duke of Normandy and king of England. Although remembered today primarily for his treacherous murder of Thomas Becket in Canterbury Cathedral, Henry was one of the most talented rulers of his age, the king who ended a period of civil conflict in England and firmly planted his Plantagenet family upon the Anglo-Norman throne.

During the spring of 1167, Dermot travelled to Aquitaine in south-west France, where he was received with great ceremony by the king. Actually, Henry II already considered himself 'lord of Ireland'. Some twenty years earlier Pope Adrian IV (the only Englishman ever to hold that office) had given Henry that title hoping it might encourage the king to intervene in Ireland and assist in the reorganisation of the Irish Church. But Henry had far more pressing problems in England and on the continent, and was thus unwilling and unable to act upon the pope's offer.

Two Irish soldiers in combat, as portrayed in a thirteenth-century English manuscript.

Castles like this one at Carrickfergus, Co. Antrim gave the Normans a decided military advantage in twelfth-century Ireland.

The arrival of Dermot MacMurrough in France, however, altered this situation. While Henry may have been reluctant to get involved in Irish affairs, he was not about to look a gift horse in the mouth. If the erstwhile king of Leinster wished to promote Norman interests in Ireland, the Norman king of England would certainly give him his blessing.

Dermot returned to Britain where he met with immediate success. Among his recruits was Richard, earl of Pembroke, better known as 'Strongbow'. As his nickname suggests, Richard was an excellent soldier; he was also eager to leave Britain, since his support of the losing side in a recent rebellion had made him something of a persona non grata with the king. To guarantee his support, Dermot made Strongbow a most tempting offer: the hand of his daughter in marriage, and with it the opportunity to inherit the kingship of Leinster.

The first of Dermot's Norman allies arrived in southeast Ireland early in 1169; Strongbow himself arrived in August with a force of just over a thousand archers, infantry and cavalry. With this compact but highly efficient group of soldiers at his side, MacMurrough quickly regained his Leinster kingdom. Indeed, Dermot seemed likely to gain the high kingship of the entire country when he died suddenly in 1171. By this time Strongbow's position was secure enough for him to enforce his claim to the throne, and succeed his father-in-law as king of Leinster. Thus did the ultimate 'stranger in sovereignty' come to power in Celtic Ireland.

Strongbow's success was followed by what was perhaps the most turbulent half-century in Irish history. Despite their miniscule numbers, the Normans were able to do what the Vikings had never done: to assume a dominant position within Celtic society. By the year 1200 a handful of Norman lords controlled three-quarters of the country. Only the most remote parts of the north and west remained outside the Norman sphere of influence.

The Normans brought considerable social change wherever they went. Primogeniture was introduced in place of the complicated Celtic system of inheritance. The *bóaire* became the *betagh*, the Irish word for 'serf', as feudal patterns began to replace the landholding system of the Celts.

One does not have to look far for an explanation of this remarkable Norman success. No attempt was made by the Celts to unite against the outsiders; there was no national solidarity. In a sense every Irish ruler was a patriot, but his *patria* remained his own local state. Amidst this anarchy, there was no need for the Normans to practise a policy of 'divide and conquer'; the natives had already done the job for them.

To this eminently favourable situation, the Normans brought considerable military skills. Everywhere they went they built strong castles of stone, the first which

Archery was as essential to Norman success in Ireland as it had been to William the Conqueror at the Battle of Hastings in 1066. This is a scene from the Bayeux Tapestry.

the country had ever seen. Their armoured knights on horseback were far superior to the native cavalry; their foot soldiers were well-trained mercenaries. The Normans also brought archery into Irish warfare, with devastating effect. Over 200 years before their famous success at Agincourt, Welsh and Flemish bowmen played a vital part in the Norman conquest of Ireland.

The first generation of Norman lords in Ireland bore striking resemblance to the Spanish conquistadores of sixteenth-century America. Both groups possessed the same reckless spirit, the same sense of pride in their achievements, the same faith in their own abilities. Celtic civilisation was simply over-matched. Witness John de Courcy, the Norman adventurer who disappeared into the wilds of Ulster with 300 men, only to re-emerge six months later as the most powerful king in that province!

The independent spirit of the Normans in Ireland did not escape the attention of Henry II. The English king began to wonder if he had created a monster by agreeing to Dermot MacMurrough's seemingly modest proposal. One thing was certain: Henry was not about to tolerate powerful, self-sufficient states on his western flank.

The situation seemed to call for drastic action; only by appearing personally could Henry hope to influence developments in Ireland. Accompanied by the largest army the country had ever seen, he arrived at Waterford in the autumn of 1171, the first English monarch ever to visit Ireland.

Henry II spent six months in the country, impressing one and all with the strength of his army and the magnificence of his court. Ambitious as many of them were, the Norman lords of Ireland knew they were no match for the most powerful king in western Europe. All pledged their fealty to Henry as their overlord, ceding him title to their lands. In turn the king recognised the lords as his vassals, regranting them their territories in return for annual rents and military support. As was usually the case in such feudal arrangements, Henry retained possession of the towns of the country, including Dublin and the other Viking ports.

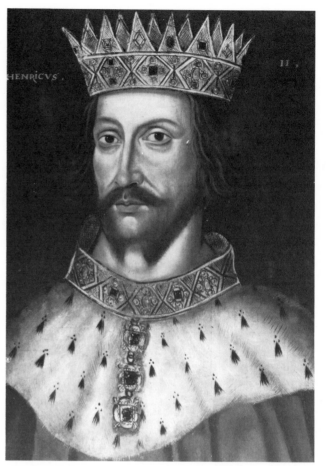

Henry II.

Perhaps the most interesting feature of this first visit of an English king to Ireland was the homage paid to Henry II by nearly all of the native 'Gaelic' rulers. Strange as it may seem, they had their reasons for accepting this foreign system of government with its foreign overlord. The Norman custom of primogeniture was a powerful attraction; many native kings hoped this would make it possible for them to pass on their crowns and their lands to members of their immediate families. Furthermore, the appearance of a potentate powerful enough to command the allegiance of the Norman lords may have convinced many Gaelic chieftains that the king was their only hope for a stable future. Perhaps Henry II could prevent further Norman encroachments.

In this hope they were sadly mistaken. Despite his position, Henry had neither the strength nor the will to keep a firm grip on Irish affairs. Once he returned to England, the Irish Sea stood as a formidable barrier between the king and his ability to enforce his policies. Unless he was prepared to organise another massive Irish expedition, there was no way he could really control Norman expansion. With dozens of continental and domestic distractions, there was no way that Henry could visit Ireland every year, or even every decade. The Normans in the country quickly grasped the realities of the situation. They learned to pay lip-service to the king, while doing precisely as they pleased in Ireland.

The royal seal of Henry II, king of England from 1154 to 1189, and the first Anglo-Norman 'lord of Ireland'.

King John became lord of Ireland in 1177, many years before he took the English throne. Henry II seems to have planned to give Ireland its own separate monarchy, since John was his fourth son and seemed to have no prospects in England when given this title. By a strange twist of fate, however, all three of his older brothers died without heirs, and he became king of England in 1199. Henry's intriguing experiment was never repeated; for the next seven centuries sovereignty over the two countries was vested in one person.

Direct control of the coastal towns did manage to give the Plantagenet kings of England a tenuous hold upon Ireland. These towns were given charters which confirmed their special relationship with the crown and outlined provisions for municipal government. This arrangement was of enormous benefit to these places, for it enabled them to develop trade independent of the control and interference of local lords.

The largest of the Irish towns, Dublin, was selected as the centre for royal government in Ireland. Gradually, a civil service which paralleled that of medieval England was developed to administer those parts of the country under Plantagenet control. A justiciar was appointed to represent the king in Ireland; while the country was given a separate exchequer and later a separate parliament.

Most of this administrative framework was laid down by Henry II's son John, who reigned as king of England from 1199 to 1216. The unpopular king of Magna Carta fame, John had been appointed 'lord of Ireland' by his father when he was only ten years old, and thus was officially in charge of the country for over thirty-five years. He visited Ireland twice (in 1185 and 1210), and kept a fairly tight rein upon both his Norman and Gaelic vassals.

The reign of King John was something of a high-water mark for Norman influence in Ireland. Norman political control reached its zenith during the first half of the thirteenth century. Considerable numbers of settlers continued to move into the eastern part of the country from England and Wales. Trade between the two British Isles increased, and improved methods of

Although standards of craftsmanship declined in medieval Ireland, Celtic motifs were still sometimes reflected in everyday objects such as this pitcher, which dates from the thirteenth century.

Conjectural reconstruction of Trim Castle as it might have appeared in the thirteenth century. The largest Norman castle constructed in Ireland, this fortress was an important government outpost on the edge of the Pale.

A medieval candlestick.

transport contributed to the rise of new inland towns such as Kilkenny and Carlow. The thirteenth century witnessed something of an agricultural revolution, especially in the south and east, where the manorial system was introduced and significant acreage was devoted to tillage crops such as oats and wheat. Contemporary European methods of crop rotation and fertilisation were introduced in many areas.

After the death of King John in 1216. however, Anglo-Norman interest in Ireland declined dramatically. Nearly two centuries would pass before another English king would visit his Irish demesne. For most of the medieval period, English kings looked east rather than west for political inspiration. This was the era of the interminable struggle between the Plantagenets and their Valois rivals in France; long after they had lost control of Normandy, English kings continued to fight for control of their ancestral homeland in northern France. Before, during and after the Hundred Years War, French affairs remained the primary foreign interest of the London government, while Ireland remained far down on its list of priorities. The Norman tide crested and passed; once again, Irish society was left to develop in relative isolation.

Improved navigational methods and better ships helped bring the two British Isles closer together, although the Irish Sea crossing remained arduous, especially in winter. This drawing shows English ships landing supplies at Waterford for a government army in 1399.

For most of the Middle Ages, the Norman lords of Ireland were left largely to their own devices. After 1215, there were fewer and fewer contacts across the Irish Sea; those few Dublin justiciars who did attempt to rule effectively found their efforts hampered by lack of financial support from London. While some emigration from England and Wales to the towns of Leinster continued, few settlers could be induced to live among the 'wilde and barbarous Irishry' of the countryside.

Despite the power vacuum created by English disinterest, no single Norman family obtained a dominant position in Ireland. One reason for this was the death without issue of so many of the first-generation Norman conquerors. Perhaps more important was the nature of Celtic society itself. The same anarchy which made possible the rapid rise of lords like Strongbow and de Courcy now prevented any single ruler from controlling the country. Ironically, lack of political unity, a fundamental 'defect' of Celtic civilisation, was now a crucial factor in its continued existence.

The original Norman colonists soon found themselves an isolated and scattered minority, surrounded by Gaelic chieftains and receiving the homage of native vassals and tenants. In such circumstances, it was perhaps inevitable that they would begin to adopt Gaelic customs and become, in the words of the now famous phrase, 'more Irish than the Irish themselves'. In his *Chronicles*, Froissart mentions one Norman squire who took an Irish wife and boasted: 'The Irish language comes as readily to me as the English tongue, for I have always spoken it with my wife and have taught it to my grandchildren.'[1] Perhaps the outstanding example of a Gaelicised Norman was Gerald Fitzmaurice, 3rd earl of Desmond (1359–98) and ruler of most of modern Munster. The earl was more than just an Irish speaker; he was also one of the foremost Gaelic poets of his age.

These 'Gaelo-Normans', however, rarely broke completely with their own tradition. Most still recognised the English monarch as their overlord, however distant and ineffectual he might be; most looked to England for social as well as political leadership. Gaelo-Norman lords sent their sons to be educated at the English colleges of Oxford and Cambridge, and dutifully attended parliaments in Dublin summoned infrequently by the Irish justiciar. Within their own territories, most of these rulers practised primogeniture and other land-holding customs developed in feudal Normandy.

Nevertheless, the Gaelo-Normans became in time a hybrid race, something of a 'middle nation' with roots in both British Isles. In his description of a thirteenth-century seige of Dublin, Giraldus Cambrensis lets one of the defenders speak for the Gaelo-Normans:

> What are we waiting for? Do we look for aid from our own people? No, for such is our position now that to the Irish we are English, and to the English we are Irish. The one island does not hold us in greater detestation than the other.[2]

As a result of the neglect of the Plantagenets, a Gaelic political revival took place during the fourteenth and fifteenth centuries. Native rulers learned to adopt Norman military techniques, arming themselves with similar weapons and building the same kind of stone castles. They even introduced a novel element of their own into Irish warfare: well-armed and well-trained Scottish mercenaries called 'gallowglass'.

By the end of the thirteenth century Gaelic armies were, on the whole, equal in strength and skill to those of the Normans. This military parity made it possible for native chieftains to recover most of their traditional territories. Families like the O'Neills in Ulster once again dominated their traditional lands, as Norman influence waned in the north and the west.

This political success was accompanied by renewed interest in Celtic cultural patterns, particularly in literature. While the *brehon* legal system never recovered from the Norman intrusion, bards and poetry flourished in medieval Ireland. It was something of a golden age for bardic poetry, when hundreds of Irish folk tales were given their modern form. In 1433 over 2,700 'men of learning' were reputed to have attended a great cultural

This famous drawing of Irish mercenaries was done by Albrecht Dürer in 1521. Note the mantle, the traditional Irish cloak worn by the figure on the left.

During the medieval period, stone tower houses like this became prominent features of the Irish countryside, serving as the homes and fortresses of both Gaelo-Norman lords and Gaelic chieftains.

But most English monarchs continued to ignore their Irish lordship. The Irish exchequer was constantly on the edge of bankruptcy; in 1411, for example, when the English government spent £22,000 fortifying its French outpost at Calais, a meagre £2,000 was provided for the administration of all Ireland.

Given such financial stringency, a gradual decline in the area under government control was inevitable. By 1400 English law could be enforced only within a thirty-mile radius of Dublin. Outside of this 'Pale' and several garrisoned towns, the justiciar was virtually powerless.

Striking evidence of this weakness was provided by the Statutes of Kilkenny, a group of laws passed by parliament, which the justiciar summoned to that town in 1366. Designed to stem the Gaelic tide which was sweeping the countryside, these statutes forbade Norman and English settlers to practise Irish customs, to

Manuscript illumination became a lost art in medieval Ireland. Those few illustrated volumes that were produced, including this fourteenth-century Psalter, reflected European motifs and techniques rather than Celtic ones.

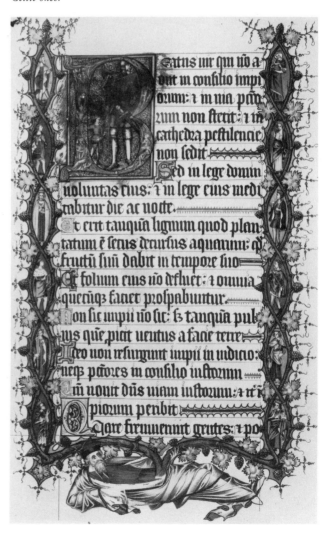

festival neld near Athlone. Great manuscript compilations of Celtic law, history and legend were produced, although these were not as lavishly illustrated as the manuscripts of the pre-Viking period.

In both political and cultural spheres, one can perceive the faint outlines of an Irish national spirit during the medieval period. The coming of the Normans did create among the Celts a shared sense of betrayal at the hands of the 'foreigners'. But this sentiment remained just that; there were no programmes for constructive, united action, no plans for a national campaign against the Normans. Gaelic chieftains continued to devote most of their energies and much of their blood to struggles with their greatest enemies: each other.

While English influence in Ireland declined greatly during the later Middle Ages, it never disappeared altogether. Dublin remained the centre of English administration, and many other coastal towns retained close links with Britain. Despite the confused political situation and the great plague of the mid-fourteenth century ('The Black Death'), the medieval period was fairly prosperous for most Irish towns. Dublin became a major European port, attracting imports and merchants from all over the continent. Wool, leather and fish were the major exports of this city of 30,000 inhabitants.

Because of their mercantile connections and the fact that much of their population was of English origin, Irish towns remained loyal to the crown, condemning the behaviour of both Norman lords and Gaelic chieftains in the countryside. The records of this period are filled with requests sent by town leaders to London, begging for soldiers and funds to protect their cities from outside raiders.

45

speak the Irish language and to have any social or economic dealings with the native population. In the circumstances of medieval Ireland, however, these laws were not worth the paper they were written on. Norman and Gael were already so intermingled that separation of the two communities was virtually impossible, even if the government had possessed the financial and military resources to attempt to enforce these apartheid statutes. Only in Dublin and a few other towns was it possible to maintain the 'purity' of the colonists, and even in these places, the bulk of the labour force was native in origin.

Reluctantly, the English government seems to have accepted this basic fact of medieval Irish life. A sixteenth-century English observer later made these comments about the Norman 'conquest' of Ireland:

> Where the country is subdued, there the inhabitants ought to be ruled by the same law that the conqueror is governed by, to wear the same fashion of attire wherewith the victor is vested, and speak the same language that the vanquisher parleth. And if any of these three lack, doubtless the conquest limpeth.[3]

Whatever its merits or defects, the Norman intrusion did bring Ireland into closer contact with European political and cultural developments than ever before in her history. Even before the Norman invasion, however, the island had moved towards the European mainstream, thanks to changes within its most important social institution: the Church.

Since the time of Patrick, the Irish Church had been the most independent in western Europe. It may have been Christian, but it was anything but Roman. Even in its 'golden age', during the eighth and ninth centuries, the Irish Church developed its own rituals and traditions. Indeed, both Irish and Vatican records indicate that there was no written correspondence between the Papacy and Irish religious leaders for over four centuries between 640 and 1080.

Along with continental concepts of monasticism, new religious orders like the Benedictines and the Cistercians brought European styles of architecture to twelfth-century Ireland. This Romanesque doorway was built into a cathedral at Clonfert, Co. Galway.

Henry of London, Archbishop of Dublin from 1213 to 1228, also served as justiciar for six years. Throughout the medieval period all Dublin archbishops were English-born.

The introduction of European monastic orders was accompanied by the foundation of convents as well as monasteries.

Begun in 1251, St Canices's Cathedral in Kilkenny shows the influence of European architectural developments in medieval Ireland.

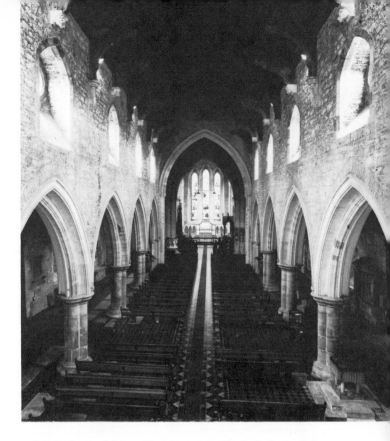

Despite its independence, the Irish Church in 1100 had entered a long decline. The zeal and fervour of the early Christian period had been dissipated; traditions of scholarship and education had been sadly neglected. Many monasteries had closed; those that remained open were usually the personal property of their abbots, who passed along their wealth and titles to their children. Monastic vows were ignored, as were religious duties. Little attempt was made to improve moral standards among the laity, who by this time had replaced Christian practices with traditional Celtic customs. Marriages were rarely solemnised; even Anselm of Canterbury was aware of the fact that in Ireland 'men exchange their wives as freely and publicly as a man might change his horse'.[4]

Early in the twelfth century, however, a reform movement began to develop within the Irish Church. The leading figure in this campaign was an Ulster monk named Malachy, who became Archbishop of Armagh in 1129. Along with many of his contemporaries, Malachy was convinced that many of the Church's problems stemmed from its lack of a proper organisational structure. Since its earliest days, the Irish Church had been dominated by abbots; bishops had usually been figures of secondary importance, and the laity had been largely ignored. Malachy called for a regular diocesan structure, as existed in most European countries, which could better serve the religious needs of the people. After many years of effort, the changes which he desired were finally ratified by a Church synod which met at Kells in 1152. The country was divided into four archepiscopal provinces (Armagh, Cashel, Dublin and Tuam) and thirty-six separate dioceses. This twelfth-century formulation has provided the basic organisational structure of the Irish Catholic Church to this day.

Malachy and his colleagues saw the isolation of the Irish Church as a major source of the country's religious problems; 'only by turning our wills and hearts to Rome,' he wrote in 1143, 'can we hope to cure what ails us.' Thanks to the efforts of the reformers, the Papacy began to play a larger role in the appointment of bishops and general administration of the Church. Malachy himself visited Rome in 1139, stopping en route at the monastery of Clairvaux in France, where the renowned monk Bernard was implementing his new system of religious discipline. The two reformers became close friends (Malachy died at Clairvaux during a second visit in 1148), and Bernard later wrote a *Life of Malachy*, in which he gave a sensitive portrait of his Irish activities:

In all churches, he ordained the apostolic sanctions and the decrees of the Holy Fathers, and especially the customs of the Holy Roman Church. Hence it is to this day that there is chanting and psalmody in them at the canonical hours, after the fashion of the whole world: for there was no such thing before, not even in the city of Armagh. . . . Malachy instituted anew the most wholesome usage of confession, the sacrament of confirmation, the contract of marriage, all of which were either unknown to the people or neglected by them.[5]

While Malachy was interested in Church re-organisation, he was also a monk, a man who admired the strict discipline and spiritual richness of monastic life. In fact he was so impressed with the monastic rule which Bernard had developed at Clairvaux that he left some of his companions there for training, and invited the monks of Clairvaux to introduce their form of monasticism in Ireland.

Bernard's followers – the Cistercians – duly came to Ireland and in 1157 a great new abbey was consecrated at Mellifont in Co. Meath. These monks were in the vanguard of a monastic revolution which swept through

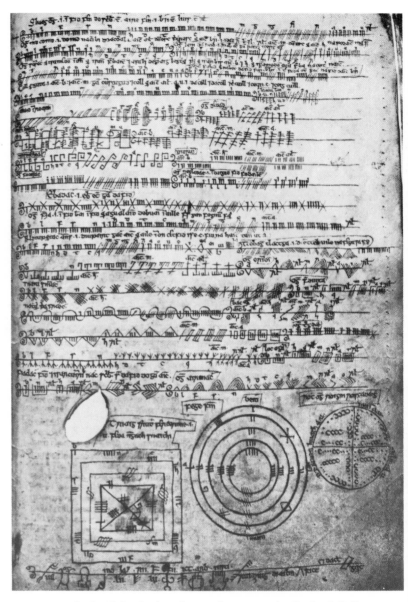

Human representation became more common in late medieval Irish art. This Madonna and Child is carved on a stone panel in the cemetery of the Catholic church at Piltown, Co. Kilkenny and dates from the early sixteenth century.

Produced in the late fourteenth century, the Book of Ballymote contained many Irish legends as well as historical and genealogical material. It also includes this unusual page written in ogham, the primitive written language of the early Celts.

The fifteenth century witnessed a tremendous increase in the number of Franciscan houses, especially in western areas. These monasteries included lay brothers as well as ordained friars, and performed a wide range of public services for the local people. Moyne Abbey, near Killala, Co. Mayo, was consecrated in 1462, and was one of the largest Franciscan houses in Ireland, with over 100 resident monks.

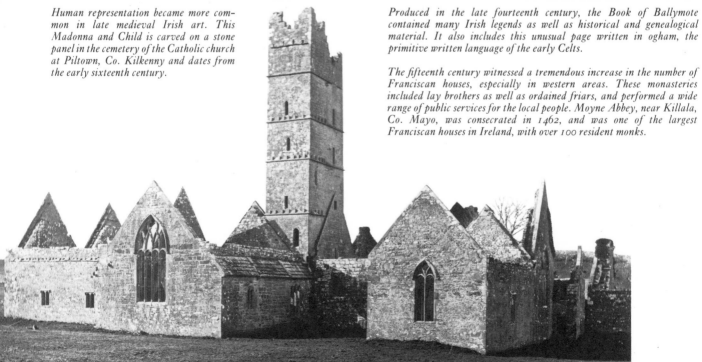

Produced during the late fifteenth century, these wooden figures of Christ at Calvary and God the Father were discovered in Fethard, Co. Tipperary. They show obvious European influence, and may well have been carved by a continental artist.

Methers, medieval Irish drinking vessels. Made of wood, they were passed round the company and people drank out of the corners.

The charter of freedom which Henry II granted to the city of Dublin in 1172.

Christ Church Cathedral, Dublin. Begun on the site of an earlier church in 1172, it was not completed until the middle of the fourteenth century. The tower dates from 1330. The cathedral was extensively restored in the nineteenth century.

Ireland during the twelfth and thirteenth centuries. During this period, all of the major European religious orders – the Benedictines, the Augustinians, and later the Dominicans and Franciscans – established houses in Ireland. By 1225 there were thirty-one Cistercian abbeys alone; by this date there were few Irish monasteries not affiliated with one of the European orders.

Two significant changes were initiated, therefore, by the religious reformers of the twelfth century: reorganisation of the Irish Church along standard European lines, and the introduction of European monasticism. Unfortunately, neither of these developments really improved the quality of the Irish Church. The reforming fire seems to have only lasted a generation or two, and did not succeed in rooting out the major problems of corruption within the Church. As early as 1221 a monk from Clairvaux, visiting Ireland, reported that 'in the abbeys of this country the severity of Cistercian discipline and order is observed in scarcely anything but the wearing of the habit'.[6] The traditional problems of Irish monasticism crept rapidly into the new European models. The secular Church fared no better. Bishoprics soon became as hereditary as abbacies, while church offices were pursued with the same ruthlessness as political titles.

Sanitary conditions in medieval Ireland left much to be desired, as they did elsewhere in contemporary Europe. This woman is picking lice from the hair of a soldier.

This drawing of Irish revenue officers at work was contained in a fifteenth-century accounts book. Note the chequered cloth on the table; the word 'exchequer' is derived from the fact that such cloths were commonly used in medieval treasuries.

Several factors were involved in the continued wane of the Irish Church. Endemic warfare did little to encourage an improvement in standards; since they brought control of some of the most valuable property of the country, church positions were naturally considered prizes in the eyes of all combatants. The Norman invasion also contributed to the religious anarchy; the Archdiocese of Dublin, for example, came under close English control, while many western dioceses were dominated by Gaelic chieftains, making Church unity virtually impossible. Furthermore, the Irish Church had the misfortune to establish close links with Rome at exactly the moment that the Papacy was entering the most sordid period in its history. While the Vatican now had considerable influence in the appointment of Irish bishops, most fourteenth and fifteenth century popes were principally concerned with gaining the maximum financial benefit from this control. Malachy's fond hopes of a purified Irish Church linked closely with Rome came to nothing when Rome itself began to set new standards for clerical depravity.

If the fifteenth century represented a low point in the development of Irish Catholicism, it also brought more complications to an already confused political situation. During this period English influence reached its nadir, as the London government was preoccupied with war in France and later thirty years of internal strife in the so-called 'War of the Roses'. Into this vacuum stepped three powerful Gaelo-Norman families: the Fitzgeralds of Desmond in Munster, the Fitzgeralds of Kildare, and the Butlers of Ormond (the modern county of Kilkenny). During the fifteenth century each of these families enjoyed a period of dominance, while all three stood above the other rulers of the country in terms of territory controlled and power wielded.

Undoubtedly the greatest of these lords was Garret Mór Fitzgerald, the 8th earl of Kildare, who was the uncrowned king of Ireland for the last quarter of the fifteenth century. The 'Great Earl' was perhaps the most powerful Irish leader since Brian Boru. Making use of skilful military tactics, careful alliances, and clever marriages, he built an Irish empire based around his own rich lordship of Kildare. Even the English government recognised the special position of this earl of Kildare; for most of his long political career Garret Mór held the office of justiciar (the official title was now 'Lord Deputy'), a position which gave him control of the towns of the Pale as well as most of the Irish countryside.

During the early 1490s, Henry VII, the English monarch who successfully concluded the War of the Roses, did make a serious attempt to restrain the Great Earl. He removed Kildare from his position of Lord Deputy, replacing him with an English official. But the outburst of lawlessness and violence which followed this replacement convinced Henry VII that he had but two options: either he must send a large army to conquer Ireland, or he must let its strongest personality maintain a degree of order there for him. Unwilling to make the

enormous financial commitment which a military expedition would require, the English king restored Fitzgerald as Lord Deputy, a position which the latter held until his death in 1513. Frustrated in his attempts to control Garrett Mór, Henry VII is supposed to have made the following analysis of the Irish situation: 'If all Ireland cannot rule this man, then he shall rule Ireland!'[7]

While Henry VII may have lamented his lack of success in Ireland, the dynasty which he founded was destined to fare considerably better. Few contemporaries of Henry VII and Garret Mór Fitzgerald could have believed that the country stood on the verge of a political revolution. During the sixteenth century the Tudor monarchs would transform Ireland from a semi-autonomous feudal outpost into an integral part of a new and expanding English empire.

This later medieval astrological chart shows the signs of the zodiac and the planets in Latin, as well as the names of the months. At the bottom is a note in Irish which explains the connection between the signs of the zodiac and the human anatomy.

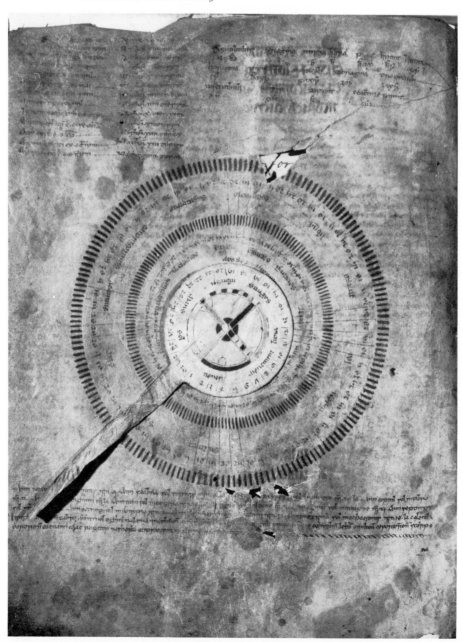

4—Conquest and Colonisation

Your Highness must understand that the English blood of the English conquest is in manner worn out of this land. . . . And contrary-wise, the Irish blood ever more and more without such decay, encreaseth.

Lord Leonard Grey, 1536.

Detail from a late sixteenth-century print, showing a typical Irish homestead. The heavy forestation was characteristic of much of the countryside until after 1600.

Lord Grey, the English Lord Deputy for Ireland from 1536 to 1540, made the above observations in a letter written to King Henry VIII. In this he was echoing sentiments that had been shared by most officials who had held this office during the late Middle Ages. During this period Ireland mattered little to English kings; it was, in the words of one historian, 'a marginal threat, a marginal problem, and a marginal asset'.[1] English political and cultural influence declined, as the fourteenth and fifteenth centuries witnessed something of a Gaelic revival.

The reign of the second Tudor king of England, however, proved to be a crucial turning point in the history of Anglo-Irish relations. Henry VIII was the most powerful monarch England had seen for centuries. Secure on the throne, supremely confident of his own abilities, Henry was determined to transform his kingdoms into a unified, centralised state, and destroy the local autonomy of magnates like the Fitzgeralds.

After centuries of neglect, the English administration in Dublin at last began to receive significant royal attention.

There were several reasons for increased English interest in Ireland during the first half of the sixteenth century. Most important was the fact that Ireland was now a genuine threat to English security. While France remained a major rival after Henry VIII succeeded his father in 1509, the new English king was aware of the growing importance of the newly-formed kingdom of Spain. Moreover, improved sailing techniques were helping to make Ireland far more accessible to these two continental powers. There was now a very real possibility that Spain or France might try to gain control of the island, and use it as a base for an attack against England. In such circumstances, Henry VIII was determined to extend his government's military and political influence in Ireland.

53

At the same time, Henry wished to alter the relationship between the English monarch and his western demesne. For over three centuries his predecessors had held the title 'lord of Ireland'. Yet this had given them little real power in the country; to a large extent, the English king was a mere figurehead. This was not good enough for Henry, nor would it suffice for his successors. During the sixteenth century the Tudors introduced a new concept of sovereignty to Ireland, one which made the English monarch ruler of the country in fact as well as in name.

During the first two decades of Henry's reign, the house of Kildare continued to dominate Irish political affairs. In 1513 Garret Óg Fitzgerald succeeded his father as earl of Kildare, and for a time proved an equally effective ruler. Gradually, however, Henry began to reduce Kildare influence in the country. Well-trained English officials were appointed to posts in the Dublin administration, and given solid financial and military backing. At the same time alliances were made with other Gaelo-Norman lords, many of whom were as anxious as the king to break the power of the Kildares.

Nevertheless, Fitzgerald remained a formidable obstacle, one whose removal might occupy Henry's entire reign. Fortunately for the king, the Kildares eliminated themselves. In 1534 Henry summoned Garret Óg to London. The earl left his lordship under the control of his twenty-seven year old son, 'Silken Thomas' Fitzgerald. Thomas's preference for gaudy apparel seems to have been matched by a volatile personality. When rumours reached Dublin that Garrett Óg had been executed (Garrett Óg was in fact alive and well at this point), the younger Fitzgerald led his forces into open rebellion against the crown.

Few metal items from this period survive. The de Burgho-O'Malley Chalice, perhaps the best, was produced in 1494.

The tomb of Piers Fitzoge Butler at Kilcooley Abbey, Co. Tipperary. He was ninth Earl of Ormond and a cousin of Anne Boleyn, Henry VIII's second wife. Throughout the sixteenth century, the Ormonds remained staunch allies of the crown.

The foyer at Bunratty Castle, the restored fifteenth-century stronghold of the O'Briens of Clare.

Produced in the late fifteenth century, the Ballylongford Cross was a product of continental influence.

Thomas soon regretted his impetuous action. The king sent the most powerful army Ireland had seen for generations to crush the revolt. Receiving little support from other Irish rulers, the Kildare rebels were easily defeated, and Silken Thomas and his five uncles were captured. In 1536 all were executed at the Tower of London, where Garret Óg had died in captivity in the meantime. Within the remarkably short space of two years, the influence of the most powerful Gaelo-Norman family in Ireland had been virtually eliminated.

After the rebellion all Kildare lands were confiscated by the crown, and given to English lords and captains who were completely devoted to the king. For the first time in living memory the boundaries of the Pale were expanded.

To indicate his increasing power, Henry VIII in 1541 had the Irish and English parliaments declare him 'king of Ireland'. Taking this new title, Henry called upon all Irish rulers to reaffirm their allegiance to him, recognising him as both their king and their landlord, by whose grace each held his own territory.

An Ulster chieftain dines with his colleagues in the open, c. 1575.

Virtually all of the Gaelo-Norman lords accepted Henry's new position; so too did most Gaelic chieftains. At first glance the adherance of the latter seems strange. Traditionally the land of a *tuath* belonged to all of its freemen, not to an individual ruler; thus in theory Gaelic chieftains were signing away the property of their people by accepting the king as owner as well as ruler of Ireland. But most probably believed that these agreements were of no lasting consequence. After all, their ancestors had made roughly similar agreements with Henry II in 1171, and then proceeded to follow traditional political customs.

The Gaelic rulers of the sixteenth century did not appreciate the difference between the Tudors and the Plantagenets. Few were aware that their submission to the new king of Ireland was more than ritual and pageantry. The English armies which Henry had in Ireland would not sail back across the Irish Sea and leave the native rulers in real control of the country. The destruction of the Kildares was not an isolated event, but the first step in the Tudor conquest of Ireland.

While the foundation for this conquest was laid by Henry VIII, its achievement was left to his daughter Elizabeth I, who ruled England and Ireland from 1558 until 1603. This was the period of Spain's ascendancy on the continent, during which a Spanish invasion of Ireland was always a threat. As a result, Elizabeth

spared no expense in her attempt to gain firm military control of the country. The Dublin administration increased tenfold; separate government departments were established to deal with affairs in each of the four provinces. Large, well-equipped English armies became permanent fixtures of the Irish scene; these were commanded by experienced and skilful generals.

Ireland had never known a centralised government with the single-minded determination of this one. Although both Gaelic and Gaelo-Norman rulers took up arms whenever they felt that English expansion threatened their local interests, their rebellions seldom brought success. The Elizabethans pursued their policy with an efficiency and ruthlessness rarely seen in earlier Irish warfare. When the earl of Desmond rebelled during the 1580s, his army was pursued and destroyed, and all of his Munster lordship was laid waste. Among the officers in the English army which wreaked this havoc was Edmund Spenser, author of *The Fairie Queene* and for twenty years an Irish colonist. He described the supression of the Desmond rebellion in the following manner:

[The people] looked anatomies of death; they spake like ghosts crying out of their graves. They did eat of the dead carrions . . . and if they found a plot of watercresses or shamrocks there they flocked as to a feast . . . in short space of time there were almost none left, and a most populous and plentiful country was left void of man and beast.[2]

A stylised engraving which shows 'Silken Thomas' Fitzgerald renouncing his allegiance to the king in Dublin in 1534.

Effigy of Piers Rua Butler, Earl of Ormond from 1515 to 1539, and his wife on their tomb in Kilkenny. Traditional rivals of the Fitzgeralds, the Butlers supported Henry VIII in his campaign against the Earl of Kildare.

Sir Walter Raleigh (c. 1552–1618) was deeply involved with Elizabethan colonial ventures both in Ireland and North America.

During the 1570s and 1580s Elizabethan armies firmly established English rule in the provinces of Munster and Connaught. During the next decade they turned their attentions to Ulster, the last bastion of Gaelic society. During the 1590s that province became the theatre for Elizabeth's longest and costliest military campaign.

While Gaelo-Norman families had successfully established lordships in many parts of Ireland they had little lasting success in Ulster. By the sixteenth century virtually the entire northern province was controlled by Gaelic chieftains, the most powerful of whom were the O'Neills of Dungannon, who exercised a rough form of sovereignty over the other rulers of Ulster.

Although there had been numerous O'Neill rebellions during the sixteenth century, the rebellion of the 1590s was something of a surprise. Hugh O'Neill, who became head of the family in 1593, had been educated at the English court and had proved consistently loyal to the crown. In fact he had served with the royal army which devasted Munster after the Desmond rebellion, and had been awarded the title 'earl of Tyrone' for his services.

A study in contrasts – Gaelic peasant and Anglo-Irish lady of the Pale, c. 1575.

Robert Parsons and Edmund Campion were two Jesuit missionaries active in Ireland around 1580. This print shows Campion's execution in 1581; Parsons escaped to Rome.

Hugh O'Neill, Earl of Tyrone, (kneeling) last of the independent Gaelic chieftains and Elizabeth's most formidable opponent.

Henry VIII (reigned 1509–1547), the Tudor king who determined to conquer Ireland.

Elizabeth I (reigned 1558–1603), the Tudor monarch responsible for carrying out the Irish conquests.

During this period English attention was focused upon the south and west; the Gaelic rulers of Ulster were left largely to their own devices. Once Munster and Connaught were secure, however, the government turned its attention to the north. The year 1593 saw English armies subdue a rebellion by a number of O'Neill sub-chieftains along the southern border of Ulster. Hugh O'Neill realised that his turn was next. Resenting English interference in what he considered his own preserve, Hugh joined the other Ulster chieftains in open rebellion in 1595.

For most of the war which followed, O'Neill and his allies held their own against the English. An excellent tactician, Hugh was able to exploit the blunders of an enemy unfamiliar with the Ulster countryside and get the most out of his own limited resources. He realised, however, that his rebellion was doomed to eventual failure without foreign assistance, and finally convinced the king of Spain to send a military expedition to Ireland. Unfortunately, this army proved to be more of a curse than a blessing when it was landed at Kinsale, Co. Cork in 1601. O'Neill was forced to march three hundred miles through hostile territory in order to link with the Spaniards. When his Ulster army finally arrived on the south coast, it was decisively beaten by an English force led by Lord Mountjoy, Elizabeth's most able general. Beseiged at Kinsale, the Spanish force eventually signed a truce with the English, and returned to the continent without having fired a shot in support of the Irish rebels.

After the defeat at Kinsale, O'Neill's forces limped back to Ulster, pursued by English troops and harried by the forces of other unsympathetic Irish lords and chieftains. Never able to regain the initiative, Hugh finally surrendered in 1603. Ironically, this submission took place during the very week that Queen Elizabeth died. But she had largely completed her mission in Ireland. For the first time the entire country was effectively ruled by an English government.

A contemporary view of the Battle of Kinsale, 1601. In this picture, the Spanish forces lay beseiged by those of the English Lord Deputy, Lord Mountjoy, awaiting the arrival of O'Neill and his allies from Ulster.

An early seventeenth-century lady's dress.

The Lord's prayer in Irish, from a Catholic manuscript published in Antwerp in 1611. The Irish remained resolute in their devotion to Catholicism.

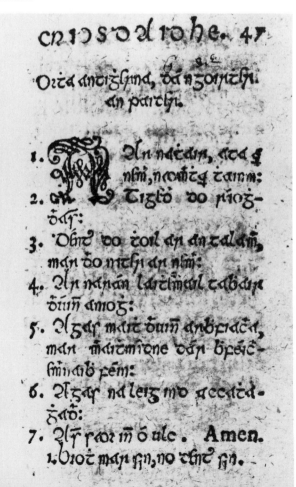

Just as the East India Company attracted some of the outstanding Britons of later generations to serve in that country, the sixteenth-century conquest of Ireland lured some of the most talented individuals in Elizabethan England. Among those who crossed the Irish Sea were the poet Spenser, Sir Walter Raleigh, and Sir Henry Sidney, father of the poet Philip. Supremely confident of their abilities as administrators, these conquerors were convinced of the superiority of their own culture. In Elizabethan eyes, the Irish adventure was but the first step in a great worldwide expansion of English civilisation. Indeed, many of the individuals who played a part in the Tudor conquest of Ireland later helped to lay the foundations for English settlement in North America.

Not surprisingly, the Elizabethans viewed native Irish civilisation with a considerable amount of disgust. They had little time for the Irish language, and little appreciation of the subtleties of Celtic landholding and political customs. 'My soul doth detest their wild shamrock manners',[3] wrote John Derricke in 1575, while another Elizabethan used verse to draw these unflattering parallels between Irish and Russian culture:

> Wild Irish are as civil as the Russies in
>   their kind,
> Hard choice which is the best of both,
>   each bloody, rude, and blind.[4]

The native Irish, for their part, showed equal contempt for certain aspects of English civilisation. In this sixteenth-century poem, translated from the Irish, the bard heaps praise upon a young warrior who is true to his traditions:

> Eoghan Bán, the darling of noble women,
>   a man who never loved English customs,
> Does not set his heart on English ways,
>   but rather has chosen the wild life.
>
> Little he cares for gold-embroidered cloaks,
>   or for a high well-furnished ruff,
> Or for a gold ring that would only be vexatious,
>   or for a satin scarf down to his heels.[5]

In earlier centuries adherence to Christianity had been one of the few elements shared by English and Irish culture. During the sixteenth century, however, even this common link was broken, as the Henrician Reformation led England towards Protestantism.

In 1534, after failing to get papal sanction for his divorce from Catherine of Aragon, Henry VIII declared himself Supreme Head of the Church of England. As the Anglican religion gradually evolved during the sixteenth century, an attempt was made to carry out a similar reformation of the Irish Church. An allied Church of Ireland was established in 1536, and all bishops and priests were required to swear religious allegiance to the English monarch. While Henry himself made few doctrinal changes, his Tudor successors borrowed many Reformation ideas from the continent, so

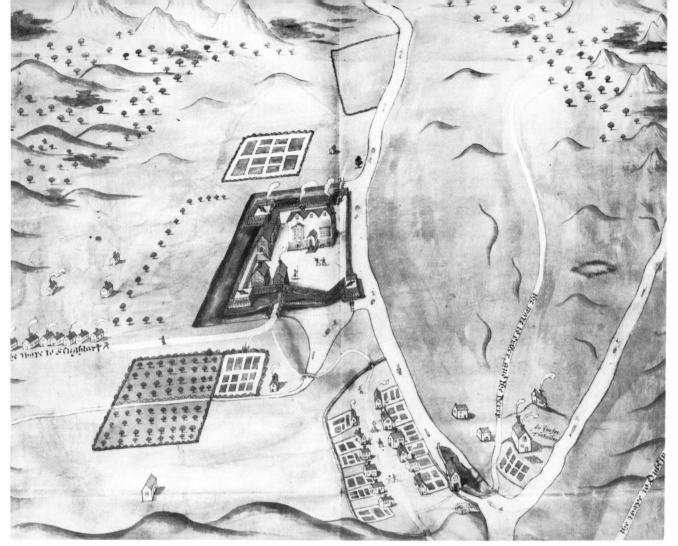

A seventeenth-century overview of Omagh, Co. Tyrone. Note the orderly layout of this Plantation town founded by Scottish immigrants.

Owen Roe O'Neill (c. 1590–1649), one of the leaders of the Catholic rebellion of the 1640s. His death was a crucial factor in the failure of this revolt.

much so that by the end of the century the Church of England differed in both form and substance from the Church of Rome.

But the Tudor attempt to extend English Protestantism to Ireland was a dismal failure. Many factors were involved: among these were the confused political situation, the generally poor quality of Irish Protestant leadership, and the reluctance of English-speaking ministers to preach and teach in Irish, the language still spoken universally outside the towns. Perhaps the most important reason for this lack of success was the Tudor policy of closing monasteries in the country. This was especially unpopular in the west, where many Franciscan and Dominican houses served as schools and hospitals as well as friaries.

Whatever other factors were involved in the survival of Irish Catholicism, religious piety was probably not a significant one. The sixteenth-century Irish Church was as riddled with corruption as any in Europe, and few laymen took their religious duties very seriously. Indeed, Irish rejection of the Anglican Church had little to do with theology. Timing was of crucial importance; if the Reformation had occurred a hundred years earlier or later, it might well have had the same impact on Ireland as on England. In the sixteenth century,

A sixteenth-century map of Galway, showing several blocks of Connaught's largest town. Note the city walls and the planted gardens.

however, all Protestant sects were doomed by their connections with England at a time when the Tudor conquest was beginning to arouse the faint stirrings of an Irish national spirit. While this emotion was far too weak to generate united political resistance in the sixteenth century, it was strong enough to produce national rejection of English forms of Christianity.

In 1579 James Fitzmaurice Fitzgerald, a cousin of the earl of Desmond, landed in Kerry with a group of 600 mercenaries whom he had recruited in Rome with papal assistance. 'This war', he announced, 'is undertaken for the defence of the Catholic faith against the heretics.'[6] Although his motley band was easily crushed by an English army then in Munster, James helped inaugurate a new era in Irish history. Twenty years later, a large Spanish army would land at Kinsale, sent by the most powerful Catholic sovereign in Europe, to support the Catholic rebels of Ulster in their campaign against Elizabeth, the Protestant anti-Christ. In future, it would be difficult to separate religious and political motives in the Irish struggle against English dominance. For the next four centuries, this connection between religion and nationalism would be a constant factor in Anglo-Irish affairs.

To a large extent the first modern invaders of Ireland – the Vikings and the Normans – were assimilated by traditional Gaelic society. But given the political and religious circumstances of the age, there was little danger that the sixteenth-century English conquerors would be similarly absorbed. To the Elizabethans, the Irish were an inferior race, whose mediocre political and social systems made them unworthy to occupy the fertile lands of the island.

The idea of replacing native landowners with English ones grew steadily more popular during the Tudor period. Several attempts were made during the reign of Elizabeth, the most ambitious being the 'Plantation' of

A contemporary Dutch drawing of a purported massacre of Ulster Protestants. Memories of the Reformation led most continental Protestants to side with their religious colleagues during the 1640s.

Munster during the 1580s. Over a thousand English settlers (including Spenser and Raleigh) were given estates, carved out of the former lordship of Desmond. But the large size of these holdings and dependence upon native tenants made them difficult to manage, especially since English control of the area was still tenuous. Most of these Munster planters abandoned their holdings during the turmoil of the Nine Years War.

The most successful colonisation attempt was a direct result of this war of the 1590s. While Hugh O'Neill and his allies had been allowed to keep most of their lands in Ulster, after 1603 many were not content to be mere landlords. In despair, Hugh abandoned Ireland for the continent, leaving in 1607 with most of his former sub-chieftains. This 'Flight of the Earls' left most of Ulster in the hands of the English government, since the lands of the exiles were declared forfeit to the crown.

The new English king was thus presented with an ideal opportunity for plantation. When he succeeded his spinster cousin Elizabeth in 1603, James I had already ruled as king of Scotland for thirty-five years. Since Ulster was so close to his own country, James naturally thought in terms of encouraging Scottish settlement there. Even before the Flight of the Earls, he had granted most of the modern counties of Antrim and Down to two court favourites, James Hamilton and Hugh Montgomery. These two men had established a thriving colony in the north-east, bringing over large numbers of merchants, craftsmen and small farmers from southern Scotland.

In view of the success of Hamilton and Montgomery, James decided to colonise those parts of Ulster abandoned by O'Neill and his allies. The province was divided into counties, and government surveyors mapped the areas to be settled. Certain locations were designated for towns. In the countryside, English and Scottish gentlemen were to be given estates of 2,000 acres at very low rent, provided that they promised to bring over tenants from Britain to work the land.

Compared to earlier Elizabethan efforts, the Plantation of Ulster was a resounding success. Over 40,000 settlers were attracted to the province between 1610 and 1630. Most of these came from the Scottish lowlands, where poor economic conditions provided a powerful stimulus for migration.

Within a generation these newcomers transformed the Ulster landscape. Small, well-tilled fields replaced the open pastures of the previous century. The large woods of Ulster were cleared, making room for hundreds of new farms. An English-style market economy developed, and new towns such as Enniskillen, Omagh and Belfast prospered.

The English had long viewed plantation as the best way to control Ireland. The Ulster Plantation, however, created almost as many problems as it solved. For one thing, it proved impossible to displace the native inhabitants completely. Despite the large number of immigrants, there were never enough Scottish or English settlers to farm every section of every estate. A

The Fair Geraldine. Elizabeth Fitzgerald was the daughter of Garret óg Fitzgerald, ninth Earl of Kildare, and the sister of the ill-fated Silken Thomas.

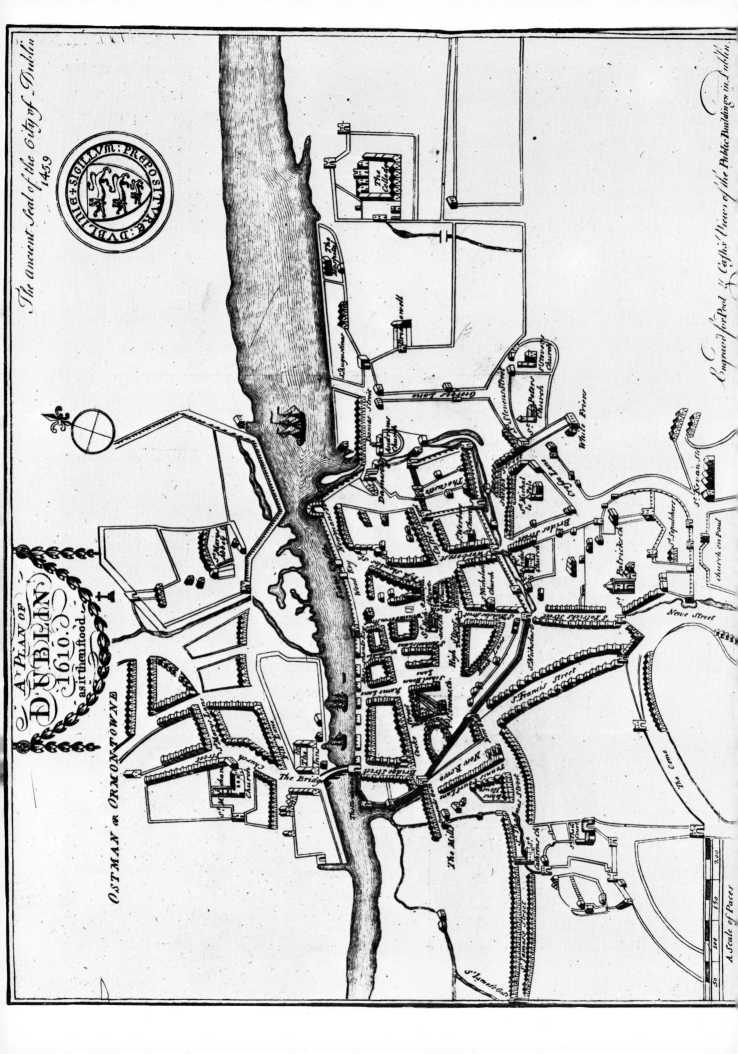

The ancient Seal of the City of Dublin 1459

SIGILLVM: PRGPOSITVRE: DVBLINIE

A PLAN of DUBLIN 1610 as it then stood.

OSTMAN or ORMONTOWNE

The Bridge

Engraved for Pool & Cash's Views of the Public Buildings in Dublin.

A Scale of Paces

50 100 150 200

Withdraw your scouring stick. · *Shorten your scouring stick.* · *Return your scouring stick.*

Recover your Musket. · *Poize your Musket and recover your Rest.* · *Rest your Musket.*

Draw out your match. · *Blow your match.* · *Cock your match.*

substantial number of Irish tenants were retained; more were hired as farm labourers. The result was that the natives remained a sizable and troublesome minority in the province, 'a political liability, but an economic necessity'. Indeed, Gaels remained in the majority in more remote areas such as Donegal and Cavan, since few settlers were willing to risk their lives in these less-secure places.

For better or worse, the Ulster Plantation introduced a new element into Irish society. The seventeenth-century Scottish settlers were a proud and ambitious people, whose culture and values differed greatly from the Gaelic inhabitants whom they had partially displaced.

Religion proved to be the distinction of crucial importance. Most of the newcomers were Presbyterians, followers of the teachings of John Calvin and John Knox. Unlike both Catholics and Anglicans, the Presbyterians eliminated bishops and priests from their

A soldier of Cromwell's New Model Army. This efficient and well-led force easily routed the Catholic Irish opposition during the period 1649–51.

The siege of Drogheda, 1649. This print shows Cromwell and his officers before the city during the preliminary bombardment.

Dublin in 1610. This map was made by John Speed.

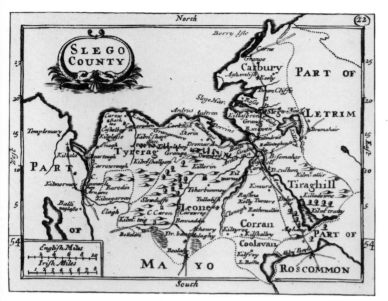

A seventeenth-century map of Co. Sligo, showing roads and towns developed largely by the English. By 1680 accurate maps of all parts of the country were available.

church structure, allowing leading members of each congregation to choose clergymen and administer the affairs of the community. Lay control was combined with emphasis on the Bible as the source of all religious inspiration, and a belief that God had 'predestined' certain souls for Eternal Glory and others for the Fires of Hell.

In the hostile Ulster colonial situation, it was easy for the average Presbyterian settler to locate this dividing line between salvation and damnation. Outsiders themselves, the Presbyterians treated the Irish-speaking natives of the province as outcasts. For their part, Ulster Catholics were just as narrow in their beliefs. In this case religious distaste was mixed with hatred for those who had taken their lands and reduced them to economic subservience.

The Catholic rebellion of 1641 was the almost inevitable result of this friction. All over Ulster, planters were driven from their homes and killed; houses and farms were destroyed, as their inhabitants fled to the safety of the walled towns. But thanks to British military superiority, the Plantation was able to survive this outburst. The settlers remained in Ulster, building a prosperous economic community that soon made Ulster the richest of the four Irish provinces. Religious animosities, however, remained. Three centuries later, Protestant and Catholic Ulstermen would harbour all the ill-will, fear and bitterness of their seventeenth-century ancestors.

The English conquest of Ireland was achieved in two distinct stages. During the sixteenth century, the Tudors took firm political control of the country. The seventeenth century, on the other hand, witnessed a conquest of another kind. Beginning with the Ulster

Plantation, ownership of land was gradually removed from native hands. By 1700 almost 90 per cent of the land of Ireland was owned by non-Catholics of British origin.

Native adherence to the Catholic religion was largely responsible for this massive transfer of property. 'Papists' became increasingly suspect in the eyes of the English Parliamentary leaders who came to dominate British politics during the seventeenth century. As a result, English officials took advantage of every legal pretext to dispossess Catholic landowners.

This process reached a peak during the 1650s, after parliament had ordered the execution of King Charles I and named Oliver Cromwell as Lord Protector. Cromwell detested Catholicism, and waged a brutal campaign against Catholic Royalists in Ireland during the winter of 1649–50. After breaking the siege of Drogheda in September 1649, he ordered that all 3,000 of its defendants be put to the sword. 'I am persuaded', he wrote to parliament, 'that this is a righteous judgement of God upon these barbarous wretches.'[7]

Given such behaviour, it is not surprising that Cromwell devised an equally drastic solution to the Irish land question. The Lord Protector gave the Catholic landowners of Leinster, Munster, and western Ulster the option of going 'to Hell or to Connaught'. Those who chose to stay out of hell were instructed to surrender their estates and remove themselves and their families to the western province, where they would be given holdings of 'similar' value. In view of the poverty of Connaught this was clearly impossible, even if the landowners already there had been willing to step aside.

Such considerations did not really trouble Cromwell. To him Ireland was nothing more than a vacant lot, one which could be used to reward various Englishmen who had helped his Parliamentary Army win the English Civil War. About six million acres of Irish land were distributed among some three thousand Cromwellian supporters.

At first Cromwell intended that these areas would be colonised in the Ulster fashion. But few Britons could be enticed to settle on these newly-acquired properties. As a result the Cromwellian confiscations of the 1650s provided merely a landlord caste for Ireland, one which depended almost entirely upon native Irish tenants. For the next two and a half centuries, the descendants of these three thousand Cromwellian landlords would form the backbone of the Irish ruling class.

The Stuart monarchy was restored in 1660, when Charles II, the new king, was invited to return by parliament. While he did promise to restore the old Irish landowners to their estates, he was unwilling to offend the English parliament, many of whose members now owned land in Ireland. As a result, most of the landlords created by Cromwell kept their Irish estates.

Despite the confiscations of the sixteenth and seventeenth centuries, Irish Catholics were not completely without influence after 1660. A certain number of the Catholic descendants of Gaelo-Norman lords and

Oliver Plunkett (1625–1681), Catholic Bishop of Drogheda who was executed by the government for treason. A man of great piety, he was canonised by the Vatican in 1976.

The new king, William III, realised that the struggle for the English throne would have to be carried to Ireland. He himself travelled to Ireland in June 1690, where his own superior military skills helped the Williamite forces win the Battle of the Boyne, fought in July 1690. Although James II fled to France soon after this battle, Irish resistance continued for over a year. Catholic hopes were finally quenched at the Battle of Aughrim (Co. Galway), fought on 12 July 1691, a date still commemorated annually by Ulster Protestants.

The War of the Two Kings was finally concluded by the Treaty of Limerick, signed in October 1691. In retrospect, the most important feature of this document was the clause which allowed the most able Irish general, Patrick Sarsfield, to emigrate to France with 12,000 of his soldiers. While Baron von Ginkel, the Williamite commander in chief, was severely criticised in England for this apparent leniency, the Irish emigration was in fact a blessing in disguise. For one thing, the flight of so many of the surviving Catholic landlords made possible the confiscation of most of the land in Connaught. By 1700 there were only a handful of Catholic proprietors in Ireland.

Robert Boyle (1627–1691), the famous physicist, who was born in Co. Waterford, where his father had enormous estates.

Gaelic chieftains had managed to retain at least a portion of their estates, particularly in Connaught. Moreover, Irish Catholics could count upon the support of Catholic France, and economic and social links were maintained between that country and the west of Ireland.

Catholic hopes received a boost in 1685, when James II succeeded his brother Charles II as king of England, Scotland and Ireland. A fervent Catholic, James was determined to restore his faith in his kingdoms, an ambition which seemed to bode well for Catholic Ireland. The English parliament and the English people, however, would not accept a return to Catholicism, and in the bloodless revolution of 1688, James II was replaced by the Protestant Dutch prince, William of Orange, husband of James's daughter Mary.

While English popular opinion drove him from his throne, James II realised that he could still depend upon Irish Catholics if he attempted to regain his position. After fleeing first to France, he landed in Cork in March 1689, accompanied by a party of loyal English supporters and a coterie of French military officers. Within a year he had raised an army of some 25,000 men from the ranks of Irish Catholics.

Irish 'Wild Geese', soldiers in the army of Swedish King Gustavus Adolphus, c. 1625.

The Treaty of Limerick sounded a death knell for the Catholic aristocracy. With Sarsfield to France went the best-educated and most politically-conscious Catholics in Ireland. Deprived of their traditional leaders, the masses were in no position to oppose the political and economic hegemony imposed by the English in Ireland.

The political turbulence of the sixteenth and seventeenth centuries brought a great deal of social change to Ireland. While the greatest transformation took place in Ulster, the entire country took on a new appearance. New towns were created, roads were built and rebuilt, and the surviving tracts of woodland were cut down. By 1700 much of the countryside looked like it does today, with green fields separated by hedges, and peasant cottages not terribly different from those still common in the early twentieth century. The system of shires introduced by the English was now firmly established, so much so that the names of the thirty-two counties were used by both strangers and local inhabitants as the basic signposts of Irish geography.

English influence was pervasive. Thanks to military superiority, administrative efficiency and unbridled ambition, the intruders had converted tenuous political control into total social and economic dominance. English landlords had displaced both Gaelo-Norman lords and Gaelic chieftains as the ruling class of the island. In virtually all spheres of Irish life, the native population was in a position of subservience.

There is a certain similarity between English attitudes towards Ireland during this period and American attitudes towards the native Indian population during the nineteenth century. Both the Irish and the Indians were considered inferior peoples who deserved nothing more than subjection. In both cases land was stolen, treaties were broken, and people were uprooted. In both cases naked force was exercised in the name of 'progress'.

The Irish, however, had one great advantage over the North American Indians: numbers. A million-odd people spread out over thousands of miles, the Indians stood little chance against the millions of Europeans invading their homelands. Three million Irish people, on the other hand, were concentrated on one small island, controlled by an alien aristocracy whose numbers never exceeded five hundred thousand. England in 1700 may have controlled the land and government of Ireland, but it possessed neither the support nor affection of most of its people. Most shared the sentiments of the seventeenth-century Gaelic poet who wrote:

May we never taste of death nor quit this vale of tears
Until we see the English go begging down the years;
Packs on their backs to earn a penny pay,
In little leaking boots, as we went in our day.

Time has o'erthrown, the wind has blown away
Alexander, Caesar, such great names as they.
See Troy and Tara where in grass they lie –
So even the very English yet might die![8]

This Ormond mansion in Carrick-on-Suir, Co. Tipperary, with its windows and non-defensive construction, was a sign of more peaceful times. It was begun in 1568.

5—Ireland in the Eighteenth Century

On Tuesday last Mr Handel's Sacred Grand Oratorio, the Messiah, *was performed at the New Musick-Hall in Fishamble-street; the best judges allowed it to be the most finished piece of Musick. Words are wanting to express the exquisite delight it afforded to the admiring crowded Audience. The Sublime, the Grand and the Tender, adapted to the most elevated, majestik and moving words, conspired to transport and charm the ravished Heart and Ear.*

from *Faulkner's Dublin Journal*, 17 April 1742.

The fact that the *Messiah* received its first public performance in Dublin gives some indication of the changes that had taken place in eighteenth-century Ireland. One hundred years earlier, the appearance of a leading composer of the English court in Ireland would have been unimaginable. Seventeenth-century Dublin was a garrison city, the provincial headquarters for what was essentially a government of military occupation. By 1742, however, this same city had become an integral part of the English world, 'the second city of the British Empire'.

A thriving seaport, a bustling community with nearly 150,000 inhabitants, Dublin was eighteenth-century Europe's fifth largest city, larger than Rome or Amsterdam. Both its physical appearance and its cultural life reflected this prosperity. Dublin in 1742 possessed nearly as many bookshops and theatres as London, while construction had already begun on many of the magnificent public buildings which have remained city landmarks to the present day.

The brilliance of the Irish capital was in large measure the work of its evolving ruling class, the so-called 'Anglo-Irish'. This group was even more of a mixed breed than its name suggests. It included descendants of Norman lords, Tudor government officials, Cromwellian adventurers, and even members of a few Gaelic families who had been clever enough shift their religious and political loyalties at the crucial moment. By the middle of the eighteenth century, however, these various fragments had fused to form a distinct social class, one which owned nearly all the land in the country as well as most of its commercial and industrial enterprises. Few sobriquets have been more accurate than the one which was coined to describe this aristocratic group: the Ascendancy.

Designed by James Gandon, the Custom House was built along the north bank of the Liffey during the 1780s at a cost of over £200,000. This magnificent edifice served as a model for the architects of the Capitol building in Washington D.C. Today it is still occupied by government offices, and remains the single most impressive public building in Dublin.

Although the Ascendancy often displayed a spirit of independence, particularly towards the end of the eighteenth century, its members never really forswore their English antecedents. Throughout the 1700s, Anglo-Irish cultural patterns remained very similar to English ones; Irish aristocrats looked to London for social leadership, just as their English counterparts in Norfolk or Devon did. Indeed, the Ascendancy never forgot how it had come by its position, or that its continued existence ultimately depended upon British military support.

Because Irish society was so dominated by this alien caste, one tends to assume that the eighteenth century was an unhappy one for most Irishmen. The truth, however, is not quite so simple. The social and economic structure of the country differed little from the contemporary European norm; if the Ascendancy controlled a disproportionate share of Irish wealth, so did the ruling classes in other European countries, be

A pillar of the Ascendancy, William Conolly (c. 1675–1729) was an important political figure who served for a time as Speaker of the Irish House of Commons. He was also one of the country's wealthiest landowners, although a totally self-made man, and built Castletown House in Co. Kildare, the most spectacular mansion constructed during the Georgian period.

Many examples of Georgian architecture survive in the streets of modern Dublin. This row of what were once elegant town houses is in Merrion Square.

they native or alien. In fact, the first seven decades of the eighteenth century was one of general economic prosperity, a prosperity which was shared in some measure by nearly all Irishmen. Throughout this time, there was only one brief period (1739–41) of serious economic depression.

The eighteenth century brought more than prosperity to Ireland. Its greatest blessing was peace. For nearly two hundred years Ireland had endured an almost endless series of wars, struggles accompanied by widespread destruction and property confiscations. But between 1691 and 1797 not a single battle was fought on Irish soil. This happy fact mattered far more to the average Irishman of the eighteenth century than the national origins of his landlord or employer.

While most members of the Ascendancy were of English origin, religion was its real badge of distinction. By 1700 it was almost impossible to claim membership of the upper class unless one was an adherent of the Protestant Church of Ireland. From this point onward,

Carton House, Co. Kildare. Designed by Richard Cassels for the Dukes of Leinster, it is a perfect reflection of the new sense of security felt by the Ascendancy in eighteenth-century Ireland. No longer did they regard their homes as fortified positions: henceforth they were to be expressions of opulence and grandeur.

James Gandon (1743–1823), the architect of the Custom House. Gandon also designed the Four Courts and the King's Inns, two other notable landmarks of Georgian Dublin.

religion became the crucial social denominator in Irish life, much as colour would later serve a similar purpose in the southern USA and modern South Africa.

This religious polarisation had become more extreme after James II's unsuccessful attempt to recover his English throne by way of Ireland. Memories of the Boyne and Aughrim were etched deeply upon the Anglo-Irish mind, where they served as fitting proof of the maxim that the Catholic Irish could never be trusted.

The Penal Laws, the anti-Catholic legislation enacted by the Ascendancy-controlled Irish parliament, were a natural consequence of the events of the early 1690s. As long as James II and his heirs remained alive and well in France, the threat of a Stuart revival remained. The Anglo-Irish lived in constant fear of this prospect; every year they expected a French army to land somewhere in the south. In such circumstances they considered the Penal Laws a necessary precaution that could prove the key to their own survival.

This legislation was framed with two broad purposes in mind: to disarm, disinherit, and discredit the Catholic population as a whole, and to exterminate the last remnants of the Catholic aristocracy. Many laws were directed against the practice of the Catholic religion. All priests had to register with the government, while bishops were forbidden to remain in the country. No Catholic was allowed to maintain a school, or send his children abroad for education. Intermarriage was discouraged; if a Protestant were to marry a Catholic, the former forfeited all titles and claims to property.

Equally important were those laws which deprived Catholics of civil rights. All but the most menial of government positions were closed to those who would not take an Oath of Allegiance accepting the English monarch as head of the Church of Ireland. Catholics were denied all voting privileges. Landowners were required to divide their estates equally among their sons; if, however, an eldest son decided to become a Protestant, he could inherit the entire property! Catholics could not purchase land, nor hold leases for longer than thirty-one years.

On paper, the Penal legislation seems a formidable catalogue of discrimination. The code was rather strictly implemented during the first three decades of the century, until the Hanoverian King George I was securely placed upon the British throne. After 1730, however, the threat of a possible Irish invasion and Stuart restoration became increasingly remote. As a result, the Penal Laws were enforced with much less

Luke Gardiner (Lord Mountjoy) was responsible for the passing of the Catholic Relief Act 1778, the most significant repeal of the Penal Laws during the eighteenth century. Ironically, he was killed fighting against the Catholic United Irishmen at the Battle of Vinegar Hill in Co. Wexford in 1798.

One by one, the Penal Laws were repealed. Those few Catholics wealthy enough to fulfil the property qualification regained the right to vote in 1793, by which date Catholics could purchase land freely and practise their religion without hindrance. By the end of the century the only real civil rights denied to Catholics were the freedoms to sit in parliament and to hold high government and army posts.

In retrospect, the most effective of the Penal Laws were those which related to land inheritance. Many Catholic landowners, forced to choose between their consciences and the continued prosperity of their families, decided in favour of the latter. While such reluctant converts displayed little zeal for their new religion, their children and grandchildren often became ardent Protestants. It is estimated that over half the Catholic landed families of 1700 shifted religious allegiance during the course of the century. By 1800 less than 5 per cent of the land of Ireland was owned by Catholics.

The conversion of so many Catholic landowners combined with the decision of many Catholic aristocrats to seek their fortune in the service of continental armies to strip the country of its traditional upper class. Into this vacuum stepped the clergy of the Irish Catholic Church. In contrast to landowners who abandoned their religion and 'Wild Geese' who abandoned their country, many Irish priests risked their freedom and their lives to keep the Catholic faith alive in the hearts and minds of the people. Preaching to the peasantry in the native language and quite willing to celebrate Mass in 'chapels' that were little better than hovels, these priests bore more resemblance to their counterparts in early Christian Rome than to their immediate Irish predecessors.

rigour. Government officials came to realise that full implementation was impossible, in view of the continued allegiance given by most Irish people to the Catholic Church. By 1751 a Catholic bishop charged with treason could admit openly in court that over twenty other bishops were operating in the country – and still be acquitted!

Composed almost entirely of Irish Catholics, the Irish Brigade was considered one of the best in the French army, and played a decisive role in the French victory at Fontenoy in 1745. Among the 'Wild Geese' who fought in that battle was one Richard Hennessy (1720–1800). He later settled in Cognac and established the distillery which still produces the brandy which bears his name.

THE IRISH BRIGADE.
CHRISTMAS AFTER THE BATTLE OF FONTENOY.

Cork grew rapidly during the eighteenth century and became a thriving port, exporting meat and butter to both Europe and America.

The ordinary people repaid this dedication with a degree of religious devotion unknown in Ireland before this period. 'The people give the fruit of their labours liberally to me', one Connaught priest told a French traveller, 'and I give them my time, my care, and my entire soul. . . . Between us there is a ceaseless exchange of feelings of affection.'[1]

During the sixteenth and seventeenth centuries, improved sailing techniques had helped make Ireland more accessible to its European neighbours. But increased English political control was only one result of this revolution in communications. Equally important was the dramatic increase in foreign trade, trade which was an important factor in the prosperity of both town and country during the eighteenth century.

Like the North American colonies, Ireland endured the British mercantile system, which demanded that local economic interests be sacrificed for the greater good of the 'mother' country. The Westminster parliament passed laws which restricted trade in those areas which were considered a threat to English merchants and producers. But such legislation did not hinder economic development as much as push it in certain specific directions. For example, the export of live cattle from Ireland was forbidden during the 1660s.

Irish merchants responded by shifting emphasis to salted beef. New markets were found in North America and continental Europe, and by 1750 provisions were the country's second most valuable export. Much of this trade in salted beef passed through Cork. By 1800 that city could claim 80,000 inhabitants, along with its reputation as the slaughterhouse of Ireland.

The eighteenth century also witnessed rapid expansion in internal trade. It was a period of great building activity, during which many of the towns of the country began to take on their modern appearance. Improved roads helped to make places such as Mullingar and Ballinasloe important commercial centres. By 1803 over 125 different towns were holding regular fairs and markets.

Most of the profits of this urban development, of course, found their way into the hands of merchants and entrepreneurs, an increasing number of whom were Catholic. The Penal Laws had not severely restricted Catholic involvement in commerce; Galway and Waterford were two cities whose business life were dominated by Catholics. A large majority of city dwellers, however, lived in poverty, collecting miserable wages and living and working in miserable conditions. Although it was the economic as well as political capital of the country, Dublin possessed some of the worst slums in Europe. 'In my week in Dublin', wrote a Frenchman who visited the city in 1796, 'I have seen more mud, rags, and wretchedness than in my whole life in Paris!'[2]

The production of linen cloth from flax was the single most important Irish industry of the eighteenth century. Little linen was produced in Great Britain; in fact the London government did much to encourage the growth of this industry by setting up an Irish Linen Board in 1711. With a virtual monopoly of the English market, Irish linen production expanded at a fantastic rate, from $2\frac{1}{2}$ million yards in 1720 to over 37 million in 1790. By 1788 linen accounted for an amazing 70 per cent of all Irish exports.

Despite its success, this particular industry remained highly localised. It was centred around the Lagan Valley in Ulster; the four counties of Antrim, Armagh, Down and Londonderry usually accounted for two-thirds of Irish linen sales. Until the development of the factory system at the end of the century, most cloth was woven by the farming families who actually grew the flax. Travelling merchants then purchased the cloth and brought it to the linen markets, which were important features of most Ulster towns. At first most finished cloth was exported from Dublin, but the growing Ulster ports of Belfast and Londonderry became equally important after 1750.

Arthur Guinness (1725–1803) very nearly commenced operations in Wales before buying the Rainsford brewery at St James's Gate in Dublin in 1759. By the end of the century, Guinness had one of the country's largest operations, and had already begun exporting stout and porter to England.

Belfast was another town which prospered during the Georgian period; its economy was based largely upon the export of linen. Industrialisation, however, was still decades away when this bucolic print was made in 1783.

Most of the farmers and merchants involved in the Ulster linen industry were Presbyterians, descendants of the Scottish settlers of the previous century. Thanks to the extra income which the sale of linen cloth provided, the average 'Scotch-Irish' farmer of the north-east was able to enjoy a much higher standard of living than his southern counterpart. Unfortunately, this helped to widen the cultural gap which religion had already formed between Catholic and Presbyterian Irishmen.

> Imagine four walls of dried mud (which the rain, as it falls, easily restores to its primitive condition) having for its roof a little straw or some sods, for its chimney a hole cut in the roof, or very frequently the door through which alone the smoke finds an issue. One single apartment contains father, mother, children and sometimes a grandfather or a grandmother. There is no furniture in the wretched hovel; a single bed of straw serves the entire family. In the midst of all lies a dirty pig, the only thriving inhabitant of the place, for he lives in filth.[3]

Nearly every Irish travelogue of this period contains similar descriptions of Irish hovels. Despite the economic progress of the eighteenth century, poverty remained the normal condition of existence for well over half of the Irish people. For the poorer class of Irish tenants and agricultural labourers life had few attractions. Many families lived on tiny plots of less than ten acres, subsisting almost entirely on diets of potatoes and milk, and raising a few pigs or sheep to pay the annual rent. Farming methods remained almost medieval.

Conditions worsened as the century drew to a close. After 1770 the Irish population began to increase at the fantastic rate of 12 per cent per decade. This phenomenal growth led to continual subdivision of already small holdings, and a further deterioration of living standards.

Not all Irish tenants, however, lived in such misery. The western part of the country was considerably poorer than the east. Many of the richer farmlands of Leinster and eastern Munster were occupied by tenants prosperous enough to be called 'strong farmers'. Working from thirty to a hundred acres, and producing marketable commodities such as wheat and dairy products, many families of this class were able to live in frugal comfort.

No matter what their economic situation, all Irish farmers shared a similar responsibility: payment of rent. Often this involved several grades of middlemen as well as the land-owner and the farmer. Non-payment invariably led to eviction, especially since the rapidly-increasing population created an increased demand for land. Even if a tenant paid his rent regularly, he usually had no guarantee of tenure; when his lease expired he might well be replaced by another tenant willing to pay a higher rent. Only in Ulster, where a large percentage of tenants were of Scottish descent, did the peasantry have any protection against such removal. The so-called 'Ulster Custom' dated back to the Plantation era, and while it had no force in law, it prevented eviction of a tenant as long as he paid his rent regularly.

The peaceful conditions of the eighteenth century stimulated internal trade. Market towns such as Kilmallock, Co. Limerick took on new commercial importance.

The production of linen from flax was a family activity, as this eighteenth-century Ulster print shows. Here the flax is being treated and prepared for spinning.

Nevertheless, most of the Irish peasantry was mired in its own peculiar form of serfdom, one which found parallels in eastern rather than western Europe. Arthur Young, the English agricultural reformer, made these observations while visiting Ireland in 1776:

> A landlord in Ireland can scarcely invent an order which a servant, labourer, or cottier dares to refuse to execute. Disrespect or anything tending towards sauciness he may punish with his cane or his horsewhip with the most perfect security. . . . Landlords of consequence have assured me that many of their cottiers would think themselves honoured by having their wives or daughters sent for to the bed of their masters, a mark of slavery that proves the oppression under which such people live.[4]

In such circumstances it is not surprising that the eighteenth century saw the growth of secret societies, groups of frustrated tenants and labourers who used intimidation, arson, and sometimes armed force against their oppressors. Secret societies bore such colourful names as Blackfeet, Whiteboys and Hearts of Oak, and tended to be most active in relatively prosperous areas where the tenantry could appreciate the difference between good and lean years. While they might terrorise exceptionally venal landlords and their agents, secret societies more often attacked tithe proctors, the agents of the Church of Ireland who collected 'contributions' from all Irishmen, regardless of religion.

These secret societies never coalesced into a national movement; their actions were always tied to particular local grievances. The eighteenth century saw no large-scale peasant revolt in Ireland. Indeed, compared to what had gone before and what was to follow, this period was a fairly comfortable one for the average rural family. Population growth did not yet outstrip the country's resources; as a result there was usually enough food for everyone. Daily life was not without its joys. Holidays, fairs and even wakes were festive occasions, spiced by music, dancing and the inevitable *usquebaugh*. Even Young was moved to comment that the people were 'infinitely more cheerful and lively than anything we commonly see in England.'[5]

77

*Living conditions for a majority of the Irish people remained abysmal.
This drawing of a peasant cottage in the west was made during the 1780s.*

*Working conditions for the mass of the people remained hard. This
engraving, made towards the end of the century, shows Irish peasants
footing turf, a back-breaking exercise but a necessary one : turf (or peat)
was the only fuel available to them.*

*John Wesley (1703–1791), the founder of Methodism, first visited
Ireland in 1747, and made several other missionary trips to Ireland. He
had little good to say about the country, and was particularly
disconcerted by the religious views of its inhabitants. 'Oh what a harvest
might be in Ireland,' Wesley wrote prophetically, 'did not the
Protestants hate Christianity worse than either Popery or Heathenism'.*

*Even for the poorer classes life was not without its lighter moments.
During the eighteenth century the 'public house' became a prominent
feature of Irish life.*

INTERIOR OF AN IRISH COUNTRY INN.

The fact that the Irish language contributed the word 'whiskey' to its English counterpart during this period reveals much about both cultures. By the end of the eighteenth century the boisterous, indolent, and often intoxicated Irishman was a stereotype of the English stage. No doubt this caricature fitted many Irishmen. But they were members of what one historian has called a 'culturally-deprived and psychologically-alienated' group.[6] It was hard to fault the average Irish worker for taking pleasure in such leisure activities in a society which offered him so few tangible economic rewards.

As a result of increased demand for land and generally high agricultural prices, rents increased sixfold during the eighteenth century. The beneficiaries were the Anglo-Irish landlords of the country, who enjoyed a degree of affluence rarely seen before in the country. Many of the 'Big Houses' which still dot the Irish landscape were built during this period. While there were a considerable number of absentee landlords, the large majority lived in Ireland, either on their estates or in town houses in Dublin and the other cities.

Many Irish landlords seem to have shared the same taste for leisure as their peasantry. One observer remarked that 'the chase, the bottle and the pipe' were the three great enjoyments of the gentry.[7] Lavish hospitality became a trade-mark of the class, and the visitor to the average Big House needed both a good appetite and the ability to consume large quantities of claret. One well-to-do Tipperary landlord even went into frugal exile for seven years so that he could entertain his friends properly upon his return. 'This is your castle', he would tell visitors, 'Here you are to command as absolutely as in your own house. From this moment you are never to know me as master of the house, and only consider me one of the guests.'[8]

The actress Peg Woffington was successively the darling of Dublin and London audiences in the middle years of the century. She was a great comedienne, an intelligent and witty conversationalist, and a celebrated mistress of, among others, the great English actor David Garrick.

The moral code was not as rigorous in Georgian Ireland as it would become in the next century, and cartoons such as this one were regularly printed and published in Dublin.

Decorative plasterwork was a major feature of Georgian architecture; as much care and attention went into interior as exterior design. This magnificent stairwell is in Belvedere House, Dublin.

Affluent societies usually produce a fair share of eccentric personalities; as the above example shows, Ascendancy Ireland was no exception. It produced Buck Whaley, a reckless gambler who managed to squander a large family fortune, but not before he had won £15,000 in 1790 from friends who bet him that he could not travel to Jerusalem and back in less than two years. More anti-social behaviour was demonstrated by George Robert Fitzgerald, a Mayo landlord who chained his father to a bear for entertainment, and committed a wide range of murderous atrocities before meeting with the hangman in Castlebar in 1789.

These examples, of course, represent only one side of the Ascendancy. Many landlords took deep personal interest in their estates, spending heavily on land drainage, fencing, liming and other improvements. Some built houses for their tenants and kept rents as low as possible so as to encourage productivity. Others, like Robert French of Galway, purchased looms and spinning wheels for their tenants, so that they might engage in linen production.

This public spirit was not confined to rural areas. In 1731 a group of 'improving' landlords joined with leading merchants to form the Dublin Society (later the Royal Dublin Society), an organisation which aimed to promote Irish agriculture and industry. One of the first European institutions of its kind, the RDS held regular exhibitions and did much to spread knowledge of the latest agricultural developments throughout the country.

The British House of Commons, 1833. In the right foreground, the Duke of Wellington stands with his right arm resting on the edge of the benches. In the centre, Daniel O'Connell is about to sit down.

The Battle of the Boyne, 1690. This painting, by the Dutch master Jan Wyck, shows the death of Marshal Schomberg, one of King William's leading generals.

A view of Dublin in 1832, by Thomas Roberts. Just north of the Liffey in this print is the Four Courts, designed by James Gandon.

Dublin remained the focal point of Anglo-Irish life. When the Irish parliament was in session every second winter, the capital was filled with gentry from all parts of the country. The Vice-Regal Lodge in the Phoenix Park was the scene of numerous state dinners and lavish balls; it was not unusual for its resident, the lord lieutenant (as the king's representative in Ireland was now called) to spend £20,000 annually on entertainment. The city offered a wide variety of evening activities, with regular performances of plays and concerts. Smock Alley, eighteenth-century Dublin's most successful theatre, was operated for a time by Thomas Sheridan, father of Richard Brinsley Sheridan.

The younger Sheridan was himself part of an extraordinary flowering of literary and intellectual life in the new Dublin. Trinity College, the university established in the city in 1591 by Elizabeth, assumed a pivotal position; every major literary and intellectual figure of Ascendancy Ireland passed through its gates at some time or other: George Berkeley became one of the most influential figures in the history of European philosophy; Oliver Goldsmith achieved eminence both as a novelist and a dramatist, while his Trinity contemporary, Edmund Burke, was one of the most prominent political thinkers in late eighteenth-century Europe. There was also, of course, Jonathan Swift. Although he spent his formative years in England, Swift was a native of Dublin and spent over thirty years in the city as Dean of St Patrick's, the Anglican cathedral. Today he is remembered for *Gulliver's Travels*, but he was also the foremost satirist of his age. Indeed, there have been few periods, before or since, when the Irish capital contributed so many figures of genius to the store of European culture.

Their position as a ruling caste helped to make the Anglo-Irish increasingly aware of their own identity, and increasingly unhappy with the manner in which

Clergyman, novelist, pamphleteer and political activist, Jonathan Swift (1667–1745) was in many ways the conscience of Ascendancy Ireland, a 'cantankerous genius' deeply involved in the affairs of his country.

Trinity College, Dublin grew and prospered during the eighteenth century, and became one of the major universities in the British Isles. The college library shown here was completed in the 1720s, and was the largest in the country.

Ireland was governed. Although their loyalty to the crown was unshakable, many Ascendancy leaders felt confident of their ability to govern Ireland effectively with minimal interference from London. Swift served as spokesman for this group, which demanded increased powers for the Irish parliament:

> Were not the *People* of *Ireland* born as *Free* as those of *England*? Is not their *Parliament* as *fair* and as *Representative* of the *People* as that of *England*? Are they Subjects of the same King? Does not the same *Sun* shine on them? And have they not the same *God* for their *Protector*? Am I a *Free-Man* in England, and do I become a *Slave* in six hours by crossing the Channel?[9]

Alone among Britain's colonial possessions, Ireland possessed a legislative assembly that predated the Tudor re-conquest. The Irish parliament was created during the Middle Ages by the English administration based in Dublin; as such, it was closely patterned upon the Westminster model. It consisted of two Houses, Lords and Commons, and while the former could and did veto bills, the House of Commons was the real legislative battleground.

The Irish House of Commons consisted of 300 members, two from each county and two from each of 118 cities and boroughs. The sixty-four county MPs were elected by those Protestants who met fairly moderate property qualifications, although electoral results usually depended upon bribes, which were freely given and taken. Most borough seats were filled by members selected by small, self-perpetuating corporations, which were invariably controlled by local gentry. Many boroughs were little more than empty fields; the deserted village of Bannow, Co. Wexford, sent two members to parliament, the same number as thriving cities such as Belfast and Cork. The eighteenth-century Irish House of Commons was hardly a democratic assembly; the country's two and a half million Catholics were completely unrepresented in parliament.

While the Irish parliament had the power to make laws for the country, there were several important restrictions placed upon it. Most severe was the fact that the chief government official in the country, the lord lieutenant, was responsible to the king and the prime minister in London; parliament had no control over their appointment or behaviour. In addition, its legislative powers were restricted by a 1494 statute (Poynings' Law) which stipulated that all Irish bills had to be approved by the king and English privy council. Furthermore, a Declaratory Act passed in 1719 gave the English parliament the right to over-rule its Irish counterpart. These restrictions were deeply resented by the Anglo-Irish, who felt that they were the best judges of what was right for the country. Although the English administration usually kept the Irish House of Commons in line through tactful combination of bribery and patronage, a formidable 'Patriot' opposition gradually developed within the assembly, and came to be led in the 1770s by Henry Flood and Henry Grattan.

Leader of the 'Patriot' party in the Irish House of Commons, Henry Grattan (1746–1820) was a key figure in the successful struggle for Irish legislative independence. Unlike most of his Ascendancy colleagues, however, Grattan realised that this was a hollow victory as long as the Catholic majority remained unrepresented. Despite his efforts, Catholics continued to be denied political participation.

The Patriots put the British government in a difficult position. Although unwilling to concede the sort of autonomy they demanded, the English realised that their position in Ireland depended largely upon the good will of the Ascendancy. Realising the delicacy of its position, the government did what it could to accommodate the Patriots and to avoid a major crisis.

Just such a problem, however, developed during the 1770s, when George III was faced with the rebellion of the North American colonies. The American Revolution forced the British government to withdraw nearly all its troops from Ireland, and leave the defence of the country in the hands of 'Volunteer' units drawn from the ranks of the Anglo-Irish. There were strong links between the Volunteers and the Irish parliament; most of the leading officers in the militia were also members of the House of Commons.

As the American war moved towards its unsuccessful conclusion, trouble in Ireland was the last thing the British needed. In 1782 the Irish parliament was granted full legislative independence, as both Poynings' Law and the Declaratory Act of 1719 were repealed, and the Westminster parliament renounced forever its right to make laws for Ireland.

On the surface, the successful campaigns of the American colonists and the Irish Patriots were very similar. Both groups fought for and obtained the right to play an effective role in the governing of their countries. There was, however, a difference of crucial importance. The Americans desired a government of and for all residents of the Thirteen Colonies; the Anglo-Irish wanted merely to confirm their position as the dominant minority within Irish society. Henry Flood said as much in 1783:

> Ninety years ago four-fifths of Ireland were for King James. They were defeated. I rejoice in that defeat. The laws that followed were not laws of persecution; they were a political necessity. What will be the consequence if you give Catholics equal powers with Protestants? We will give all toleration to religion. We will not give them political power.[10]

During the last quarter of the eighteenth century, the Irish House of Commons was known as 'Grattan's Parliament', in honour of the most prominent Patriot

A Volunteer regiment gathers in Dungannon, Co. Tyrone, in 1782. The presence of this Ascendancy militia in Ireland during the period of the American Revolution was largely responsible for the British decision to concede wider powers to the Irish parliament.

But Grattan's Parliament was an edifice built on sand. Despite the efforts of Grattan and a few other MPs, it rarely exercised its new powers in constructive fashion. Traditional vested interests remained strong. No real reforms were made of the electoral system; no real attempt was made to wrest power away from the English administration based at Dublin Castle. Most Irish MPs had no real interest in the functions of their assembly, preferring the glitter of the social scene and patronage plums to legislative duties at College Green.

Grattan's Parliament was destined to be short-lived. Within two decades, both the native Irish and the British government would decide that continued political control of Ireland by the Ascendancy was both impractical and intolerable.

leader. Legislative independence set the real seal on the golden age of the Anglo-Irish, the Ascendancy, who for a century had presided over a country at peace, and had transformed Dublin into one of Europe's most elegant capitals.

Preceded by his beadle, the Speaker of the Irish House of Commons arrives to open a parliamentary session. Completed in 1735, the Irish parliament building on College Green was in its day the most splendid in Europe, 'much beyond that heap of confusion at Westminster', observed Arthur Young. After the Act of Union was passed in 1800, the building was sold to the Bank of Ireland, which still owns it.

6—The Birth of Nationalism

1   Men are born and remain free and equal in rights. . . .
2   The aim of every political association is the preservation of the
natural and inalienable rights of man; these rights are liberty, property,
security, and resistance to oppression. . . .
3   The source of all sovereignty resides essentially in the nation; no
group, no individual may exercise authority not emanating expressly
therefrom.

Declaration of the Rights of Man, Paris, 27 August 1789.

Arthur Dillon (1750–1794) commanded a crack regiment of the Irish Brigade and fought for the French against the British in America and the West Indies. He met his own death on the scaffold as a royalist sympathiser during the Reign of Terror.

Ad. Varin sculp.

Arthur DILLON

Servit la France dans la guerre d'Amérique.

GOUVERNEUR DE St CHRISTOPHE

Député, 1789. Vainqueur en Champagne, 1790.

Né à Braywick (Irlande), 1750.

+ sur l'échafaud, 1794.

Perhaps the most important single event in modern European history, the French Revolution presented Europeans for the first time with a government in which all citizens could participate. During the 1790s loyalty to the French nation replaced personal allegiance to the monarch as the guiding political principle in that country.

For two centuries there had been close ties between Catholic Ireland and Catholic France. Long after Sarsfield's regiment sailed for France in 1689, thousands of Irish volunteers continued to serve with the Irish Brigade, one of the most highly-regarded units in the French Army. Those Catholics who could afford to do so evaded the eighteenth-century Penal Laws by sending their children to French and Belgian colleges for education. Large quantities of wool continued to be smuggled to the continent from the west of Ireland.

Most of these connections, however, were with the France of the *ancien régime*. Most of the 'Wild Geese' in the French army remained loyal to Louis XVI until the bitter end; many Irish officers followed the king to the guillotine during the Reign of Terror.

During the 1790s, the anti-clerical policies of the French revolutionary government cost it further goodwill among Irish Catholics. Irish priests saw their former teachers and classmates stripped of power and position, and resolved that the French 'disease' would not infect their parishioners.

Ironically, the democratic ideals of *liberté, egalité, fraternité* received their greatest support from the Presbyterians of eastern Ulster. The Presbyterian Church had long nurtured a democratic tradition among its members, with self-governing congregations who despised authoritarian figures, be they Catholic popes or Anglican bishops. As the French Revolution became progressively more radical and anti-clerical, it received more and more support from the tenant farmers of Antrim and Down, and from the artisan class in the burgeoning city of Belfast.

PHŒNIX LODGE.

ost Humbly Dedicated to His Grace the Duke of Portland, Lord Lieutenant *of Ireland – by Tho.*

Published as the Act directs 1.st January 1783, by J.Walter Charing – Cross London, for the Author J.Milton in Dublin

Laid out at the city's edge during this period, Dublin's Phoenix Park was one of the largest in Europe. It contained the Vice-Regal Lodge, built in 1751 and extended in 1782, the official residence of the lord lieutenant in Ireland.

In Dublin the French Revolution received a certain amount of support from educated Protestants, as well as from a few middle-class Catholics. Although the Ascendancy as a group was totally opposed to democracy, there were some members of Protestant professional and commercial families who wanted significant changes made in the way that Ireland was governed. These radicals resented landlord dominance of the Irish parliament, and wanted wholesale reform that would make that legislature more democratic: abolition of 'rotten boroughs' (underpopulated 'towns' which sent MPs to parliament in spite of their size), increased representation for cities, and extension of voting rights to a wider section of the population.

The most influential of the Dublin radicals was a personable young barrister named Theobald Wolfe Tone. Despite his Protestant background, Tone sympathised completely with the Catholic struggle for equal citizenship. Indeed, in 1791 he was appointed secretary of the Catholic Committee, a pressure group formed by Catholic lawyers and merchants in Dublin to press for removal of the Penal Law which denied Catholics the right to vote. Under Tone's stewardship, the Committee achieved its main objective in 1793, when the London government, anxious to minimise its Irish difficulties while at war with France, forced a reluctant

Born and raised in Ireland, Edmund Burke (1729–1797) was one of the leading British political figures of his age, a powerful orator whose fame spread all over Europe. Despite his philosophical opposition to the French Revolution, Burke was at heart a liberal and gave strong support to those who demanded Irish political reform.

While stagecoaches connected Ireland's major cities by the end of the eighteenth century, methods of transport remained primitive, especially in remote western areas where roads were little more than dirt tracks.

Irish parliament to remove this disability. Catholics who met the property qualifications could now vote in parliamentary elections.

This concession satisfied most members of the Catholic Committee. Prosperous men with considerable wealth and property, they were as horrified as their Anglo-Irish counterparts by the increasingly radical course of events in France. Like the Ascendancy, these Catholic leaders had no desire to share political power with the masses.

Wolfe Tone was more sympathetic to democratic reform. He was also less than happy with the existing political connection between Great Britain and Ireland, a link which he once referred to as 'the never-failing source of all our political evils'.[1] While he was never the advocate of complete Irish independence which later nationalists claimed he was, Tone was interested in creating a new spirit of brotherhood among the Irish people. He despised the sectarian divisions of his society, and had little time for bigots of any religious persuasion. As he wrote in 1794, Tone hoped 'to unite the whole people of Ireland, to abolish the memory of all past dissensions, and to substitute the common name of Irishman in place of the denominations of Protestant, Catholic and Dissenter'.[2] It was, to say the least, an ambitious undertaking.

In 1791 Wolfe Tone had travelled to Belfast to establish links between the Dublin radicals and their Presbyterian counterparts in that city. One result of this contact between the two groups was the foundation of the Society of United Irishmen. The new organisation called for sweeping parliamentary reform, including universal manhood suffrage, and the ending of all forms of religious discrimination.

At first the United Irishmen functioned as a legal political association, with branches in most of the major towns. But by 1794 Britain was at war with France, and increasingly suspicious of the society's connections with French radicals. The organisation was proscribed and driven underground. This caused a decline in the number of members, but a hard core remained. These radicals now became convinced of the futility of peaceful political reform, and began to consider armed revolution as the only possible alternative.

In such circumstances it was almost inevitable that the French government and the United Irishmen should seek to make use of each other. In 1796 Wolfe Tone travelled to France, where he convinced the Directory that an Irish invasion could be the first step towards French military victory and the establishment of republican government in the British Isles.

These two prints were among the thirty drawn by English caricaturist George Cruikshank during the 1840s to illustrate an anti-nationalist history of the 1798 rising. All of the illustrations focus upon either Protestant gallantry (above) or Catholic atrocities (below).

In December 1796, 15,000 French troops under the leadership of General Hoche set sail for Ireland. Tone, who travelled with the expedition, had arranged that a general uprising would accompany the French landing. But fog and storm combined to disperse the armada long before it reached its destination. Only fourteen of forty-three ships reached Bantry Bay in the far south-west. Weather conditions remained so bad that even these chose to return to France rather than risk a landing, and with them went any real hope of a successful Irish rebellion.

Even before the failure of the Hoche expedition, the British government had decided to trust to more than nature for the defence of Ireland. Although the war with France kept much of the British army occupied elsewhere, a substantial military force was created in Ireland with the assistance of the Protestant gentry and tenants loyal to the crown. Now there was no talk of independence by the Ascendancy; the Anglo-Irish fully appreciated that their survival depended upon repulsion of the French threat and suppression of the United Irishmen. The latter was carried out with ruthless enthusiasm by the new militia during 1796 and 1797. Houses were burned, suspects were tortured, and brutality became the order of the day. During this period the country experienced its own Reign of Terror, which claimed several thousand innocent victims.

In fact these military efforts proved counter-productive. The climate of repression brought new recruits to the United Irishmen. Many of these were Catholic tenants who had little appreciation of the ideology of Wolfe Tone and the other leaders, but fully understood that the organisation offered them their best opportunity to lash out at the government and the hated gentry. It was no coincidence that the society prospered in Leinster and eastern Munster, the very areas where secret societies were traditionally most active. Despite Tone's hopes, the United Irishmen began to take on a markedly sectarian character.

Theobald Wolfe Tone (1763–1798), the spiritual father of modern Irish nationalism.

Like most major civil disturbances, the 1798 rebellion visited its share of woe upon Irish women, as this contemporary cartoon suggests.

THE NEWRY GIRL

The banner of the Mayo Legion, raised by the French when they landed at Killala in 1798. Unfortunately, the ragtag army that rallied around this flag was no match for British regulars at Ballinamuck.

Perhaps the most talented of all the United Irishmen leaders, Henry Joy McCracken (1767–1798) was a Protestant cotton manufacturer from Belfast who took to heart the ideals of the French Revolution. Sectarian rivalries, however, doomed the cause in Ulster. After a feeble rebellion in Antrim in June 1798, McCracken's small force surrendered and the Ulster leader was executed.

Although still reluctant to embark upon an actual rebellion without French help, the Executive Committee of the United Irishmen in Dublin decided that a rising should take place in May 1798. This scheme was known to the government, however, almost as soon as it was organised, since by 1797 nearly one-third of the Dublin leaders were in fact British spies. In March most of the others were arrested. From this point onwards the society was a headless beast, whose actions depended almost entirely upon local circumstances.

Thus in May, the government was faced with major disturbances only in two widely-separated parts of the country. The more serious revolt occurred in Wexford, where several thousand rebels under the command of Father John Murphy managed briefly to take control of the county. The rising in Wexford had all the qualities of a religious war, as the Catholic tenantry wreaked vengeance upon their Protestant overlords. Captured soldiers and local gentry were repaid in kind for the depradations of the previous two years. But sheer numbers were not enough. Poorly-armed (most carried only pikes) and badly organised, the rebel force was crushed by a government army at Vinegar Hill in June 1798. The victors took few prisoners.

The second rebellion took place in the Ulster counties of Antrim and Down, the original strongholds of the United Irishmen. Several thousand Presbyterian farmers and linen-workers revolted in each county, but both rebellions were very quickly defeated. Although the leaders were executed, the government treated these rebels much more leniently than those in Wexford. Most were allowed to return to their homes after giving pledges of future loyalty. These pledges were more secure than either side imagined. 1798 was destined to be the last occasion when a large body of Irish Protestants protested the British connection.

No sooner had these revolts been put down than the government was faced with another problem in a most unlikely quarter: Connaught. The western province had remained at peace during the previous years of turbulence, as sheer poverty combined with strong clerical influence to give the United Irishmen negligible support. But in August 1798 a small French force of a thousand men landed in Mayo. It captured the imagination of the local peasantry; many joined the French, who easily defeated the few government troops stationed in the west. But reinforcements quickly gave the British and Anglo-Irish the upper hand, and the invading army was forced to surrender in September. Defeat brought destruction to most of the tenants who had been reckless enough to side with the French, and to many unlucky bystanders.

Through all the events of 1798, Wolfe Tone had remained in France, where he had managed to convince the Directory to send the token force that landed in Mayo. One last expedition was sent in September, but this third French fleet was defeated at sea, off the coast of Donegal in the north-west. Among the prisoners taken was Wolfe Tone. Brought to Dublin for trial, he took his own life in November while awaiting execution.

The 1798 rising is usually considered one of the great milestones of Irish history. It reintroduced, after a century of peace, a tradition of political violence; an estimated 30,000 persons were killed between 1796 and 1798. Furthermore, this period saw the concept of nationalism introduced for the first time to the general population. Until the 1790s the word 'Irish' had merely implied membership of a particular social group; now for the first time, it had definite political connotations. The pike, the colour green, and the rebel ballad all became potent symbols of this new force:

> I care not for the Thistle,
> And I care not for the Rose,
> When bleak winds round us whistle,
> Neither down nor crimson shows,
> But like hope to him that's friendless,
> When no joy around is seen,
> O'er our graves with love that's endless
> Blooms our own immortal green![3]

Perhaps the most significant consequence of 'ninety-eight' was its impact upon Protestant Ulster. The ideals of the United Irishmen, as we have seen, received enthusiastic support among the Presbyterian working-class farmers and labourers of Antrim and Down. But these were the two most Protestant counties in Ireland. In the rest of Ulster the numbers of Catholics and Presbyterians were roughly equal. Here there was competition between the two groups for jobs and land. Here the United Irishmen ideal of brotherhood remained an abstract concept.

Lord Cornwallis (1738–1805), of Yorktown fame, came to Ireland as Lord Lieutenant to supervise the passage of the Act of Union through the parliament in Dublin. He found it an unpleasant task. 'I long to kick', he wrote, 'those whom my public duty obliges me to court'.

John Fitzgibbon, Earl of Clare (1749–1802), a powerful political figure who threw his support behind the Act of Union. Like many Ascendancy leaders, he was convinced that closer ties with England were necessary to buttress the Anglo-Irish position in the face of Catholic demands in Ireland.

The late eighteenth century had witnessed the growth of secret societies in Ulster as well as in other parts of Ireland. Instead of combating landlords and tithe proctors, however, these northern agrarian groups directed their fury at each other. Peep O' Day Boys protected Presbyterian interests, while the Defenders 'defended' those of Ulster Catholics.

Such animosities led in 1795 to Ulster's first modern riot, the so-called Battle of the Diamond, fought in the streets of Armagh. On this occasion the Defenders were completely routed. Soon after, the victorious Protestants formed the 'Orange Society', a group which took its name from King William III's Dutch homeland, in honour of his victory over the Catholic King James II in the early 1690s. This society soon outgrew its Armagh origins; by 1798 it was organised on a national level, attracting support from a majority of Irish Protestants. While the group they formed was technically a defensive organisation, Orangemen did not shun violent confrontations. Many joined the militia groups which the government formed in 1796 and 1797. All remained dedicated to the twin Orange aims of maintaining Protestant supremacy and minimising concessions to Catholics.

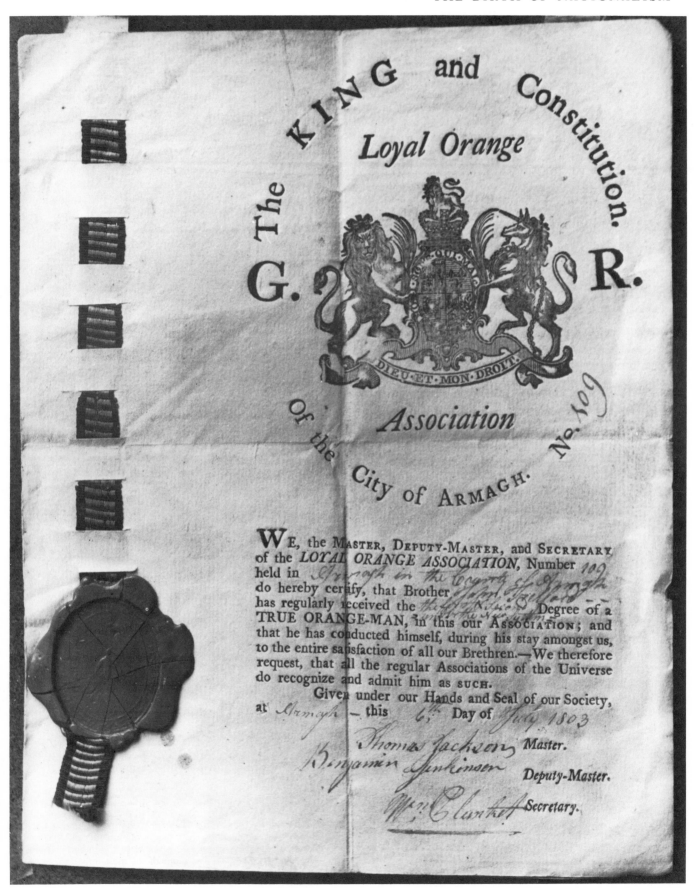

The KING and Constitution.

Loyal Orange

G. R.

Of the City of ARMAGH.

Association

No. 109

WE, the MASTER, DEPUTY-MASTER, and SECRETARY of the *LOYAL ORANGE ASSOCIATION*, Number *109* held in *Armagh in the county of Armagh* do hereby certify, that Brother *John Stafford* has regularly received the *first Orange* Degree of a TRUE ORANGE-MAN, in this our ASSOCIATION; and that he has conducted himself, during his stay amongst us, to the entire satisfaction of all our Brethren.—We therefore request, that all the regular Associations of the Universe do recognize and admit him as SUCH.

Given under our Hands and Seal of our Society, at *Armagh* — this *6th* Day of *July 1803*

Thomas Jackson Master.

Benjamin Jenkinson Deputy-Master.

Wm Clarke Secretary.

Early membership badge for the Armagh branch of the 'Loyal Orange Association'.

Orangeism thus competed with the Society of United Irishmen for the allegiance of working-class Presbyterians in Ulster. The Orange Order got its greatest support from those parts of the province where Catholics were most numerous, in counties like Armagh, Tyrone and Cavan. But the events of 1798 drove even the Protestants of Antrim and Down into the Orange camp. The original democratic ideals of the United Irishmen seemed lost in a swelling tide of Catholic protest. The peasant risings in Wexford and Mayo resembled religious crusades, and convinced many Ulstermen that the Catholic masses would make most unpleasant bedfellows if and when Ireland became independent.

In most of Ireland the leaders of the rebellion became the heroes of ninety-eight, and the founding fathers of modern nationalism. Among the Presbyterians of Antrim and Down, however, the United Irishmen and their principles died in 1798. Sectarian enmity was a lasting result of the events of that year. In future the colour of one's banner – orange or green – would matter far more than the content of one's thought.

The year 1793 saw the beginning of a twenty-year military struggle between France and Great Britain for supremacy in western Europe, the last of the great wars between these two traditional rivals. As we have seen, Ireland played an important role in the early part of this conflict. France sent three separate expeditions to the country during the late 1790s, hoping to gain a foothold for later conquest of Britain. Despite the failure of all three, the London government continued to fear a possible alliance between her two most dangerous enemies. The domestic events of 1798 seemed further proof of the shallowness of Irish loyalty to the crown.

In 1799 William Pitt, the British Prime Minister, announced his plans to abolish the Irish parliament. At first glance, this seems a strange development, especially since the Anglo-Irish who controlled the Irish parliament had proved their complete dedication to the British cause during the 1798 rebellion. But the government feared the institution, not the individuals connected with it. Pitt put this argument forward:

Suppose, for instance, that the present war, which the parliament of Great Britain considers to be just and necessary, had been voted by the Irish parliament to be unjust, unnecessary, extravagant, and hostile to the principle of humanity and freedom. Would that parliament have been bound by this country? If not, what security have we, at a moment the most important to our common interest and common salvation, that the two kingdoms should have but one friend and one foe?[4]

Published   1828 by   *College Green Dublin?*   J. Le Petit 21 Grafton Str? Dublin.

A Brocas print of College Green, dated 1828. Samuel F. Brocas (c. 1792–1847) was one of several outstanding graphic artists who produced Dublin scenes during this period.

A 'hedge-school' in operation in the Irish countryside. Such gatherings were most common in Munster, where they helped keep alive a sense of separate Gaelic identity.

MASTER BEN.

The abolition of the Irish parliament proved to be an onerous task. Most Irish MPs were reluctant to surrender their positions of power and influence; others feared that elimination of the Ascendancy legislature would strengthen the status of Irish Catholics. But British influence eventually prevailed, and an Act of Union became law in 1800, as the Irish parliament voted itself out of existence. Many of these votes had been bought; such compensations cost the British government over a million pounds. Bribery, however, was not needed to make the Anglo-Irish realise how completely dependent they were upon British military support. In the end many Ascendancy MPs voted for the Union because they saw it as their only realistic hope for survival.

In 1801 thirty-two Irish lords and 100 Irish MPs took their seats in the new parliament of the United Kingdom of Great Britain and Ireland in London. Most of the notorious 'rotten boroughs' that had been represented in the Irish House of Commons were eliminated. The new House of Commons contained two members from each Irish county, and one each from thirty-one towns plus Trinity College. Due to their relatively small

93

Charles Bianconi (1786–1875) came to Ireland from Italy in 1802 and established a remarkable coach system that covered nearly 4,000 miles daily. 'Bians', as his long cars were called, were a familiar sight in most parts of the country.

numbers, however, Irish influence was minimal in the new legislature. There were 576 MPs in the House of Commons; Irish members formed only 17 per cent of this total.

A new flag, the Union Jack, flew over Westminster in honour of this parliamentary fusion; it was an ingenious combination of the traditional flags of England, Scotland and Ireland. Actually, the changes of 1801 were more of form than substance. The British executive operating from Dublin Castle carried on the government of the country much as it had for the past century. Irish MPs at Westminster quickly adapted to their new role as British politicians; within a few years they were split along the same party lines as their English comrades. Indeed, the whole Union issue mattered little to the people of the country. Only in Dublin, where the entertainment of Irish MPs and lords had been an important industry, was there any popular support for a separate Irish parliament. 'The mass of the people of Ireland', wrote Marquis Cornwallis, lord lieutenant of Ireland from 1798 to 1801, 'do not care one farthing about Union.'[5]

One tragedy of the Act of Union was that it did not include provision for repeal of the last of the Penal Laws, the restriction which banned Catholics from parliament and prevented them from holding high government office. In fact, Pitt had intended that full Catholic Emancipation would be granted soon after the parliamentary union. However, the combined opposition of the Tory Party, the Irish Ascendancy, and King George III (who once referred to Catholics as 'human cockroaches') forced the Prime Minister to postpone these plans. His untimely death in 1806 combined with the Napoleonic Wars to push the question of Catholic Emancipation into the background. Ascendancy MPs, determined to keep the 'rabble' out of politics, used their best efforts to make sure that the idea stayed there.

There were Irish Catholics, however, who did not consider themselves part of this rabble. After all, the chairman of the Catholic Committee of the 1790s, a Dublin merchant named Edward Byrne, had left the not-so-penurious sum of £400,000 in his will. Nevertheless, the Catholic bourgeoisie had been reasonably satisfied with the concessions which had been obtained during the 1790s, including the right to vote and the establishment of a government-supported Catholic seminary in Maynooth, Co. Kildare. Few of these middle-class Catholics had participated in the 1798 rebellion, and most continued to give loyal support to the British government in the years after the Union.

By 1820, however, a new generation of well-to-do Catholics had grown up in Ireland. Ambitious men who were not prepared to accept permanent exile from political life, these young lawyers and professional men formed a Catholic Association in 1823, hoping to win the right to sit in parliament and the chance to hold government posts.

With few contacts in English government circles and even less popular support, the new organisation met with little success. At the end of its first year the Catholic Association had less than a hundred members. At this point one of its leaders, a prominent Dublin lawyer named Daniel O'Connell, proposed a shift in emphasis. O'Connell suggested a dramatic reduction in the Association's annual dues, so that the ordinary farmers and labourers of the country could become members. By enlisting the support of the masses, O'Connell hoped to make the Catholic Association so large that the government could no longer afford to ignore it. The acceptance of his proposal by his colleagues marked the beginning of a new era in Irish politics.

The departure from Howth of the first steam packet to Britain in 1816, an important milestone in Anglo-Irish relations. Note the crowd of 'spalpeens' bound for harvest work across the Irish sea. Emigration became an increasingly attractive proposition as the century progressed.

A Petrie print showing the Royal Canal on the outskirts of Dublin. Completed in 1817, the Royal Canal connected Dublin with the Shannon and along with the Grand Canal was an important commercial artery until the development of railways.

Born in Kerry in 1775, Daniel O'Connell could claim a most unusual background. His family was part of that rarest of Irish species, the Catholic aristocracy. The O'Connells of Kerry were landlords, one of the fifty-odd Catholic landholding families in the country, and part of the 'hidden' Ireland of south-west Munster. For over two centuries the O'Connells had maintained their positions by keeping as low a political profile as possible.

Young Daniel was raised in the household of his uncle Maurice, an entrepreneur who combined farming and smuggling to achieve an economic affluence enjoyed by few other Irish Catholics. O'Connell grew up speaking Irish; no doubt he had contacts with the last of the Gaelic bards, who during his youth still wandered throughout southern Munster, trying to maintain the Celtic traditions which were now nearly two millenia old.

Like most other young Catholics of his station, O'Connell was sent to France for his education; his contact there was another uncle who served as a general in the French royal army. But young O'Connell returned home in 1794, having witnessed all the early turbulence of the French Revolution. This left him with a lifelong abhorrence of physical force, and more admiration for British political methods than French ones. He established a successful legal practice in Dublin, and was soon involved in a wide range of political activities. A tireless worker with a dynamic personality, O'Connell was perhaps the outstanding orator in the British Isles. A continental visitor left this description:

> He is a tall, handsome man, and a most persuasive speaker. He has received from nature an invaluable gift for a party leader: a magnificent voice, united to good lungs and a strong constitution. It is almost impossible not to follow his powerful speeches with interest or to refrain from laughing at his wit. His manner is winning and persuasive; altogether he looks much more like a general of Napoleon's army than a Dublin barrister.[6]

Once the Catholic Association had made its decision to appeal to the masses, O'Connell put his considerable abilities to great use. He travelled all over the country, encouraging Catholics of all classes to join the organisation. So many took his advice that by 1825 the Association claimed over 300,000 members. This successful appeal swelled its treasury, as ordinary tenants and labourers contributed a penny a month – the 'Catholic Rent' – to the Emancipation cause.

In 1826 the leaders of the Association decided to use these funds to support pro-Catholic candidates in the forthcoming general election. They decided to concentrate efforts in four county constituencies: Louth, Monaghan, Roscommon and Waterford.

In each of these four counties, Catholics formed a majority of the electorate. Fairly moderate wealth qualifications gave the right to vote to many strong farmers. Only rarely, however, had these prosperous tenants been able to vote in a truly free fashion. There were still many ways in which a landlord could intimidate his tenantry and as a result, his influence was crucial in a parliamentary election.

In 1826 the Catholic Association made a direct attack against the political power of Irish landlords. O'Connell spoke to huge crowds in each constituency, exhorting those farmers who had the franchise to ignore the dictates of their landlords.

In this task he had the assistance of the Catholic clergy, who were beginning to exert a temporal as well as spiritual influence upon Irish society. Their efforts met with success, as all four pro-Emancipation candidates were elected.

'Does he blaze'? Dueling was an Anglo-Irish tradition, and many a man's reputation depended upon the answer to this question. The most famous nineteenth-century duel, however, involved a prominent Catholic: Daniel O'Connell. Honour demanded that he defend himself when challenged in 1815; that he did, as this print shows. The resulting furore over this particular duel, which resulted in the death of D'Esterre, his opponent, sounded the death knell for the custom.

'Hair Trigger Dick', the landlord whose kindness towards animals rivalled his cruelty towards his tenants. Richard Martin owned an enormous estate in Galway and his fondness for dueling earned him his intriguing sobriquet.

The champion of downtrodden Catholics, O'Connell maintained a large estate and elegant home at Derrynane, Co. Kerry, shown here in a late nineteenth-century photograph. 'Whatever happens', he remarked to a road worker during the Emancipation campaign, 'you will still be breaking stones'.

O'Connell speaking to a rain-sodden crowd from the balcony of his Dublin town house in 1844. By this time the Liberator's fame as an orator had spread to every corner of Europe.

By now events in Ireland had attracted considerable attention in London. But the Tory Party, staunchly opposed to Catholic concessions and allied with the Irish Ascendancy, remained in power. In 1828 the duke of Wellington, the hero of Waterloo, became Prime Minister. Born in Dublin, Wellington himself was a product of the Anglo-Irish upper class. An archconservative who had little but contempt for the Irish masses, he was determined to resist Catholic demands.

Undaunted, the Catholic Association decided on a direct confrontation with the government. Since the election of pro-Catholic candidates had not brought success, perhaps the election of a Catholic would. When one of the County Clare seats became vacant, Daniel O'Connell himself was put forward as a candidate.

The Clare election was held in June 1828. Since there was no secret ballot, voters had to go to Ennis, the county seat, to declare their choice. For days the streets of this town were filled with happy crowds, singing and chanting 'Hurrah for O'Connell' at every opportunity. In view of his enormous popularity and the Catholic majority among the Clare voters, the electoral result was a foregone conclusion.

The government now found itself faced with two equally unpalatable alternatives. While the Tories abhorred Catholic Emancipation, they knew that refusal to admit the newly-elected MP for Clare to the House of Commons would risk almost certain civil war. Reluctantly, Wellington placed peace before principle. An Emancipation Act was was rushed through parliament, removing the last of the Penal Laws from the statute book. In February 1830 Daniel O'Connell became the first Irish Catholic to hold a legislative position since 1692. One of Europe's first experiments in mass political protest had been carried to a successful conclusion.

The victory of the Catholic Association owed much to the personality of its outstanding leader. Few historical figures have exerted such a captivating influence over the masses. O'Connell, however, was no saint; he was a proud and ambitious man who sought both fame and fortune. By 1830 he was one of the wealthiest men in Ireland, and the owner of a 40,000-acre estate in his native Kerry. While he transformed the Catholic Association into a popular movement he remained an elitist at heart.

Indeed, Emancipation was essentially a victory for the Catholic elite. Most of O'Connell's devoted followers would never cast a parliamentary vote. In fact, nearly all of the strong farmers whose support had carried the Catholic Association to victory lost the right to vote as a result. At the same time as it granted Catholic Emancipation, the government pushed a Disenfranchisement Act through parliament. This quintupled the wealth qualification for voting, with the result that the Irish electorate was reduced from 110,000 to a mere 16,000 voters. That O'Connell accepted this reactionary measure with only the mildest of protest tells much about the man's political priorities.

Yet despite his failings, O'Connell was responsible for a major breakthrough. For the first time in modern Irish history, the ordinary people had exerted considerable influence upon the course of political events. O'Connell helped to give them pride in who and what they were, and guaranteed that in future their opinions would never be so easily ignored as in the past.

But the fact that this first mass movement in Irish politics was so closely connected with the Catholic religion did nothing to lessen the sectarian divisions in Irish society. Ulster Presbyterians viewed Emancipation with both fear and loathing. Catholic action was accompanied by Protestant reaction. The early nineteenth century witnessed an evangelical Protestant revival in Ulster, led by demagogues whose fanatical zeal knew no limits. The foremost of these was Henry Cooke, a Presbyterian minister whose anti-Catholic sentiments rivalled those of Oliver Cromwell.

Rising agricultural prices made it possible for tenants in the richer parts of the country to attain a measure of prosperity, and sturdy houses built in this style became increasingly common.

Daniel O'Connell in the regalia of Lord Mayor of Dublin. He was the first Catholic to hold this office since 1689.

This militant religious spirit had considerable political impact. The Orange Order grew and prospered as 'lodges' were formed in nearly every Ulster community. It was no coincidence that there was an upsurge in Orange activity during the 1820s, the decade of the Emancipation campaign.

In future, nearly all Catholic or nationalist successes would be met with violent protest from the Orange Order. Perhaps a connection between Catholicism and nationalism was inevitable in a country where over 80 per cent of the population was Catholic. Nevertheless, this link did much to make Irish Protestants feel both excluded and threatened.

One of the major social developments of the 1830s was Father Theobald Mathew's (1790–1856) Temperance Crusade. While he convinced thousands to 'take the pledge', alcohol continued to hold a prominent place in the lives of most Irishmen.

Although he was to remain actively involved in Anglo-Irish politics for the next two decades, O'Connell's later career was something of an anti-climax. During the 1830s he led a group of thirty-odd Irish Catholic MPs at Westminster. They became deeply involved in British political affairs, usually siding with the Whigs and supporting many liberal causes such as parliamentary and welfare reform.

Tithe reform was the great issue of the 1830s and this decade witnessed a dramatic upsurge in the activities of secret societies determined to strike against this hated tax which supported the Church of Ireland. The government did manage to defuse the issue in 1838, when it reduced tithes by 25 per cent and included them with rent payments to landlords, who would then pay the Anglican ministers. Although this did away with the hated tithe proctors, there was still much resentment over payment of 'donations' to the Established Church.

FATHER THEOBALD MATHEW'S PLEDGE CARD.
The centre shows Daniel O'Connell receiving the pledge from Father Mathew.

With the final elimination of Penal legislation, the Catholic Church came to play an increasingly dominant role in Irish society. The people remained devoted to the Church that had suffered with them through earlier troubles.

Ribbonmen meeting in a barn in Monaghan, 1851. Throughout the nineteenth century, secret societies remained a factor in rural Ireland, especially in Ulster and Munster.

An unflattering British view of O'Connell's Repeal campaign.

THE IRISH OGRE FATTENING ON THE FINEST PISANTRY.

The romantic nationalists. John Blake Dillon (1816–1866), Thomas Davis (1814–1845) and Charles Gavan Duffy (1816–1903) founded the Nation *newspaper in 1842. In its early years it was effectively the voice of the Young Ireland movement.*

By 1840, O'Connell had grown impatient with the intrigues of Westminster, and set sights upon winning another great popular reform: the repeal of the Act of Union. Once again, he hoped to mobilise the general population in support of this campaign to re-establish an Irish parliament. A Repeal Association, modelled upon the Catholic organisation of the 1820s, was founded in 1841. Although nearly seventy, O'Connell was still a tremendous speaker, and 'monster meetings' were held throughout the country, where huge crowds of up to 100,000 people gathered to hear the Liberator's call for Repeal.

This 1840 cartoon highlights the growing tension that existed in nationalist circles between the O'Connellites who counselled peaceful methods and the Young Irelanders who favoured more drastic action.

For a short time it seemed as if the events of the late 1820s were repeating themselves. But in 1828 O'Connell's election to parliament had forced the government to act; in the early 1840s the Repealers had no such political leverage. As long as the government remained resolutely opposed to Repeal, there was no constitutional method of changing its opinion. Violent rebellion was the only real option. However, this was a course of action which O'Connell, a parliamentarian and admirer of British civilisation, always rejected. Without any means of provoking a non-violent crisis, the Repeal Association gradually faded in importance.

By the mid-1840s the organisation had serious internal problems. Many of its younger members – men who had been mere children when the Liberator had won Catholic Emancipation – objected to the group's adherence to constitutional methods. They felt that O'Connell's career offered ample proof of the limits of parliamentary success, and looked more to the example of other nationalist leaders in contemporary Europe.

In 1846 these 'Young Irelanders' broke away from the Repeal Association and set up the Irish Confederation, a group that was prepared to countenance the use of violence. Led by men like Charles Gavan Duffy and John Mitchel, they began to plan for the day when they too, like Wolfe Tone and Father Murphy, could 'strike a blow for Ireland'.

The controversy between the O'Connellites and the Young Irelanders was destined to be, however, merely a storm in a teacup. The vast majority of Irish people had little interest in their political debates. More pressing matters claimed their attention in 1846. That year brought the island to the greatest social calamity in its history.

THE IRISH REVOLUTION, AT LAST! OR MILESIAN MORALFORCE VERSUS PHYSICAL FORCE!

7—The Famine

For about a century and a half, the potato has been the only food of the peasantry of Ireland. A very limited portion of land, a few days labour, and a small amount of manure will create a stock upon which a family may exist for twelve months. . . . Nearly every soil will produce potatoes; they have been seen growing from almost barren rock on the side of a mountain, and in the bog where the foot would sink many inches in the soil. . . . On the whole, it is perhaps to be lamented that the use of 'Ireland's root' has been so universal in the country, and that the people have been so well contented with it that they have made no exertion to mix the potato with varied food.

Mrs Anna Maria Hall, *Ireland: Its Scenery and Character*, 1843.

During the first four decades of the nineteenth century, the Irish population increased at a phenomenal rate. An estimated four million people lived in the country in 1800. In 1841, however, an official census revealed that Ireland had 8,175,124 inhabitants. In forty brief years, the population had doubled.

The reasons for this kind of spectacular population explosion are among the most difficult problems with which historians are presented. But if any single cause can be advanced in the case of early nineteenth-century Ireland, it must be the universal cultivation of the potato as a subsistence crop. By providing the basis of a secure diet for the mass of the people, the potato encouraged early marriages, which in turn yielded larger families. This meant that the gap between generations was being reduced and that more children were born in each decade.

Today the potato is considered something of an Irish national vegetable. Potatoes, however, were unknown in Ireland before the 1590s, when the first plants were introduced from North America. According to tradition, Sir Walter Raleigh brought the first potatoes into the country, and showed his Cork tenants how to cultivate the crop.

The new vegetable quickly became a staple of the agricultural economy. Potatoes grew well in the damp Irish climate, better than most other tillage crops. They possessed high nutritional value, and quickly became a ubiquitous feature of tenant diets. By the early nineteenth century, potatoes were the daily food of millions of Irish people.

Perhaps the greatest attraction of the potato in Ireland was its high yield per acre. Even in the nineteenth century, one acre of average farmland could produce six *tons* of potatoes annually. Because so little acreage was needed to support a family, nineteenth-century tenants were encouraged by these high yields to subdivide their holdings among all their sons. As a result Irish farms began to shrink in size with each succeeding generation, so much so that by 1841 over 300,000 Irish families lived on farms of less than five acres.

Even the cottiers, the landless labourers of the countryside, grew increasingly dependent upon this crop. Many leased small plots each year from other tenants, where they grew enough potatoes to support their families while hoping to earn enough money to pay the rent by working for other farmers. This custom of seasonal leasing, called 'conacre', became quite common after 1800. Most conacre plots were less than an acre in size; over 130,000 Irish families lived on such miniscule farms by 1841.

The rural landscape, Co. Roscommon. During the 1840s such congested areas had population densities greater than those of many cities.

The British government was not blind to the possible consequences of this increased dependence of the tenantry upon potatoes. 'If the present trend towards subdivision continues', reported a government commission in 1845, 'and the present reliance upon the potato continues among the peasantry, calamity would seem an almost inevitable consequence.' But while government commissions recorded such observations, few European governments felt obliged to interfere with 'natural' economic developments in the *laissez-faire* atmosphere of the mid-nineteenth century. Even if the government had wanted to act, there would have been considerable opposition from the peasantry which saw the sub-division of holdings as a blessing which allowed all one's children to stay at home. Indeed, those 'improving' landlords who recognised the dangers of the situation were usually very unpopular with their tenants if they tried to restrict sub-division.

While small farms devoted almost entirely to potatoes were found in all parts of the country, they were most common west of the Shannon. There both tenant and cottier laboured in a rural landscape that was increasingly crowded. In County Mayo, for example, there were 475 people for every square mile of arable land. Even today, few cities are as densely populated.

Connaught did in fact have much of the congestion of an urban area. In 1841 the province supported three times its present population; an incredible 64 per cent of Connaught farms were less than five acres in size. It was solely because of the potato that this society was able to

An early nineteenth-century print showing the well-heeled Irish landlord receiving his rent from his downtrodden tenant. Dress styles provided a clear indication of social status during this period.

maintain any sort of crude equilibrium. But most of its farms were too small to support their occupants on any other crop if something happened to the potato. Tragically, in 1845 something did.

Ireland was not the only European country which experienced rapid population growth during the first half of the nineteenth century. The population of Great Britain, for example, also doubled during this period. What made a large increase so disastrous for Ireland was the fact that it took place in a climate of general economic stagnation.

The relative prosperity of the eighteenth century faded after the end of the Napoleonic Wars. Irish agricultural prices fell dramatically in the decades which followed, so much so that even strong farmers found their positions difficult. There was a marked decline in overseas demand for linen, as cotton proved a cheaper and more popular fibre. Exports of salted beef also dwindled, as many markets were lost to American producers. Cork, the city which had been the centre of the provisions trade, lost most of its eighteenth-century importance.

The nineteenth-century Irish countrywoman, with the pot on the fire and a basket full of 'praties'.

Wakes were a major social event in rural Ireland, where women would 'keen' the deceased, and men could gather for some serious drinking.

Improved transportation made it possible for Dublin firms to dominate much of the country's commercial life. This was especially true in the brewery and distillery trades.

DUBLIN AND KINGSTOWN RAILWAY.
The Tunnel from the Excavation, looking towards Dublin.

The first Irish train took to the rails between Dublin and Kingstown (now Dun Laoghaire) in 1834, only five years after Stephenson's 'Rocket' had won the Liverpool to Manchester railway prize.

During the first half of the nineteenth century, there was a crucial parting of the ways, as the economies of the two British Isles became increasingly different. During this period, Great Britain underwent tremendous economic expansion, an expansion which brought both industrialisation and urbanisation to that country. Ireland, on the other hand, remained what it always had been: a predominantly rural country, with few cities or industries, where a large majority of the population depended on farming for its livelihood.

Many factors were responsible for Ireland's failure to experience an industrial revolution during the nineteenth century. One missing ingredient was invest-ment capital; few men of wealth in Ireland were prepared to risk their money on new ventures. Irish landlords generally shunned non-agricultural enterprises, while most merchants confined themselves to profitable commercial activities rather than more risky industrial projects. The lack of an efficient banking system, which might have provided entrepreneurs with easier access to capital, also hindered development. Another crucial factor was Ireland's lack of iron and coal, the two resources invariably linked to industrial development in the nineteenth century. Without these raw materials, the country was considered an economic No Man's Land by many British and Irish investors.

A modern drawing of Kingsbridge Station, Dublin, one of the finest pieces of Victorian architecture in Ireland. Completed in 1848, it is a perfect example of the confidence and arrogance of the new railway age. It is interesting to bear in mind that it was built at a time when rural Ireland was in the throes of the Famine. It was re-named Heuston Station in 1966.

Only the Lagan Valley in eastern Ulster was able to overcome these formidable disadvantages. As we have seen, this area had already enjoyed economic prosperity during the eighteenth century, when it had been the centre of a thriving Irish linen industry. Its progress after 1800, however, depended more upon individual businessmen than local products such as linen. Their talents in the face of very adverse circumstances made it possible for Ulster to enjoy its own industrial revolution during the first half of the nineteenth century.

The linen industry went into serious decline after 1780. Its demise was directly connected with the great textile inventions made in England during this period. While machines such as James Hargreaves' spinning jenny and Edmund Cartwright's power loom revolutionised production, and led to the construction of hundreds of mills and factories in England, they were designed to spin and weave cotton, and were unsuitable for linen, a more delicate fibre. As a result cheap cotton cloth produced in the factories of Lancashire easily outsold Irish linen produced by hand.

Ulster business leaders, however, did not despair. Entrepreneurs such as Robert Joy travelled to England, learning the new techniques and purchasing cotton spinning and weaving machines. In Ulster they set up their own cotton mills in the Lagan River Valley, using the water of that river as their main power source. Soon

One of the city's most prominent hotels during the nineteenth century, the Shelbourne is still a Dublin institution.

THE SHELBOURNE HOTEL is the best suited for Families, possessing all the advantages of a Town and Country Residence, having Stephen's-green and the Wicklow Mountains in front, and the Leinster Lawn in the rere.
The Terms will be found adapted to the state of the times.
Nos. 27, 28, and 29, Stephen's-green, North, and No. 12, Kildare-street.
MARTIN BURKE, Proprietor.

HIGH STREET, BELFAST, FROM DONEGALL ARMS, 1851.

By 1851 the sleepy village of Belfast at the mouth of the River Lagan had become Ireland's fastest-growing city.

Ulster was producing most of the cotton garments sold in Ireland. By 1811 over 30,000 people were employed in the factories of that province.

This prosperity proved tenuous, however, as the great British manufacturers were still able to produce better quality cloth at lower prices. The position of Ulster producers became especially critical after 1825, when the tariffs which had protected the Irish cotton industry were removed.

Eastern Ulster might then have suffered the same economic fate as the rest of the country, had it not been for a timely coincidence. Just as the northern cotton industry was sagging, new techniques were developed which made it possible to produce linen cloth by machine. In 1828 Thomas Mulholland set up the first flax mill in Belfast; by 1850 dozens were operating in the Lagan Valley.

Mechanisation brought about a renaissance for the Ulster linen industry. Old markets were recovered, while new ones were also secured. Towns such as Bangor and Portadown blossomed overnight, while Belfast could claim nearly 100,000 inhabitants by the middle of the century. Thackeray visited the Ulster capital in 1842, and described it as 'as neat, prosperous, and handsome a city as need be seen. . . . It looks hearty, thriving and prosperous, as if it had money in its pockets and roast-beef for dinner'.[1]

The rebirth of the linen industry benefited rural as well as urban areas. The production and sale of flax once again brought prosperity to the farmers of eastern Ulster. Nor was linen the only industry which flourished; in the north east a score of subsidiary enterprises were successfully launched, ranging from button-making to cloth-dying. All contributed to the economy of the province, and helped immunise much of Ulster from the tragic events which the 1840s brought to the rest of Ireland.

The *Freeman's Journal* of 14 October 1845 carried the following melancholy comment:

> We regret to find that the accounts we receive tend to confirm the apprehension that there is a considerable failure in the potato crop, and that the disease which has caused it is not on the decrease.

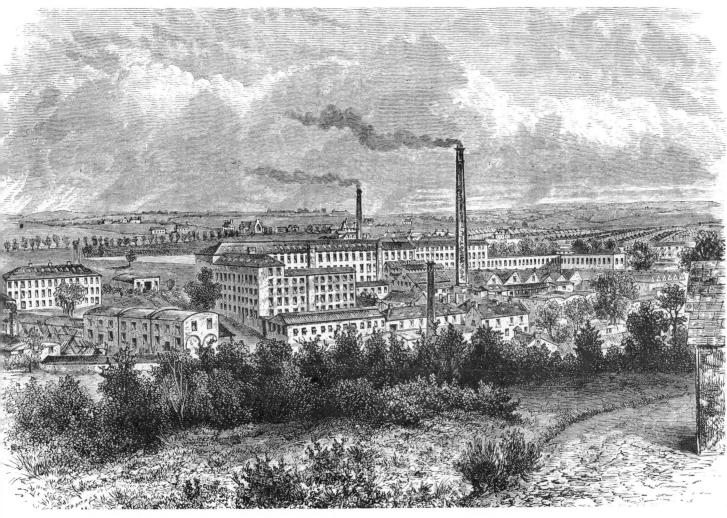

Linen mills blossomed in the Lagan Valley during this period. This particular complex was built at Bessbrook, Co. Armagh.

Economic expansion in Belfast brought social problems. As people flowed in from rural areas, pressure for jobs gave rise to sectarian rivalries between Catholics and Protestants, which hitherto had been principally confined to the countryside.

The summer of 1845 had been unusually warm and damp in Ireland. We now know that these climatic conditions were directly responsible for the failure of the potato crop in that year. The decay was caused by a parasitic fungus, *Phytophthora infestans* (a close relative of bread mould), which attacks potatoes in very humid weather. Today this blight can be prevented by spraying the crop with one of a variety of copper compounds. In 1845, however, the cause of the disease was unknown; many blamed it upon foul vapours in the air, or invisible insects in the soil.

Despite the economic importance of the potato, the blight of 1845 did not arouse a great deal of concern. There had been many potato failures before, the most recent being in Mayo in 1831 and Donegal in 1836. While the national nature of this new infestation was peculiar, only about one-third of the total crop had been destroyed. Most families had enough potatoes to get them through the winter; local charity assisted the remainder. It was a lean season, but everyone was confident that the following summer would bring a bountiful harvest.

The spectre of death haunted many Irish cottages during the Famine years.

Instead, 1846 brought utter disaster. Humid conditions once again allowed the fungus to flourish, and this time over two-thirds of the total potato crop was destroyed. The blight was most severe in the West, the part of the country which could least afford such widespread failure. In many parts of Galway and Mayo the blight was total; virtually no undamaged potatoes were recovered.

Desolation in Skibbereen, Co. Cork, 1848.

The following winter brought unparalleled misery. Because they depended so completely upon the potato, hundreds of thousands of families had neither their usual food nor money to purchase alternative supplies. To make matters worse, the winter of 1846–7 was one of the coldest and wettest of the nineteenth century. Thousands of miserable huts and cottages were filled with shivering wretches, literally starving to death. A visitor to north Mayo in March left this frightful description:

> We entered a cabin. Stretched in one dark corner, scarcely visible from the smoke and rags that covered them, were three children huddled together, eyes sunk, voice gone, and evidently in the last stage of actual starvation. . . .
> Crouched over the turf embers was another form, wild and all but naked, scarcely human in appearance. Moaning piteously was a shrivelled old woman, begging us to give her something, partly baring her limbs to show how the skin hung loose from her bones. . . .
> We visited over fifty of these tenements. The scene was one and invariable, differing little but in the number of sufferers. They did but rarely complain. When asked what was the matter, the answer was alike in all: '*Thá shein uchrais*' ('I am hungry'). We truly learned the meaning of that sad word 'uchrais'.[2]

The scene was repeated throughout the western part of the country. John Mitchel, one of the Young Irelanders, made this melancholy report after visiting Galway during the same month:

Death wagons in Co. Cork, 1847.

Why do we not see the smoke curling from these lowly chimneys? Surely we ought by this time to scent the turf fires. But what (may Heaven be about us this night) what reaking breath of Hell is this oppressing the air?

There is a horrible silence; grass grows before the doors. We stop before the threshold of our host of two years ago, put our head, with eyes shut, inside the door jamb and say with shaking voice *God save all here*. No answer. Ghastly silence and a mouldy stench as from the mouth of burial vaults. Ah! They are all dead; they are all dead![3]

By a cruel twist of fate, the summer of 1847 was fair and dry; this led to a blight-free harvest that autumn. But distress continued, since so few potatoes had been planted; after two consecutive failures there had been a shortage of seed potatoes. The good 1847 crop did lead to increased sowing in 1848 but the humidity of that summer brought back the fungus. In the West the destruction was again nearly total; the winter of 1848–9 brought renewed suffering.

Never before had the potato crop failed in three out of four consecutive years; never before had there been blight on anything like the scale of 1846 and 1848. The country recovered very slowly from this holocaust; there was partial failure in 1849, and again in 1851. By that time over a million Irish people had died; another million had emigrated. 'Characteristic of this country', wrote Friedrich Engels when he visited Ireland in 1856, 'are its ruins. The most ancient are all churches; after 1100 churches and castles; after 1840 the houses of peasants. I never thought that a famine could have such tangible reality.'[4]

Soup kitchens operated by private charities did what they could to alleviate the suffering.

The behaviour of the British government during the Famine has always been a subject of controversy. By modern standards it did virtually nothing to relieve the sufferings of a starving nation. But the *laissez-faire* principles to which English political leaders adhered were popular all over Europe; few governments of the period would have behaved differently. Lord John Russell, Prime Minister during most of the crisis, gave this statement of contemporary economic philosophy in a letter written in 1847:

> It must be thoroughly understood that we cannot feed the people. . . . We can at best keep down prices where there is no regular market and prevent established dealers from raising prices much beyond the fair price with ordinary profits.[5]

It has often been asserted that Russell would have taken a far different attitude if England rather than Ireland had been affected by this natural disaster. Whether or not this is true is completely beside the point. The Great Famine could never have occurred in Britain, or for that matter in any other country in north-west Europe. Only in Ireland did such a large proportion of the population depend upon a single crop; only in the west of Ireland did a purely subsistence economy survive into the nineteenth century. The Famine had many of the qualities of a medieval plague, and demonstrated just how different the country was from its neighbours.

While this difference helps to explain why the British failed to deal effectively with the catastrophe, the British governments of the 1840s by no means deserve complete exoneration. After all, an efficient Irish civil service provided London with copious statistical information about the country; no fewer than 114 Commissions and sixty-one Special Committees reported to parliament on Irish conditions during the first forty-five years of the nineteenth century. In many ways the British government was better informed than its modern Irish counterpart. In these circumstances its failure to act more decisively was certainly reprehensible.

Ireland, of course, was never the primary concern of the British government; domestic and European events usually commanded more attention, even during the Famine years. It is significant that neither Russell nor his predecessor, Sir Robert Peel, visited Ireland during the gravest crisis in its history; indeed, no British Prime Minister ever visited Ireland during his term of office until 1916. Not for the first or last time, British misconceptions were a major impediment to the solution of Irish problems.

Even those landlords who wanted to help their tenants were often unable to do so because of their own financial difficulties. Here a Monaghan landlord tries to explain to his tenants why he cannot afford to reduce their rents.

PAT IN A FIX.

"I'm to go wid you, am I? Faith and you see nothin'
suspicious-looking about me, sure!"

The prosperous members of these Boards usually shared the typical Victorian attitude towards poverty, viewing it as more of a disease than an economic problem. To cure it, most workhouses were made as uncomfortable as possible. The Guardians went out of their way to discourage 'customers', since the emptier the workhouses, the lower the taxes needed to support them. Men, women and children were housed separately. Buildings were badly heated, while paupers received only two meals (usually porridge or soup) per day. Not surprisingly, most of the Irish peasantry and city poor despised the workhouses, and did everything in their power to keep away from them.

Despite their Dickensian flavour, however, the workhouses did much to alleviate suffering during the Famine years. One measure of the severity of the crisis is the fact that most Irish workhouses were filled from the winter of 1846–7 onwards. Indeed, conditions were so crowded that disease was rampant. During that winter the government empowered Poor Law Unions to provide 'outdoor relief' to those who could not be accommodated at the workhouse, even providing some of the funds for this programme.

Attempts by the Young Irelanders to stage a rebellion in 1848 were hampered by police knowledge of their activities, thanks to spies in the organisation.

The effects of the Famine: this map shows the percentage population decline per county between 1841 and 1851.

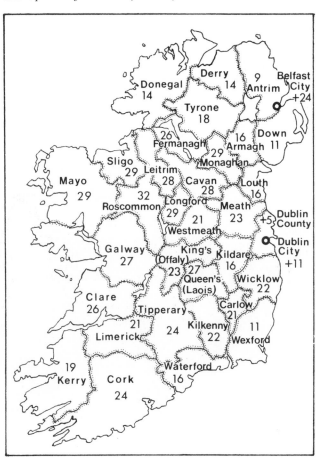

The distress in Ireland did not go completely unrelieved. Despite the official attitude of benign neglect, many groups and individuals did attempt to alleviate the general misery. Foremost among these were the Quakers, the Society of Friends, who set up soup kitchens in towns throughout the country. While many ruthless landlords used the Famine as an excuse to clear their congested estates, others bent over backwards to help their beleaguered tenantry, reducing and remitting rents, and sometimes paying the price of passage for those who wished to emigrate. So many landlords went bankrupt during these years that special legislation was passed through parliament in 1849 to facilitate the transfer of property.

The most significant assistance, however, was provided by the workhouses. These had been established as a result of an 1838 law which divided the country into ninety-two districts known as Poor Law Unions. Each Union was required to maintain its own workhouse, where local paupers could be fed and housed. Funds to maintain these institutions were provided by special taxes paid by landlords and strong farmers. These men elected a Board of Guardians, usually of about a dozen members, to administer each Poor Law Union.

For the duration of the Famine, well over a million people received some form of assistance every day; included in this total was an amazing 80 per cent of the population of Galway and Mayo. While these pioneering ventures in social welfare were limited, they did prevent a desperate situation from becoming even worse.

Undoubtedly the greatest legacy of the Famine was the fact that it made emigration an Irish tradition. What had been a trickle became a human flood in the years after 1845. To many of its people, Ireland became a land without resources, a land without a present or a future. Over 300,000 left in 1851 alone. More than any other country in the world, emigration became an overwhelming factor in the social fabric. It is estimated that one out of every two persons born in Ireland between 1830 and 1930 left the island to make his permanent home elsewhere.

But the Famine transformed Irish society in many other ways. It brought near total destruction to the cottiers, the class of landless labourers which had been so numerous in western areas. There was a swing away from tillage; more and more farms were devoted to grazing sheep and cattle. The perfidious potato declined drastically in importance.

Subdivision of farms stopped almost completely. Farmers began giving their holdings intact to only one of their sons; the unlucky others usually had no choice but to emigrate. Those who remained behind, both male and female, had few opportunities. One result was an increase in the number of people remaining single and a trend towards later marriages. By 1900 the average age at marriage for men in rural Ireland was 39; for women it was 31. Both of these figures were far higher than any others in Europe.

The Famine left a deep psychological scar upon the the collective Irish memory. For the time being at least, they were, in the words of Matthew Arnold, 'a beaten race'. Perhaps this explains why the holocaust did not produce any mass revolt of the peasantry and why a feeble attempt by the Young Irelanders to spark off a nationalist uprising in 1848 ended in fiasco. The Famine was a crisis of mind as well as of body. While the populace blamed the British for their sufferings, they were too dispirited to translate this resentment into positive action.

One measure of this apathy was the staggering decline of the Irish language in the half-century after the Famine. In 1841 Irish was still the vernacular of two million Irishmen; in 1891, however, the total number of Irish speakers numbered less than half a million, and many of these used English more regularly.

The Young Ireland rebellion of 1848 got no further than the Widow McCormack's homestead in Co. Tipperary. The rebels were easily routed and most of the leaders were deported to Australia.

THE AFFRAY AT THE WIDOW M'CORMACK'S HOUSE, ON BOULAGH COMMON.—(SEE PAGE 88.)

Despite the efficiency which this illustration suggests, Irish emigration remained a haphazard affair, and there were few real controls put upon either ship owners or the emigrants themselves.

What happened? For one thing, the Famine had been most severe in the same western areas where Irish had been extensively spoken. Many took the language with them to Boston or Birmingham. Those who stayed behind encouraged their children to learn English, the language so many would need when their turn came to leave.

Equally important was the fact that the Irish language had long ceased to be the proud medium of an independent Celtic culture; instead, it had become a symbol of the poverty of the people who spoke it. 'The Famine', wrote Douglas Hyde in 1891, 'knocked the heart out of the Irish language.'[6] It had a similar impact

upon society as a whole. Writing in 1855, a Dublin antiquarian named George Petrie captured the spirit of the 'new' Ireland:

> The green pastoral plains, the fruitful valleys, as well as the wild hillsides and the dreary bogs had equally ceased to be animate with human life. 'The land of song' was no longer tuneful. . . . This awful, unwonted silence, which, during the Famine and subsequent years, almost everywhere prevailed, struck more fearfully upon their imaginations, as many Irish gentlemen informed me, and gave them a deeper feeling of the desolation with which the country had been visited, than any other circumstance which had forced itself upon their attention.[7]

'Farewell to Galway'. An emigrant ship, bound for America, 1850.

DEPARTURE OF THE "VICEROY" STEAMER FROM THE DOCK QUAY, GALWAY.

8—Tipperary So Far Away

Our ship is now waiting, her anchor she's weighing,
Farewell to the land that I'm going to leave;
My Betsy has parted with father and mother,
With me for to cross o'er the wide western wave.
So hasten dear Betsy, my dear blue-eyed lassie,
Bid farewell to Mother and come with me;
I'll do my endeavour to make your heart cheery,
Till we reach the green fields of Americay.

Anonymous.

Emigrants take a welcome respite on deck during the long voyage to
Australia, c. 1855.

BETWEEN DECKS IN AN EMIGRANT SHIP—FEEDING TIME: A SKETCH FROM LIFE

AWFUL WRECK OF THE QUEEN VICTORIA.

Shipwreck remained a constant threat to nineteenth-century travellers. This ship, the Queen Victoria, *sank off the coast of Newfoundland in 1849.*

The tragedy of the Famine forced millions of Irish people to follow the example set by the composer of this melancholy ballad. When compared to the desolation and despair all around them, the 'green fields of Americay' seemed a most attractive prospect.

Going to America in the middle of the nineteenth century, however, was no easy matter. Only a handful of steamships plied the Atlantic during the 1840s and 1850s. The vast majority of emigrants travelled aboard sailing ships, which took between four and ten weeks to make the crossing. There was a wide variety of ships, ranging from sleek, smooth-riding 'packets' to clumsy, ill-fitted boats that took cargoes of timber or cotton to Europe and carried emigrants as ballast on their return to North America. Whatever the quality of the vessel, rough seas could make any passage unpleasant, causing even the stout-hearted to curse Columbus for having discovered America.

The average cost for cabin and provisions on board a packet was £15 per person. Since this represented several years' wages for the ordinary labourer, most emigrants had no choice but to travel in 'steerage' aboard the poorer class of vessels. The steerage was the central part of the ship's hold, where hundreds of emigrants were crammed together in conditions not very different from those of the slave traders of a century earlier. For £4 or £5 the traveller was given a 5½ by 2 foot berth – and little else.

Most steerage passengers had to provide their own food; often they were forced to eat as well as sleep in their berths. Ventilation and lighting were poor, especially in rough weather. Water was almost always in short supply, and little if any was available for sanitary purposes. A reporter of the London *Times* commented in 1847: 'The Black Hole of Calcutta was a mercy compared to the holds of these vessels.' One traveller who made a transatlantic crossing in the steerage during the same year wrote:

Before the emigrant has been a week at sea he is an altered man. How could it be otherwise? Hundreds of poor people, men, women, and children of all ages, from the drivelling idiot of ninety to the babe just born, huddled together without light, without air, wallowing in filth, and breathing a fetid atmosphere, sick in body and dispirited in heart.

No cleanliness was enforced, and the beds were never aired. The master during the whole voyage never once entered the steerage, and would listen to no complaints. Once or twice a week ardent spirits were sold indiscriminately to the passengers, producing scenes of unchecked blackguardism beyond description.[1]

117

An optimistic group of Irish immigrants pose for the camera before docking in New York City.

Much depended upon the quality of the captain and crew, and the scrupulousness of the ships' owners. While both the United Kingdom and the USA had regulations that specified the number of passengers emigrant ships could carry, these were not strictly enforced until the late 1850s. As a result many ships sailed grossly overloaded.

Such conditions only exaggerated the ever-present threat of disease. Many ships of the 1840s were struck by cholera epidemics. One of these, the *Larch* from Sligo, lost 108 of its 440 passengers before landing in Quebec in 1847; over 100 more died in quarantine after landing.

An Atlantic crossing could have its brighter moments. Some ships made the voyage without incident, such as the *Cultivator* which brought its 945 passengers from Liverpool in 1854 with only a single fatality. Even the most stormy passages had their patches of fine

weather, when passengers could spend the day on deck, dancing, gaming, and listening to the music of a fiddler. The sea had a beauty all its own, especially during the summer months. Nevertheless, the risks were very real. In 1847 almost one in six of those who travelled from the British Isles to North America died as a result of shipwreck or disease. The willingness of millions of Irish people to travel at such odds is one measure of just how desperate conditions were in post-Famine Ireland.

Between 1845 and 1859 nearly two million Irish people settled in the United States of America. These were not, however, the first Irish-Americans. From the beginning of the eighteenth century, there had been a small but steady movement of people from Ireland to the New World. Most of these early settlers were Ulster

Immigrants waiting to pass through customs inspection at Ellis Island in New York harbour, c. 1880.

Harper's Weekly, *the literary magazine of the American establishment, consistently printed anti-Irish cartoons such as this one which appeared in 1883.*

Protestants, ambitious men and women anxious to colonise America in the same way that their Scottish ancestors had undertaken the Plantation of Ulster. These 'Scotch-Irish' newcomers played a significant part in the development of the American colonies and the formation of the United States.

Few of these early Irish-Americans were Catholic, although several wealthy Catholic families took part in the foundation of the colony of Maryland after the Williamite Wars. Among these were the Carrolls of Waterford, whose descendant Charles gained the triple distinction of being the wealthiest, the longest-lived, and the only Catholic signatory of the Declaration of Independence in 1776. He died in 1837. A cousin of Charles, John Carroll, became the first Catholic bishop in the USA in 1789.

The Famine generation of emigrants differed greatly from these early Irish settlers. Almost entirely Catholic, they were a much poorer group. While most earlier emigrants had come from fairly prosperous tenant or merchant families, the 'children of the Famine' were mostly small farmers and cottiers from the devastated areas of the south and west. In contrast to the Scotch-Irish, who had distributed themselves fairly evenly throughout the country, the new wave of emigrants settled primarily around the north-eastern cities of New York, Boston, Philadelphia and Pittsburgh. Here they formed the major part of the labour force which stoked the fires of the American Industrial Revolution.

THE BALANCE OF TRADE WITH GREAT BRITAIN SEEMS TO BE STILL AGAINST US.
650 Paupers arrived at Boston in the Steamship *Nestoria*, April 15th, from Galway, Ireland, shipped by the British Government.

Irish squatters in the northern end of Central Park in New York City, 1869.

Since so many emigrants arrived in destitute condition, they naturally occupied the lowest rungs of the economic ladder. Largely without trades or skills, most Irishmen became labourers, helping to build and rebuild the old colonial cities that were now undergoing rapid expansion. The rewards for their labour were slight: desperately low wages and the dubious honour of residing in the first modern American slums.

In city after city, the Irish found themselves forced to live in wretched hovels and crowded tenements. The filth and squalor of this environment led naturally to disease and high mortality rates, giving Ralph Waldo Emerson ample justification for his comment that he had 'never seen a grey-haired Irishman'.

Although they had a reputation for indolence in their native land, Irish-Americans rarely shirked hard work. One type of employment to which they were drawn was railway building. 'Hibernian brawn' helped build most of the railways of the eastern and midwestern USA. It also helped to draw the Irish out of the north-east. Irish railway builders were reasonably well paid for their back-breaking work; many chose to settle in the new cities of the midwest such as Chicago and St Louis. Others were drawn west in the California Gold Rush of the 1850s. The unlucky majority returned to the railways, or went to work in the growing metropolis of San Francisco.

By 1900 some four million Irish people had settled in the USA. Three-quarters of these had settled in the eight states of Massachusetts, Connecticut, New York, New Jersey, Pennsylvania, Ohio, Illinois and California. Not surprisingly, these were the most industrialised states of this young and expanding nation. Despite their rural background, the Irish in America became very much an urban people.

How does one explain this transformation? No doubt the poverty of many of the newcomers prevented them from going further than a few miles from where their boat left them. Furthermore, many Irish 'farmers' had been little more than potato planters; thus they lacked the agricultural skills necessary for farming in America. Most important of all may have been the fact that life in densely-populated rural Ireland was very different from life in rural America. In a letter home, one Irish farmer in Missouri eloquently summed up this difference:

> I could then go to a fair, or a wake, or a dance … I could spend the winter's night in a neighbour's house cracking jokes by the turf fire. If I had there but a sore head I would have a neighbour within every hundred yards of me that would run to see me. But here (in America) everyone can get so much land that they calls them neighbours that live two or three miles off.[2]

Without doubt the Irish are among the world's most convivial races; they like and need to be with other people. Given their extroverted nature, it is not surprising that most preferred the slums of Boston to the wheatfields of Kansas.

Few immigrant groups have settled in America without incurring the wrath of those who were there

Born in Co. Mayo, William Brown (1777–1857) emigrated to Latin America, where he helped found the Argentine navy and served as its first admiral.

Eliza Lynch (1835–1886) left Ireland for Paris during the 1850s, where she met and became the consort of Francisco Solano Lopez, future President of Paraguay. She returned with him to South America and played a crucial role in the war of the Triple Alliance in which Paraguay's forces were decimated by the armies of Argentina, Brazil and Uruguay. After the death of Lopez in this conflict, she returned to Europe and died in penury in Paris.

In the nativist agitation of the 1850s, Irish and German Catholics were considered serious threats to the freedom – and sobriety – of American society.

before them. The Irish were no exception. They were accused of taking jobs away from 'native' Americans; of adding indigent thousands to the welfare rolls; of depressing the national wage scale by working for very low wages. Moreover, the Irish were responsible for introducing Catholicism to America on a large scale, a fact that was neither forgotten nor forgiven by Protestant nativists.

Thousands of Irish immigrants found employment in domestic service in urban America.

A USEFUL FAMILY.

"We'll jist suit ye, Ma'am. I can wait at the table, an' tend the horses; my wife 'ill be cook, an' the childers 'ill mind the door, an' clane the knives and forks."

Anti-Catholic and anti-Irish feeling surfaced as early as 1831, when a Boston mob burned down a Catholic convent in that city. During the same decade a book titled *Maria Monk's Awful Disclosures* became a national bestseller. This purported to be her story of life within a Montreal convent where she was held for several years against her will. It was a catalogue of illicit liaisons between nuns and priests, and gave grisly details of the secret murder of the offspring born of these unfortunate unions. Maria Monk was in fact a pickpocket and prostitute who put together her totally-fabricated story with the help of several over-zealous nativists. Yet this did not prevent the pornographic tome from selling. Her *Awful Disclosures* went through twenty printings and sold 300,000 copies before 1860. The book was still being quietly circulated a hundred years later, during the Presidential campaign of an Irish Catholic named John Kennedy.

The nativist movement reached a peak during the 1850s when riots between 'No Popery' mobs and German and Irish Catholics became almost monthly occurrences in the major cities of the USA. In 1854 an anti-Catholic, anti-immigrant political group – the American Party – was founded in Boston. Supporters of the American Party were better known as 'Know-Nothings', since the group had developed from a secret society whose members were sworn to declare 'I know nothing!' if questioned about its activities.

The Know-Nothings enjoyed spectacular success during the mid-1850s, winning eight seats in the American Senate and capturing control of both the governorship and the state legislature in Massachusetts. In 1856 former President Millard Fillmore ran for the office on the American Party ticket, and captured 22 per cent of the popular vote.

The progress of events in the 1860s did much to help Irish-Americans rise above the scorn of the nativists. During the Civil War Irishmen demonstrated their patriotism by enlisting in the Union army in large numbers; altogether 144,221 persons of Irish birth served in the army of the northern States. Not all of these served willingly, however. A discriminatory draft law which allowed those conscripted to buy their way out of service for $300 greatly upset the lower-class Irish, and led directly to massive riots in New York City in 1863.

After the war other immigrant groups, such as the Italians, Jews, and Chinese, began to replace the Irish at the bottom of American society, becoming the most dangerous 'aliens' in the eyes of the nativists. Most importantly, however, the Irish quickly demonstrated that they could wield enough political clout to enfeeble the protests of the most rabid Know-Nothings.

Few Irish settled in the rural areas of North America; those who did were usually Ulster Protestants. Many nineteenth-century Ulster emigrants went to Canada, where they could make homes in the New World, yet maintain their links with the British crown. Like other Irishmen, they did not forget their origins. This intriguing photograph shows a tiny orange parade in a prairie village in the Canadian province of Manitoba, c. 1890.

The city of Chicago developed a strong Irish flavour, and Regan's public house was but one of hundreds of such establishments in that city.

A nativist comment on the rise of the Irish in New York City politics.

Sport was one area in which Irish-Americans excelled, and successful athletes were catapulted to the centre stage of American society. None were more successful than John L. Sullivan (1858–1918). Born in Boston shortly after his parents arrived from Ireland, Sullivan won the heavyweight boxing title in 1882. He was champion for ten years, before being beaten by another Irishman, 'Gentleman Jim' Corbett.

In nineteenth-century America the Irish possessed one great advantage over other immigrant groups: they spoke the English language. The Irishman's grasp of English, combined with his experience of parliamentary methods at home, helped make him a keen student of American politics. This education was not long in paying dividends. By 1880 Irish-American politicians dominated the governments of Boston, Chicago, San Francisco and a dozen other industrial cities.

The Irish achieved their most impressive political success in New York City. New York remained the focal point of Irish-American life; in fact the East Side of Manhattan was the largest Irish community in the world for much of the nineteenth century. As early as 1850, the New York Irish had managed to convert this numerical strength into political power.

The instrument of this transformation was Tammany Hall. The Society of St Tammany (Tammany had actually been a seventeenth-century Indian chief) was founded in 1789 as a fraternal order for Protestant working men in the city. Within a few years, however, Tammany Hall had become the effective Democratic Party organisation in New York City. Its leader, the Grand Sachem, usually was more powerful than the mayor; he had the power to make and unmake political careers at both state and local level.

Ironically, the original Tammany Hall organisation did not allow Catholics to become members. But the attraction which the Democratic Party had for Irish newcomers, as the party of 'the common man', forced New York Democrats to change their nativist policies. As nine out of every ten Irish voters registered as Democrats, Tammany Hall had no choice but to open its doors to the swelling Irish electorate.

By the late 1840s the Irish of New York City had their own political leader: Mike Walsh. Born in Cork in 1815, Walsh grew up in New York and became a radical journalist, founding a newspaper called *The Subterranean* which, as its title suggests, espoused the cause of the city's lower class. Walsh's greatest talent was oratory ('He is America's answer to Dan O'Connell', one New York paper commented) and his outstanding abilities as a speaker led him into politics. The activities of Walsh and his supporters, nicknamed 'the Spartan Band', marked the first direct involvement of the New York Irish in Tammany affairs. Walsh eventually became a Congressman, and by the time of his death in 1859, the Irish were an integral part of the Democratic Party machine in the city.

For the rest of the century, the Irish were the dominant influence in Tammany Hall. Most of the city ward bosses were Irish, while leading figures such as

I remain as usual *Mike Walsh*

Mike Walsh, at Tammany Hall, in 1843

DRAWN FROM LIFE & ENGRAVED BY S.H.GIMBER.

PUBLISHED BY 1801 MENTOON, 83 PINE ST NEW YORK.

'Honest John' Kelly and 'Boss' Croker held the powerful office of Grand Sachem for long periods.

In New York City, as elsewhere, the American Irish developed their own particular political style. To most Irish politicians, government was more than a public trust; it was an opportunity to set right the economic and social balance of American society. In short, they spent public money to insure that the Irish 'have-nots' became the 'haves' of urban America.

Spending was to the Irish political leader as frugality was to his Yankee counterpart of half a century earlier. Most Irish mayors embarked on huge public building programmes, which besides improving city conditions provided thousands of jobs for Irish labourers. At the same time the civil service positions at their disposal became ideal sinecures for relatives and friends in the Irish community. As late as 1933, for example, 7,000 of New York City's 20,000 policemen here had been born in Ireland or had parents born there.

While this 'Robin Hood' approach to government was usually short-sighted and invariably corrupt, it did help to give the Irish a more secure position in American society. Politics was the vehicle by which the

Mike Walsh (1815–1859), the journalist and political agitator largely responsible for the Irish takeover of the Tammany Hall organisation in New York City.

A telling comment upon the operation of the Tammany Hall machine during the 1870s.

"You have the liberty of voting for anyone you please; but we have the liberty of counting . . ."

Irish moved into a position of total acceptance; within two generations the outcasts became the Establishment in urban America.

While most Tammany-style leaders did concentrate on feathering their own nests, they were also responsible for bringing a very important change to American politics. More than any other group, they helped dispose of the *laissez-faire* creed of the mid-nineteenth century. Lord John Russell may have washed his hands of the Famine, but Irish-American politicians were not about to ignore the plight of the 'children of the Famine' in the New World. For all their faults, they did plant in American urban politics the idea that city governments should actively attempt to improve the living conditions of their citizens.

During the nineteenth-century diaspora of the Irish people, emigrants took up new lives in all the continents of the world. Irish men and women settled in such distant places as Australia, South Africa, and the

pampas of the Argentine. Not all went so far away. Thousands of Irish people found their New World in the cities of Great Britain.

This movement of population across the Irish Sea was not a new development. For centuries there had been a constant interchange of people and ideas between the two British Isles, especially since the governments and economies of the two islands were so closely intertwined. In terms of numbers perhaps the most significant movement involved migratory workers from the west of Ireland. For decades before the Famine such 'spalpeen' labourers had crossed the Irish Sea at harvest time to work on farms in England and Scotland. Indeed, this seasonal migration has continued to this day in parts of County Donegal.

As in America, however, the Famine provided the real impetus for permanent Irish settlement in Great Britain. Between 1841 and 1861, nearly half a million people emigrated to England, Wales and Scotland.

There were several reasons why a prospective emigrant might choose to go to Britain instead of the USA. One did not have to risk the misery of an ocean crossing. At the same time the cost of getting across the Irish Sea was minimal; for a time during the 1840s it was actually possible to travel between Britain and Ireland for free, since many English sea captains found that

Born in Wexford, Thomas Meagher (1823–1867) was exiled to Australia after his involvement with the Young Irelanders in 1848. He escaped to America in 1852, and became a prominent figure in New York legal and political circles. During the Civil War he organised an Irish Brigade within the Union army; this unit fought with distinction and Meagher attained the rank of general.

passengers who loaded and unloaded themselves were the most inexpensive ballast for their return journeys from Ireland. Added to this low cost was the knowledge that one did not have to endure the permanent separation from relatives and friends that was so tragic a reality for those who chose to go to America.

In Britain as in America the Irish became an urban people. They took jobs in the factories and mines of the English Midlands, in the coal and iron mines around Glasgow, and on the docks at ports such as Liverpool and London. By 1861 over 100,000 people of Irish birth lived in and around the city of Liverpool.

Living conditions in the Irish sections of English cities were as miserable as one might expect. Actual Irish neighbourhoods differed little from the fictitious ones of Dickens's *Oliver Twist*. A parliamentary investigator described the Rookery of St Giles, a notorious Irish slum in London, in the following fashion:

> Rows of crumbling houses flanked by courts and alleys, culs de sac etc. in the very densest part of which the wretchedness of London takes shelter. Squalid children, haggard men with long uncombed hair, in rags with the short pipe in their mouths, many speaking Irish, women without shoes or stockings, wolfish-looking dogs; decayed vegetables strewing the pavement, low public houses, linen hanging across the street to dry.[3]

Anti-Irish sentiment was not a modern development in Britain. This cartoon of 1804 indicates how deep such feelings were ingrained even at the beginning of the century.

Irish spalpeens en route to Britain for harvest work.

Given such circumstances, no jobs were too humble for the 'Paddies'. While thousands of Irish women went into domestic service, the men were drawn to the building trades. As in America, they found a special place in British society as railway builders. The 'railway navigators' or 'navvies' were the aristocrats of the working class, receiving double or triple wages for undertaking such arduous and dangerous tasks as tunnelling and bridge building. Dressed in their black serge waistcoats and smoking their 'píobs', the navvies were a hard-working, hard-drinking and reckless group. But they laid the foundations of industrial Britain, often by removing as much as ten tons of heavy, wet clay per day per man.

Irish navvies made up about 40 per cent of the total in Britain but employers quickly learned that mixing Irish and English or Scottish labourers in the same work gangs meant trouble. Both in Britain and America, Irish workers did much to earn themselves the nickname of 'fighting Irish'.

The Irish in Britain were welcomed with anything but open arms. Most Englishmen agreed with the Liverpool merchant who stated in 1846 that 'the Irish give infinitely more trouble, and are infinitely more riotous and disorderly in the streets, than any other class of persons, or than all others put together.'[4]

As in America, riots between immigrant and local mobs were common occurrences; the Scots of Glasgow even made something of a local sport out of 'hunting the Barneys'. Of course, the Barneys proved well able to give as good as they got.

Feargus O'Connor (1794–1855) was a leading figure among the Irish in Britain and played a major role in the organisation of the Chartist movement, establishing the Northern Star, *the most prominent radical newspaper, in 1837.*

Tea break for Irish building workers in Liverpool, 1895.

Queen Victoria and Prince Albert officially open the Dublin Exhibition of 1853, organised by the Royal Dublin Society to promote Irish agriculture and industry. The painting is by James Mahony.

This painting by J. Humbert Craig shows a Sunday morning scene in Co. Cork. Entitled Returning from Mass, it conveys the sense of bleakness that descended on rural Ireland in the post-Famine years.

Railway workers, most of them Irish, gather for a group portrait beside the Union Pacific track in Colorado, 1869.

Belfast grew in leaps and bounds during the nineteenth century. This is a view of Castle Place, c. 1890.

The Irish in Britain found themselves in the most peculiar position of all the emigrants. While Irish men and women in other countries could mix love of homeland with affection for their new home, those who went to Britain found themselves in the land that controlled the government and economy of Ireland and was, in the eyes of nationalists, responsible for most of her troubles. A curious love-hate relationship was a natural result, and prevented most from ever being fully accepted into British society.

Throughout the nineteenth century the USA remained the destination of nearly three-quarters of those Irish who emigrated. Of all the different immigrant groups which went into the American racial stew, few demonstrated such unremitting dedication to their native land. Sentimental homesickness became a trademark of most Irish-Americans, even those who had never set foot on the Emerald Isle:

> Columbia the free is the land of my birth,
> And my paths have been all on American earth,
> But my blood is as Irish as any can be,
> And my heart is with Erin far o'er the sea.[5]

This poem, printed in *The Irish-American Almanac* for 1882, expressed sentiments that were shared by most Americans of Irish descent. They were made more intense by the fact that so many held the British government responsible for the Famine and the tidal wave of emigration which it produced. Millions of minds and hearts were resolved never to forgive this injury.

Ironically, the British government contributed to Irish-American nationalism in an even more direct fashion, by deporting most of the leading nationalists who had participated in the abortive 1848 uprising. Although many of the Young Irelanders were sent originally to Australia, most ended up in the USA during the 1850s. There they provided a hard-core nationalist leadership which sponsored numerous newspapers, journals, and political organisations.

The most important of these groups was the Irish Republican Brotherhood, established in New York City in 1858. This was a secret society in the separatist tradition of the Young Irelanders, aiming at the overthrow of the British government by force and the establishment of a completely independent Irish Republic. Soon they took up the nickname 'Fenians', from the Irish word 'fianna' which means 'soldiers'.

The two most important leaders of the IRB, James Stephens and John O'Mahony, had both taken part in the 1848 fiasco. Stephens spent much of the next decade in Paris, where he became absorbed in the techniques and methods of the revolutionaries who traditionally made that city their home. After 1858 Stephens was in charge of the Fenian movement in Ireland, and organised this along strict military lines, with himself as 'Head Centre'. O'Mahony was given responsibility for the Brotherhood in America.

The Fenian organisation in Ireland was riddled with spies, making it possible for the British government to keep fairly tight control over the movement. This police swoop in 1865 led to the arrest of many IRB leaders in Dublin.

In the USA the Fenian movement grew in leaps and bounds during the early 1860s. The military spirit of the IRB had great appeal to the thousands of Irish-Americans serving in the Union army. Picnics and parades drew large crowds to Fenian rallies in cities throughout the country. O'Mahony and other IRB leaders spoke confidently of sending an army of 200,000 veterans to Ireland when the Civil War ended.

In Ireland, however, the movement made far less headway. As a secret society condoning the use of violence, the IRB incurred the wrath of the Catholic hierarchy. Stephens himself proved to be an arrogant and pompous leader, whose behaviour alienated many of his colleagues and supporters. Moreover, most Irish people were simply not interested in the Fenians and their message of national rebellion. As always, most were too busy trying to keep themselves and their families alive to worry about who governed the country. Even at their peak the Fenians could never count upon the active support of more than a few thousand people in Ireland. The real heart of the movement remained across the Atlantic.

In 1866, however, serious problems developed within the American organisation. A group led by a wealthy New York merchant named William Roberts split with O'Mahony over the latter's policy of using American funds to promote a rising in Ireland. Roberts favoured more direct American action; he put forward a grandiose plan for a Fenian attack on Canada to show the British government the strength of the organisation.

While the logic of the Roberts plan remains incomprehensible, such a direct approach did have great appeal to the Civil War veterans in the IRB. Accordingly, an intricate plan was drawn up, calling for a three-pronged Fenian sweep across the Canadian border. 'We promise', declared Commander 'Fighting Tom' Sweeney, a former Union Army general, 'that before the summer sun kisses the hilltops of Ireland, a ray of hope will gladden every true Irish heart. The green flag will be flying independently to freedom's breeze, and we will have a base of operations from which we can not only emancipate Ireland, but also annihilate England!'[6]

In June 1866 the attacks took place. A Fenian army of 800 men crossed the Niagara River near Buffalo, New York. They captured the village of Fort Erie before the startled Canadian government sent forces to drive them back across the border. Several days later another Fenian army of similar size moved into Canada from Vermont, but was easily repulsed by the now-enraged Canadians.

As the British government had supported the southern States during the Civil War, the American government rather enjoyed the diplomatic inconvenience which the American Fenians caused the British and Canadian authorities. But even Washington had to draw the line at this armed invasion of a peaceful neighbouring country by a private army, the only time in American history, incidentally, that this has ever happened. Most of the retreating Fenians were arrested

One of the more bizarre Fenians, William O'Donoghue (1843–1878) was a native of Sligo and a seminary student who became obsessed with the idea of destroying British-controlled Canada. After the invasion fiasco of 1866, he moved north to what is now Manitoba, and took a leading role in an abortive rebellion by French-speaking settlers in that area against the central Canadian government. He was captured in 1871 and deported to the USA, where he ended his days peacefully as a school teacher in Minnesota.

The Catholic clergy strongly condemned the activities of the Fenians. This hostility helped prevent the republican movement from gaining a broad base of popular support, especially in rural areas.

HIS RIVERENCE. "AH THIN, MISTHER BULL, IF THE BOYS HAD LISTENED TO ME THEY'D BEEN OUT OF THAT ONTIR

The first volley.

The dead and wounded.

House and barn where Colonel Donnelly and men were concealed.

Hill held by the

PLACE FROM WHICH THE FENIANS FIRED ON THE CANADIANS, BRIDGE AT THE AMERICAN BOUNDARY-LINE—VIEW TAKEN FROM THE CANADIAN CAMP.

A scene from the abortive Fenian attack against Canada in 1866.

British army unit firing on a group of Fenians at Tallaght, outside Dublin, during the 1867 Rising. The rebels were easily and quickly defeated.

John Philip Holland (1841–1914) was a native of Clare whose early attempts to develop a ship that would operate under water were financed by the Fenians in America. The US Navy got wind of his activities and helped him develop his first submarines during the 1880s.

by American border police. But the fear of an Irish-American backlash at the polling booths was so strong that all of the Canadian invaders were quietly released over the next six months.

The American split and the failure of the Canadian invasions had serious effects upon Fenian activities in Ireland. Irish-American enthusiasm waned, as did the supply of money and arms. Thus, when the Irish

rebellion, long-promised by Stephens, finally took place in March 1867, the result was a foregone conclusion. Thanks to its numerous spies within the organisation the British government knew exactly where and when the IRB planned to strike. Further handicapped by a big snowstorm on the night of the rising, the few scattered bands of poorly-armed and poorly-trained Fenians were easily routed by the police and army.

In both America and in Ireland the Irish Republican Brotherhood seemed to have little to show for its efforts. The 1867 rising in Ireland had been a complete fiasco, while the American movement had splintered to the point of disintegration. Indeed, the separatist tradition might well have 'died' after 1867 had it not been for an incident that took place in the third great Irish nation: Great Britain.

The IRB had always commanded strong support from the Irish living in the cities of Britain. In September 1867 a group of thirty Fenians in Manchester attacked a prison van that was carrying two of the IRB leaders who had been involved in the rebellion of the previous March. In the scuffle both men were successfully freed, but only after a policeman in the van had been killed, probably accidentally by a ricocheting bullet. Three of the men involved in the ambush, William Allen, Michael Larkin, and Michael O'Brien, were captured and sentenced to death for the murder, even though none of the three had even fired the shot that had killed the police sergeant.

The attack on the prison van in Manchester in September 1867 which led to the death of a policeman and the trial of the 'Manchester Martyrs'.

The British government now made a major blunder. Instead of commuting the death sentences as it had wisely done after both the 1848 and 1867 risings in Ireland, the government chose to order the execution of the three Fenians. Allen, Larkin, and O'Brien were duly hanged in Manchester in November 1867.

These executions produced repercussions throughout the Irish world. Nearly all Irish people were outraged by this treatment of the 'Manchester Martyrs'; even Church leaders opposed to the Fenians sent letters of protest to London. Massive demonstrations were held all over Ireland and in Irish communities around the world, demanding the release of all Fenian prisoners in British jails. A song was composed in honour of Allen, Larkin, and O'Brien; entitled 'God Save Ireland', it became something of an Irish national anthem for the next half-century:

God save Ireland cried the heroes,
God save Ireland said they all,
Whether on the scaffold high
Or the battlefield we die
Oh what matter, when for Erin dear we fall.[7]

Although the Irish Republican Brotherhood became a relatively unimportant organisation after 1870, the separatist tradition remained alive. America continued to be its spiritual home. Funds continued to pour into the treasuries of those groups which were pledged to ending British rule in Ireland. The most important of these was probably Clan na Gael, led by John Devoy, an Irish Fenian deported to America in 1871. Newspapers such as Patrick Ford's *Irish World* continued to attract a wide readership in urban America. Wherever they were around the world, Irish exiles maintained their interest in their native land, and resolved to play a part some day in making it free and independent.

Exiled Irish nationalists in the United States were responsible for organising and financing the dynamiting campaign which rocked major British cities from 1881 to 1885. In their most dramatic exploit, they managed to cause an explosion in the House of Commons at Westminster. The bottom right-hand corner of the drawing shows the government bench, including Gladstone's seat.

The 'Cuba Five' – a group of five Fenian prisoners deported from Britain aboard the S.S. Cuba in 1871. The beardless young man on the left was John Devoy, who became a guiding force for Irish-American nationalism over the next half-century. Seated, on the right, was Jeremiah O'Donovan Rossa, later to be the main organiser of the dynamite campaign in Britain.

9—Wheels Turning Full Circle

For twelve years past, extensive improvements have been in progress in the harbour of Belfast....

Illustrated London News, 21 July 1849.

1849 may have been a year of calamity for much of Ireland, but it brought continuing prosperity to the thriving communities of eastern Ulster. Two dozen linen mills operated in the Lagan Valley; thousands of looms in farmers' cottages produced fine cloth that was exported to all parts of the globe. Belfast, the centre of all this industrial activity, was already Ireland's premier port, even though the city itself was only a quarter the size of Dublin.

In the two decades after the Famine, the Ulster linen industry continued to expand. The American Civil War cut Europe off from its primary cotton source, and led to increased demand for linen. Weaving became fully mechanised, and bleaching and dyeing factories produced large quantities of finished cloth. Production reached unprecedented levels; over 255 million yards of cloth were exported from Ulster in 1866.

During this same period Belfast became one of the major shipbuilding centres in the British Isles. That such an industry could succeed in Ulster, where there was no iron or coal, was almost miraculous, and owed much to the talents of two men. One of the outstanding ship designers of the century, Edward Harland, joined with a Liverpool financier named Gustav Wolff to purchase a struggling Belfast shipyard in 1858. The new company prospered from the start, thanks to Harland's engineering abilities and Wolff's shipping contacts. Harland & Wolff gained a reputation for top-quality work, and received orders from most of Britain's leading shipping lines. By the end of the century the company employed over 9,000 men at its massive complex on Belfast Lough, where production had reached 100,000 tons annually. The extraordinary success of Harland & Wolff overshadowed that of another firm, Workman & Clark. By 1900 these two Belfast shipyards were among the top five in the British Isles.

Belfast residents celebrate the opening of the new ship channel, July 1849.

Edward Harland came to Belfast in 1858 and was largely responsible for transforming the shipyard purchased by himself and Gustav Wolff into one of the largest and most prosperous in the world.

The growth of the linen and shipbuilding industries stimulated a score of other enterprises in the Lagan Valley. Spinning and weaving machinery was manufactured and exported to all parts of the world, while activities such as shirt and rope-making also became important. All of these industries brought people into Belfast. In less than a century this provincial town became the Irish Manchester; by 1900 it had over 350,000 inhabitants.

Contemporaries were quick to recognise what was taking place in eastern Ulster. A Young Irelander named Thomas Francis Meagher visited Belfast in 1848 and made these observations:

> I congratulate you, citizens of Belfast, on escaping the ruin that has overtaken every other town in Ireland since the Act of Union. Your fate has been as singular as that of Robinson Crusoe, and your ingenuity in making the most of a desert island has been no less remarkable.[1]

But the Ulster capital was not without its problems. Like its counterparts in the English midlands, the city experienced severe growing pains during the nineteenth century. Thousands of its residents were crowded into dismal slums, and worked long hours in dreary and unhealthy conditions. But these 'normal' problems were compounded by one more peculiar to Northern Ireland: ill-feeling between Catholic and Protestant Ulstermen.

Located on the border between Ulster's two most Presbyterian counties, Belfast had always had a strongly Protestant character. Industrial expansion, however, combined with rural distress to bring large numbers of Catholics into the city; by 1850 these formed over 30 per cent of the population. Competition for jobs added another layer of bitterness to the traditional rivalry between the two religious groups. Catholic and Protestant neighbourhoods were rigidly divided, and street fights between the two groups became increasingly common, especially on holidays such as St Patrick's Day and the Twelfth of July. The celebrations of 12 July 1857 were followed by ten days of continuous rioting during which several dozen people were killed.

Religious tension in Ulster was heightened by the activities of Protestant zealots, whose diatribes against the 'Papists' did much to incite mob frenzy. Both Anglican and Presbyterian clergymen were involved in what amounted to an anti-Catholic crusade. The most prominent Presbyterian preacher was 'Roaring Hugh' Hanna, while the Church of Ireland produced the

As this poster indicates, the nineteenth-century Ulster linen industry served markets all over the world.

Much of the work force of Ulster's linen mills was female.

As Belfast grew, so did tendencies towards violence within the Catholic and Protestant communities. This particular scene is from the riots of 1872.

The first train comes to Mallow, Co. Cork, 31 March 1849.

A native of Carlow, William Dargan (1799–1867) was the great Irish railway pioneer. He built the first line between Dublin and Kingstown in 1831. Over the next two decades he organised construction of more than 600 miles of railway, dozens of bridges and viaducts, and the Ulster Canal that connected Lough Erne with Belfast.

equally volatile Thomas Drew. Both of these ministers were involved in the Belfast riots of 1857, during which the Reverend Dr Drew delivered the following sermon:

> Of old time lords of high degree, with their own hands, strained on the rack the limbs of delicate Protestant women, as priests dabbled in the gore of their helpless victims. The cells of the Pope's prisons were paved with the calcined bones of men and cemented with human gore.... The Word of God makes all plain, and puts to eternal shame the practices of such persecutors, and stigmatises with enduring reprobation the arrogant pretences of Popes and the outrageous dogmata of their blood-stained religion![2]

In such circumstances Belfast quickly became a city divided against itself. Perhaps it is fitting that there has never been a single word used to describe residents of that city; Dublin has its Dubliners, and London its Londoners, but there is no such thing as a 'Belfaster'. In urban as well as rural Ulster, sectarian rivalries hindered the development of any sort of community spirit.

Although only eastern Ulster was truly industrialised, all Ireland did enjoy the benefits of one of the major technological advances of the nineteenth century. The first Irish railway was opened in 1834 between Dublin and Kingstown (Dún Laoghaire). While Dublin and Cork were linked in 1849, most railway construction was carried out during the 1850s and 1860s. By 1870, Ireland possessed a superb rail network, which consisted of over 2,000 miles of track and linked all of the major population centres.

Railway development produced some important changes in Irish society. Quick transport encouraged farmers to produce fresh food products such as eggs and milk; as a result, dairy farming became increasingly popular in some areas. Towns along rail routes prospered, as local industries benefited from easier access to both markets and raw materials. After the Famine modern-style shops became commonplace in every provincial town; these dispensed a wide range of tinned and packaged goods which railway development made available to the general population for the first time. It was during this period, for example, that tea, hitherto a luxury item, became something of a national beverage.

Dublin served as the focal point of the Irish rail network. Railways carried Dublin-produced biscuits, whiskey and shoes to all parts of the country. The Guinness brewery, for example, built a national reputation for quality, and was able to use cheap rail transport to undersell most provincial competitors. While it never became a great industrial city, Dublin became the distribution centre for domestic commerce.

Railways made a subtle contribution to the development of an Irish national spirit, since they enabled both people and ideas to move rapidly around the country. Dublin newspapers took on national importance, as they could now be delivered to most other Irish towns on the same day as they were published. For the first time, leisure travel became possible for people of all classes; farming families who rarely left their own parishes now went to Dublin, Belfast or Cork several times a year.

The first transatlantic cable linked Valentia, Co. Kerry and Newfoundland in 1865. The crew of the Great Eastern *are shown here at work laying the telegraph link.*

PREPARING FOR THE FINAL ATTEMPT TO GRAPPLE THE LOST CABLE.—FROM A SKETCH BY OUR SPECIAL ARTIST.

137

*Sackville Street, since renamed after Daniel O'Connell, c. 1850.
'Nelson Pillar' in the background was erected to commemorate the
British admiral's victory at Trafalgar, and it remained a Dublin
landmark until it was blown up in 1966.*

Local grievances captured wider attention while it now
became possible for national organisations to operate
efficiently at the town and parish level. Many of the
political and cultural movements of the late nineteenth
century would have enjoyed far more limited success
had railways not provided such an effective communications network.

The second half of the nineteenth century was an age
of triumph for the Irish Catholic Church. During this
period the Church fully emerged from the shadows of
the Penal Laws, and developed its modern structure.
Solid stone buildings replaced the humble 'chapels' of
the previous century, and patterns of regular religious
observance were re-established. The Church came to
dominate Irish society as it had never done before.
Sunday Mass became the focal point of social life for the
80 per cent of the population that was Catholic. Women
were especially fervent in their religious devotion; many
of their prayers were directed to the Virgin Mary, who
assumed new liturgical and symbolic importance during
this period.

The new eminence of the Church considerably
altered the position of the Irish clergy. No longer were
they men of meagre means, forced by the Penal Laws to
live 'on the run'. Each parish now had its Parochial
House, where the local priest lived more like a member
of the Ascendancy than the tenants who were his
parishioners. Irish Catholics were quite anxious to see
their priests live in style; in this way they could show
both their landlords and the government that the 'PP'
was the ultimate authority in the Irish countryside.

The nineteenth-century Irish Church developed an
almost feudal structure. The laity accepted without
question the religious teachings of their priests, who in
turn pledged complete loyalty to their bishops. The
twenty-seven prelates who comprised the Irish
Hierarchy set the spiritual and moral tone of the Irish
Church. They maintained strict control over the
national seminary at Maynooth where the large majority
of Irish priests were trained; this helped to ensure that
the opinions of the individual priest reflected those of
the Hierarchy.

The leading Catholic churchman of this period was
Paul Cardinal Cullen, who served as Archbishop of
Dublin between 1852 and 1878. Cullen spent most of his
early career in Rome, and was a personal friend of Pope
Pius IX. During his long episcopate he did much to
reorganise the Irish Church along Vatican lines, and was
one of the staunchest supporters of the doctrine of Papal

An early nineteenth-century view of St James's Gate, Dublin, the site of Arthur Guinness's brewery, the largest in the British Isles.

While conditions remained poor in some areas, rising agricultural prices brought considerable comfort to many farmers in the eastern part of the country. The 'grazier' shown in this Jack B. Yeats print was typical of this class of tenant, who prospered by raising cattle and sheep in the rich lands of Leinster and Munster.

An Irish parliamentary candidate at the hustings, 1869. As in England, nineteenth-century Irish elections were often raucous affairs whose outcomes depended upon bribery and/or the munificence of the candidates.

Infallibility, proclaimed in 1870. By that date the Irish Church was under more direct Vatican control that at any time in its history.

At home, education was the issue which occupied the attention of Irish bishops for much of the nineteenth century. In 1831 the government had established a National Board of Education to provide the country with a primary school system open to all children. Largely financed by the government, these schools were intended to be non-denominational; children of different faiths could receive separate religious instruction after school hours.

This attempt at social integration, however, was opposed by both Catholic and Protestant church leaders. Some of the former, such as Archbishop John MacHale of Tuam, preferred no schools at all to 'godless' ones. Cardinal Cullen would tolerate such institutions only if they provided 'a Catholic education, based on Catholic principles, with Catholic masters and use of Catholic books.'[3] Faced with such powerful opposition, the government was forced to capitulate. By 1870 nearly all Irish primary schools were affiliated with religious groups.

Despite this religious segregation, the national school system was largely responsible for the dramatic improvement in standards of literacy that occurred during the nineteenth century. This was perhaps the British government's greatest contribution to Irish life during this troubled period. Thanks to this financial support, most Irish children got at least a rudimentary education. By 1911, 88 per cent of the population could read and write.

John MacHale (1791–1881), Archbishop of Tuam who was a dominant figure in the Catholic Hierarchy during the middle decades of the century.

Freed from the restrictions of the previous century, the Catholic Church began to flex its ecclesiastical muscles during this period. This photograph shows a massive new church under construction in Cahirciveen, Co. Kerry, c. 1880.

The British government attempted to establish a national system of non-denominational primary education, but its efforts were frustrated and ultimately defeated by religious leaders, both Protestant and Catholic, who insisted upon controlling the education of their flocks.

Very few, however, went on to secondary schools, since the government provided little financial backing for post-primary education. Nearly all nineteenth-century secondary schools were fee-paying institutions run by religious groups and open only to those children whose parents could afford the costs. Most of the few exceptions were schools run by the Christian Brothers, a religious order founded in Waterford in 1804. These provided secondary education for talented boys of limited means. Many future political and business leaders got their basic education with the 'Brothers'.

The vast majority of the people remained completely devoted to the Church and its doctrines. Here a group of Donegal parishioners have gathered for the dedication of a holy well, c. 1885.

The British government did make a serious attempt to support Irish university education. Prior to 1845 there were only two universities in the country (Trinity College, Dublin, and the Catholic seminary at Maynooth, Co. Kildare), each of which catered for a single religious community. Hoping to break down the sectarianism that was so much a part of Irish life, the government in 1845 established three 'Queen's Colleges', one each in Belfast, Cork and Galway, with the intention that these would provide university education on a non-denominational basis.

The plan, however, met with the immediate opposition of the Catholic Hierarchy. Archbishop MacHale and his colleagues would not tolerate any educational institution which did not allow the bishops to set curriculum guidelines and to control the appointment of teaching staff. The proposed colleges were considered serious threats to faith and morals, and Catholics were admonished to avoid them. Most did; only the Queen's College at Belfast flourished, since Ulster Presbyterians were able to take advantage of its facilities. Those Catholics who did pursue a university education attended the independent Catholic University in Dublin, founded in 1854.

An uneasy stalemate continued for the next fifty years. The Queen's Colleges were largely avoided by those whom they had been designed to serve; Cardinal Cullen proudly boasted in 1869 that only thirty-seven Catholics were attending the three 'godless' colleges. Although the medical college of the Catholic University was spectacularly successful, lack of funds and non-recognition of its degrees severely hindered that institution.

During this period a series of compromises were negotiated between the Catholic Hierarchy and the British government, culminating in 1908 with the establishment of the National University of Ireland, which incorporated the floundering Queen's Colleges at Cork and Galway with the Catholic University in Dublin, and gave Irish bishops the control over appointments and curriculum which they demanded. By that date Irish third-level education was roughly divided along sectarian lines, with Protestants attending Trinity College in Dublin, Queen's College in Belfast, and Magee College in Derry, and Catholics studying at the three constituent colleges of the National University at Cork (UCC), at Dublin (UCD) and at Galway (UCG).

The university question was one which mattered little to most nineteenth-century Irishmen; after all, only a mere 3,000 students attended Irish colleges in any given year. Nevertheless, the failure of the government's attempt to establish an Irish university system that would bring together young people of all religious persuasions reveals much about the nature of nineteenth-century Irish Catholicism. While not as obvious as the hysterical sermons of Protestant zealots like Hanna and Drew, the Church's opposition to non-denominational education was equally fanatical, and did an equal disservice to Protestant and Catholic Irishmen. Church policy revealed both an intolerance and a parochialism that would remain outstanding features of Irish Catholicism for the next century.

Rural Ireland enjoyed a modest degree of prosperity in the decades after the Famine. Harvests were generally good, and agricultural prices high. While large numbers continued to leave the country, emigration acted as something of a safety valve, allowing those who remained at home to enjoy a higher standard of living.

This prosperity was abruptly shattered during the 1870s. By this time shipping improvements had made it possible for grain and beef produced in America to be sold on European markets, helping to drive down Irish agricultural prices. Further problems were created by a series of bad harvests which occurred over the last several years of that decade. Faced with falling prices and declining crop yields, many Irish tenants found it increasingly difficult to meet their rent obligations.

As in the 1840s, this agricultural crisis of the late 1870s most seriously affected the western part of the country. In the west farms were still smaller and poorer than elsewhere. Here too there were many landlords who were determined to clear their congested estates and devote more acreage to grazing. 1878 was a particularly bad year and there were large numbers of evictions that autumn and winter.

In February 1879 a group of Mayo tenants threatened with eviction contacted James Daly, editor of a Castlebar newspaper that was sympathetic to the plight of the beleaguered peasantry. Daly helped organise a public meeting at Irishtown, the village where these particular tenants lived. Held in April, the rally was a tremendous success, as over 10,000 people turned out to demonstrate their support for the threatened farmers.

The idea of mass protest spread like wildfire and dozens of similar meetings were held throughout the county. This tenant movement found an outstanding leader in Michael Davitt, a Mayoman and former Fenian just released from English prison. It won another important convert when Charles Stewart Parnell, a leading nationalist MP, agreed to work for the tenant cause.

In October 1879 a National Land League was formed. This organisation pledged itself to three major aims: fixity of tenure, fair rent, and free sale (the right of one tenant to transfer his holding to another without landlord interference). The battle for these tenant rights was to be fought on two fronts: in parliament and in rural Ireland itself.

During the spring and summer of 1880 branches of the Land League were set up in nearly every rural parish in the country. Tenants swore to stand together against both evicting landlords and those who took over farms from evicted tenants. James Daly outlined the League's attitude towards such 'landgrabbers':

O'Kelly

...p of angry tenants disrupt an auction at which an attempt is being ...o dispose of the livestock and property of an evictee. Note the ...s.

...he was usually the best educated man in his parish, the local priest ...ave considerable secular influence over his people. Here a group of ...s consult with their parish priest during the Land War.

An eviction scene in Co. Clare, on the estate of Captain Hector Vandeleur, in 1888.

143

A British view of the Land War, published in Punch *in 1881.*

A group of Mayo men and women give dramatic force to their boycott of
a local tradesman, 1881.

Sunday afternoon at Sandymount Green, Dublin, c. 1900.
The tomb of Father Theobald Mathew, temperance crusader, Cork, c. 1900.

This picture was painted for the 1911 calendar of the Women's National Health Association of Ireland. The nationalist image of an independent, idyllic, rural Ireland is perfectly expressed here.

The militant nationalism of the late nineteenth and early twentieth centuries employed propaganda posters like this to influence public opinion.

Michael Davitt (1846–1906), Fenian turned social reformer, who played a decisive role in the Land War and founded the Land League.

While not frequent, clashes between angry tenants and government forces did occur during this troubled period. This particular confrontation resulted in several deaths near Belmullet, Co. Mayo in 1880.

Let you mark such a man. Do him no injury, but shun him as you would the devil, for he is the enemy of the people. Let the man who goes behind your backs to take your farms be the black sheep of the parish.[4]

By the end of the summer this policy of social ostracisation had proved remarkably effective. One of its many victims was the agent of a Mayo landlord whose own name was destined to enter the English vocabulary:

Garrisoned at home and escorted abroad, Mr Boycott and his family are now reduced to one female domestic. Farm labourers, workmen, herdsmen, stablemen, all went long ago, leaving the corn standing, the horses in the stable, the sheep in the field, the swedes, the carrots and potatoes in the ground. The baker in Ballinrobe is afraid to supply them with bread, and the butcher refuses to send them meat.[5]

While the Land League did not condone the use of violence, outbursts were inevitable in the charged atmosphere of the period. Many of the old secret societies were revived; hayricks were burned, animals were shot, and a handful of landlords were assassinated. Altogether, over 2,800 agrarian incidents were reported in 1880.

For the first time, Irish landlords found themselves confronted by what amounted to a social revolt. After 1880, their positions became increasingly untenable.

This massive campaign of civil disobedience did not escape the attention of the British government. A variety of police measures were tried, although none proved particularly effective.

Fortunately for both Britain and Ireland, the general election of 1880 produced a change of government, and brought to the Prime Ministership the English politician most sympathetic to Land League demands. Although a devout Protestant with no Irish connections, William Gladstone considered the pacification of Ireland his greatest political mission. During an earlier term as Prime Minister, Gladstone had brought about the disestablishment of the Church of Ireland, which terminated all state support for the Anglican community in Ireland. Now he proposed a dramatic solution for the Irish land problem.

The Land Act which Gladstone pushed through parliament in 1881 was an important milestone in the development of modern Irish society. It guaranteed the three 'F's to Irish farmers: fixity of tenure, fair rent and the right to sell freely their holdings. A system of Land Courts was established to fix just rents in those cases where tenant and landlord disagreed. Both sides were obliged to abide by the decisions of these courts, which almost always produced some reduction in rent levels. Not since the Emancipation struggle of the 1820s had a campaign of mass protest produced such dramatic results. In effect, the Irish tenant now became a joint owner of his holding; as long as he paid his rent, there was no way that he could be removed.

But as with so many British concessions of the nineteenth century, this one was granted too late. If the three 'F's had been conceded a decade or two earlier, they might have brought peace and stability to rural Ireland. While the 1881 Land Act did help to end the most violent forms of agitation, most Irish tenants were not completely satisfied. After 1881 the leaders of the

The final quarter of the nineteenth century was in a sense a last hurrah for the Ascendancy. The three children of Lord Rossmore shown here were part of the last generation to grow up in the fast-vanishing world of Anglo-Irish dominance.

The Land Courts established by Gladstone's reform legislation of 1881 did much to pacify the country by providing tenants with a forum to air their grievances and (usually) a means by which their rents could be reduced.

tenant movement directed their efforts towards a new goal: the complete abolition of the landlord system.

The nineteenth century was not a happy time for the Irish Ascendancy. The ruling class of Georgian Ireland saw its position of dominance gradually whittled away. Catholic Emancipation and the gradual extension of the franchise had destroyed its political influence; the peasantry now looked to their priests and to land reformers for leadership. At the same time the Ascendancy's economic position had been shattered. Landlords were now mere collectors of rent from lands over whose destinies they no longer had any control.

In such circumstances it is not surprising that the Anglo-Irish developed very defensive attitudes about the country which they had once considered their own. Business and personal connections across the Irish Sea were strengthened, as the Ascendancy began to consider

The drawing room, c. 1900.

itself as more of an English garrison than an Irish aristocracy. Many shared the sentiments of Lord Kitchener, the British military commander of World War I fame, who gave this reply when a friend alluded to his birth in Co. Kerry: 'Because one is born in a stable, one is not necessarily a horse.'[6]

Of course, not all of the Anglo-Irish agreed with Kitchener's perception of his birthplace. Among the exceptions were William Butler Yeats, Douglas Hyde, and Charles Stewart Parnell, all of whom played a vital part in the formation of modern Irish society. Nevertheless, a majority felt uncomfortable in a country whose citizens considered them alien interlopers, and were at last in a position to give real force to their opinions.

The Irish Ascendancy depended upon the British Army to maintain its tenuous position at the top of Irish society. This Anglican church service is being conducted at a camp in Tipperary.

The demise of the Ascendancy was not without a touch of irony, for it was the English Conservative Party, the most steadfast political ally of the Anglo-Irish, that drove the final nail into their economic coffin. The Conservatives controlled parliament for most of the last two decades of the nineteenth century, a time when Irish nationalist sentiment became increasingly vocal and troublesome. Determined to maintain the Union at all costs, the Conservative leadership attempted to buy Irish support by eliminating the landlord system altogether. A series of land purchase measures were enacted, and the government provided long-term low-interest loans to Irish tenants to enable them to buy their holdings.

While this programme failed to stop the growth of Irish nationalism, it did produce an agrarian revolution. The pace of change accelerated after 1903, when the

Golf, the great new sport, Donegal, 1902.

Conservative government announced that it would pay a 12 per cent bonus to those landlords who would dispose of all their properties at once. Most chose to take advantage of these highly favourable terms; over ten million acres changed hands. By 1910 the Irish landlord was 'an increasingly *rara avis*'.

This massive transformation in Irish land-holding patterns undid the work of centuries of confiscation. While the Anglo-Irish were never completely eliminated (a considerable number chose to remain in Ireland, and to this day families like the Guinnesses and the Gouldings dominate Irish business and commerce), their control of Irish life was at an end. The success of the tenant campaign destroyed the last bulwark of Ascendancy power: land ownership. The Anglo-Irish had surrendered their political power to the British government in the Act of Union of 1800; now they handed over their economic polity to the Irish tenantry. 'An age is the reversal of an age'[7], wrote Anglo-Ireland's greatest poet. Yeats's statement seems a fitting epitaph for an Ascendancy which by 1900 had largely lost its privileged position.

Garden party at Kilruddery, Co. Wicklow, 1902.

10—Nationalism and Unionism

The struggle for the sod of Ireland involved a combat for every other right of the Irish nation. The lordship of the land carried with it the ownership of government. The usurpers of the national claim to the possession of the source of employment, of food and of social distinction extended their power over every other privilege and right. . . . The contest for the recovery of the soil of Ireland was waged, therefore, against all the internal agencies and external forces of this buttressed feudal garrison.

Michael Davitt, 1904.

The courtyard at Dublin Castle, headquarters for the British administration in Ireland.

The struggle of the Irish peasantry to gain possession of the land that they worked was not unique; many European countries experienced similar rural campaigns during the nineteenth century. In Ireland, however, the landowners were regarded as part of an alien caste, a group whose origins and behaviour patterns were completely different from those of the masses. As a result the struggle for land became entwined with the nationalist struggle. In 1879 Charles Stewart Parnell, a leading Irish Nationalist MP, and John Devoy, the most prominent Irish-American political leader, joined forces with Michael Davitt to present a united front against the landlords. This alliance, known as the 'New Departure', symbolised the close connection between movements for social and national reform. It also marked the willingness of the nationalist leaders to become involved actively for the first time in a purely social agitation.

Despite near-unanimous sympathy for Davitt and the Land League, there was severe disagreement among Irish nationalists over how independence should be achieved and how an independent Irish nation-state should be governed. While there were many shades of opinion, two general policies could be distinguished. That of the moderates called for the use of non-violent methods, and patience rather than impetuous behaviour. These constitutional nationalists were prepared to work through parliament, until such time as electoral reform gave them maximum political leverage.

Like Daniel O'Connell earlier in the century, many of these men were prepared to accept continued Irish membership in the United Kingdom, as long as the country obtained a separate parliament with responsibility for domestic affairs. This was a concept which became known as 'Home Rule'.

At the other end of the political spectrum were those radical nationalists who looked to the rebels of 1798 and the Fenians of the 1860s for inspiration. They called for complete Irish independence, for an Irish Republic with no British connections. Many were convinced that constitutional methods were futile, and argued in favour of violent rebellion as the only effective means of ending British rule in Ireland.

Despite the rhetoric of the republicans, the Home Rule approach commanded much wider public support during the late nineteenth century. Many factors worked against the radical nationalists. They were denounced by the Catholic Hierarchy ('Hell is not hot enough,' wrote one bishop after the Fenian Rising of 1867, 'nor eternity long enough, to punish these miscreants.'[1]), at a time when clerical condemnation was a veritable kiss of death, especially in rural areas. There was also general disapproval of their penchant for violence; while they might sing patriotic ballads with fervour, few Irishmen really believed that dying for their country was a worthwhile endeavour. Most important of all, British-ruled Ireland was not Tsarist Russia; there were ways that the ordinary people could exert influence upon the course of political events. The success of the Land League was but one manifestation of the power of the masses. Another was the rise of an Irish Home Rule Party at Westminster, elected by a significant portion of the adult male population; gradual extensions of the franchise insured that this political group was truly representative of the people.

Joseph Biggar (1828–1890), the MP for Co. Cavan who was responsible for inaugurating the obstructionist campaign waged in the House of Commons by Irish members during the late 1870s.

Parnell's rise to political power was closely tied to his involvement with the Land League. This match-box dating from the early 1880s is eloquent testimony to the nature of the 'New Departure'.

By 1885 Parnell was unchallenged leader of one of the best-organised and most efficiently operated political parties in Europe.

One of the most traumatic events of this period was the assassination of Lord Frederick Cavendish, the Chief Secretary, in May 1882. He was murdered in the Phoenix Park along with T.H.Burke, the Under Secretary, by members of a secret society called the Invincibles.

For the last quarter of the nineteenth century, therefore, the republicans remained in the shadows, while the Irish Home Rule Party dominated the political stage. The only source of consistent support for the republicans was the Irish community in America. One leader of the Irish Republican Brotherhood in Dublin remarked in 1874 that the entire Irish membership of that organisation would easily fit into a medium-sized concert hall. Nevertheless, the Fenian tradition did not die; republicans held themselves in readiness for a favourable opportunity to rise against the British connection.

The careers of few modern historical figures seem as contradictory as that of Charles Stewart Parnell. A Protestant landlord from Co. Wicklow, he became the leading figure in a tenant-right movement that drew most of its support from Irish Catholics. A member of a prestigious Anglo-Irish family, he dominated an Irish Home Rule Party which sought to break the parliamentary union with Britain so highly valued by most members of the Ascendancy.

Parnell's own personality complicates any attempt to unravel these paradoxes. A lone wolf with few close friends, he left no memoirs and few explanations of why he acted as he did. His intense Anglophobia may well

have derived from his American-born mother, who had sheltered fugitive Fenians after the 1867 rising. At times his behaviour seemed Machiavellian; on occasions he was accused of making cynical use of Irish national ambitions merely to advance his own political career. But whatever his motives, Parnell proved to be the most popular Irish leader since O'Connell. A poor public speaker, who disliked rubbing shoulders with the masses, he was in many ways the antithesis of the Liberator. But perhaps his amazing success was the result of popular realisation that this self-confident aristocrat was the ideal leader for a constitutional struggle against a British enemy whom he knew and understood so well.

Contrary to popular legend, Parnell did not establish the Home Rule Party. When he entered parliament in 1875, this party already controlled fifty seats, and was led by a Dublin lawyer named Isaac Butt. But Butt had proved an overcautious and largely ineffective leader. Despairing of his methods, a small group of Nationalist MPs decided to use the weapon of the filibuster to draw British attention to Irish demands. Parnell immediately allied himself with these obstructionists, who disregarded the gentlemanly rules of the House of Commons and disrupted parliamentary business by making long speeches and tabling dozens of time-consuming

A dramatic moment in British constitutional history: Gladstone presenting his Irish Home Rule Bill to the House of Commons in April 1886.

amendments to every bill. While the government eventually managed to get around the obstructionists, Parnell and his colleagues won widespread Irish support as men who had forced the British to pay more attention to nationalist demands.

While the obstructionists never broke away from the main body of the Home Rule Party, Parnell quickly proved the most able member of this group. He further advanced his career in 1879 by becoming actively involved with the Land League and its boycotting campaign. He spoke at public meetings throughout the country, advising farmers to 'keep a firm grip on your homesteads' when threatened with eviction. These activities won him great popularity among the masses and combined with the timely death of Isaac Butt in 1879 to carry him to the leadership of the Home Rule Party at the remarkably young age of thirty-four.

Once in control, Parnell immediately began to reshape the party. In 1882 a National League was established, replacing the Land League which had been proscribed by the government. The main purpose of this organisation, however, was not land reform; with branches in every parish, the National League was designed to provide solid support for the Home Rule Party at the local level, and to give Parnell political leverage in every constituency. He also instituted a pledge system which bound all elected MPs to vote en bloc; this became so successful a means of enforcing party discipline that it was later adopted by the main British political groups. Using these methods, Parnell became 'the Chief', the boss of one of Europe's first modern political machines.

By 1885 the Home Rule Party was the most effective political grouping Ireland had ever seen. The general election of that year returned 85 Home Rule MPs, all of whom were totally committed to their leader. With this phalanx behind him, Parnell for a time held the balance of power at Westminster, and both Conservative and Liberal leaders offered concessions in return for his support. For the first time since the Act of Union, the Irish tail was able to wag the British dog.

Success came in December 1885, when the seventy-six year-old leader of the British Liberal Party, William Gladstone, announced his support for Irish Home Rule. With the backing of Parnell, Gladstone became Prime Minister, and presented his Home Rule Bill to parliament in June 1886. Gladstone's name had been connected with a number of Irish reforms, including the Disestablishment of the Church of Ireland and two substantial land acts. Now he was convinced that Home

Rule was in the best interests of both Britain and Ireland:

> We stand face to face with what is termed Irish nationality. Is this an evil in itself? I hold that it is not. . . . I hold that there is such a thing as local patriotism which, in itself, is not bad but good. The concession of local self-government . . . is the way to strengthen and consolidate unity.[2]

Not all of Gladstone's Liberal Party colleagues shared these sentiments. A small section of the party agreed with the Conservatives that preservation of the existing parliamentary arrangement was essential for British prosperity and imperial prestige. The result was the defeat of this First Home Rule Bill in the House of Commons by the narrow margin of 341 votes to 311. British public opinion, however, seemed more hostile to the proposal; in the general election which followed this government defeat, the Conservatives swept to a comfortable victory.

Except for one brief interlude (1893–4), the Conservative Party was to remain in power for the next twenty years, effectively stifling any possibility of Irish Home Rule. Conservative strength in the Commons was reinforced by the overwhelming Conservative majority

Katharine O'Shea (1845–1921), Parnell's 'Kitty', who unwittingly precipitated his downfall in 1890.

While campaigning in the 1891 Kilkenny by-election, Parnell is pelted with stones by crowds infuriated by the O'Shea affair. It was an implausible ending to an implausible career.

in the House of Lords; even if Gladstone's proposal had passed the Commons in 1886, it faced a certain Lords veto. In fact, this was precisely what happened to the Second Home Rule Bill, put forward by the aged Liberal leader during his last brief term in office in 1893.

The Conservative victory in 1886 meant that the influence of the Irish Party was severely reduced. While this was one reason for Parnell's less active role in parliamentary politics after that year, another was his deepening romantic involvement with Mrs Katharine O'Shea, the wife of a former Home Rule MP. They had lived together on occasions since 1881 and now, in 1886, decided to do so permanently. They had three children together, one of whom had died in infancy. Katharine's husband, Capt William O'Shea, had apparently acquiesced in this liaison for some years, but in 1889 he suddenly brought divorce proceedings against his wife and named Parnell as co-respondent. Parnell made no attempt to deny the affair – indeed he welcomed the prospect of a divorce which would leave him free to marry his beloved 'Kitty'.

Unfortunately for Parnell, this was the age of the Victorian double standard. Politicians might quietly maintain their mistresses, but public opinion would not tolerate blatant breaches of the established moral code. The Liberal Party, with its strong evangelical Protestant element, abhorred his behaviour and put pressure on Gladstone to sever his alliance with Parnell. Gladstone informed Irish Party leaders that future co-operation would be impossible as long as Parnell remained as leader. The Irish Parliamentary Party, after a protracted and impassioned debate, decided that the Liberal alliance was more important than their leader and rejected 'the Chief' in 1890.

Parnell refused to accept his dismissal, and embarked upon a campaign of political redemption in Ireland, contesting three by-elections. But by this time a more formidable enemy than the Liberal Party had presented itself: now Catholic clerical influence was working against 'the adulterer'. Furthermore, a large section of the Irish electorate agreed with the party leadership that Liberal goodwill was an overriding political consideration. As a result Parnell was defeated in all three by-elections. His health, never strong, gave way during the last one: he contracted pneumonia and died suddenly on 6 October 1891.

The trauma of the divorce case and the decline and fall of Parnell – as meteoric as his rise – left the Home Rule Party floundering in shocked disorder. The party split into Parnellite and anti-Parnellite wings during the 1890s and personal squabbles among his former lieutenants nearly destroyed the marvellous political machine which he had created. Not until 1900 did a single leader emerge who commanded the allegiance of all nationalist MPs, when John Redmond was selected as the leader of the re-united party.

The divisions within the Home Rule Party during the 1890s did not hamper the nationalist cause as much as continued Conservative control of the House of Commons. The Conservatives were committed to maintenance of the Anglo-Irish union at all costs, and never wavered in this determination. The Conservative government did make a number of Irish reforms; land purchase schemes were implemented, increased powers were given to local government authorities, and a separate government department was formed to deal with the enormous economic problems of the west. The Conservatives hoped that these measures would succeed in 'killing Home Rule with kindness'.

But in late nineteenth-century Ireland, good government was no substitute for self-government. Despite the chaos within the Home Rule Party, Irish national consciousness became even more intense during the 1890s. There was new interest in things that were distinctly Irish, in dance, sports, ballads, stories and the fast-dying Irish language.

This 'Celtic Renaissance' added a new dimension to the traditional concept of nationalism. Political leaders like O'Connell and Parnell had not cared greatly about Irish culture; now, however, political independence was considered more of a means than an end in itself. A young nationalist named Patrick Pearse expressed sentiments which were shared by many of his contemporaries: 'What we desire is an Ireland not free merely, but Gaelic as well'.

This new nationalist spirit found expression in many areas. There was revived enthusiasm in Irish history and in the glories, real or imagined, of the ancient Celtic past. This interest was reflected in the literature of the period, much of which dealt with ancient myths and legends. Of more relevance to ordinary Irishmen were the activities of the Gaelic Athletic Association. Founded in 1884, the GAA was directly responsible for organising the traditional Irish sports of hurling and Gaelic football. These sports proved extremely popular; the first All-Ireland finals were held in 1887, and by the end of the century club and county matches were being watched by thousands of spectators every Sunday.

As part of their policy of 'Killing Home Rule with Kindness', the Conservative government financed railway schemes in undeveloped parts of the country. This is the famous Lartigue monorail, constructed in North Kerry during the 1890s.

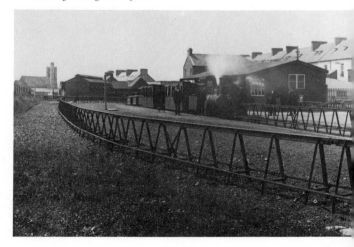

The interior of a comfortable farmer's cottage in Co. Down, c. 1895.

The Celtic revival of the late nineteenth century brought renewed interest in the glories of the past, and the publication of dozens of sentimental histories like this one (above right).

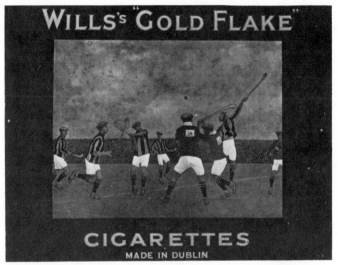

A drawing of an early hurling match between Kilkenny and Cork used to illustrate a cigarette advertisement. Note that all the players are wearing caps.

A rare photograph showing Douglas Hyde, founder of the Gaelic League, walking with a priest and four children on Inishmore, the largest of the Aran Islands. Irish was still the spoken language on these islands off the west coast of Galway.

'Know, that I would accounted be
True brother of a company
That sang, to sweeten Ireland's wrong,
Ballad and story, rann and song.'

William Butler Yeats
(1865–1939)

The Playboy of the Western World *by John Millington Synge (1871–1909) sparked a tempest of indignation when it was first performed at the Abbey Theatre in 1907. Nationalist audiences preferred dramas that sang the praises of the Irish race and ignored its defects of character.*

This renewed interest in Celtic cultural patterns extended to the Irish language itself. In 1893 the Gaelic League was established by two linguistic scholars, Douglas Hyde and Eoin MacNeill, with the aim of preserving and restoring the language. Books were published, lessons were given, and trips to the 'Gaeltacht' regions of the west were organised for those who wanted to learn Irish.

Gaelic League enthusiasts were faced with an uphill struggle. Less than 15 per cent of the population spoke Irish in 1890, and nearly all native speakers lived in the remote and poor regions along the western seaboard. While they did not succeed in restoring the language as the national vernacular, the efforts of the Gaelic League members did prevent its extinction. They also contributed their part to the growing sense of national awareness; witness these observations made by a young Gaelic Leaguer who visited western Galway in 1908:

> It was the nearest thing to heaven, really. To meet this language of your country again, to hear people speaking it. The first peasants that I heard coming out with all the verbal forms – the irregular verbs, the affirmative forms and the negative forms that I'd learned out of a book at school, to realise they were alive! And I heard this old fellow; I could have gone down on my knees and worshipped that man.[3]

There were some Irishmen, however, who felt no such kinship for the Irish-speaking peasants of the west. To the average Ulster Protestant, the Gaelic language was an alien tongue, and the glories of the Celtic past were products of an equally foreign civilisation. Not surprisingly, the imagery and symbolism which was fascinating the younger generation of Irish nationalists elicited little response among Ulstermen who looked east rather than west for inspiration.

The political aspects of Irish nationalism were equally unpalatable. Ulster Protestants had practical as well as sentimental objections to any form of Irish independence. The northern province owed much of its industrial success to the fact that Britain and Ireland were ruled by the same government. Belfast's trade links were across the Irish Sea; there were few Irish markets for the linen and ships produced in Ulster. Many northern businessmen felt certain that independence would bring both Anglo-Irish tariffs and industrial ruin.

Religious animosities, so constant a feature of northern social life, added yet another dimension to Ulster anti-nationalism. Part of a religious majority in the United Kingdom, Ulster Protestants knew that they would become a minority in any independent Irish state, and feared that a Catholic-dominated legislature in Dublin would pursue anti-Protestant policies. Home Rule might well prove to be Rome Rule.

Religious tension had not abated in nineteenth-century Ulster. While secret societies declined in importance in most parts of the country, the Orange Order became an increasingly powerful force in the north east, becoming an important feature of Ulster Protestant society. It was a remarkably classless

In this powerful turn-of-the-century English caricature, a disconsolate Queen Victoria is comforted by her other 'children' while Ungrateful Paddy is portrayed as the only member of the imperial family not satisfied with the blessings of British civilisation.

The majority of Irishmen were not separatists. This photograph shows a volunteer battalion of the 5th (Irish) King's Regiment outside St Patrick's Church, Liverpool, prior to their departure for the Boer War, 1900.

A labourer and his family from Tory Island, off the coast of Co. Donegal, pose for the camera, 1885.

Slowly but surely mechanisation came to Irish agriculture. In this photograph a crowd of Ulster labourers stand beside the threshing machine that would make many of them redundant.

While nationalist sentiment grew increasingly strong, it was by no means the only popular emotion. Many Irishmen, Catholic and Protestant, felt great admiration for 'their' Queen and thousands turned out in Dublin to welcome Victoria when she came to Ireland in 1900.

organisation, whose membership included landlords, industrial magnates, clergymen, shipyard workers and tenant farmers, men with but one thing in common: their religion.

The Orange Order was seldom far removed from the Catholic-Protestant riots which continued to be regular features of the Belfast social calendar. The First Home Rule Bill was greeted in that city with the worst urban disturbances in its turbulent history. Over 30 people were killed and hundreds wounded in a series of riots which dragged on throughout the summer of 1886.

At this point, however, many Ulster Protestants decided that it was time to take their struggle off the streets and into the House of Commons. In 1886 the Unionist Party was founded, with the almost exclusive aim of maintaining the political connection between the two British Isles. In the general election of that year, candidates representing this new party captured sixteen of Ulster's thirty-three parliamentary seats. Obviously, the Unionists could count upon the loyal support of most Irish Protestants.

While it was much smaller than the Home Rule Party, the new Unionist Party was far from insignificant.

A chaotic scene from the Belfast riots of 1886, perhaps the worst in the city's long history of strife.

Arthur Balfour, the former Conservative Chief Secretary for Ireland, doffs his cap in Belfast as a Unionist procession – complete with a burning 'Home Rule Bill' – passes the reviewing stand, 1893.

During the 1890s the co-operative movement began to have some impact upon Irish agriculture. This farmer's co-op creamery operated in Charleville, Co. Cork.

John Redmond (1856–1918) the Wexford MP who re-united the Home Rule Party in 1900 and very nearly realised his party's greatest ambition in 1914.

Faces of Belfast, 1911.

Indeed the Unionists exerted almost as much influence at Westminster as the Nationalists. A natural alliance was quickly formed between the new group and the British Conservative Party, which shared its opposition to Home Rule and had respect and affection for the 'loyalists' of Ulster. From 1886, therefore, the political battle lines were rigidly determined; the Home Rule Party stood with the British Liberals against the Unionists and their Conservative allies.

In 1886, at the time when the first Home Rule Bill was before parliament, one of the leading figures in the British Conservative Party had visited Belfast. Lord Randolph Churchill (whose son Winston was destined to be considerably more famous) was a fervent opponent of Home Rule and was given a hero's welcome by the Protestant population of the city. In return, Churchill declared his support for the Unionist cause in no uncertain terms: 'Ulster will fight', he cried, 'Ulster will be right!'

But for the two long decades of Conservative government, the Unionists had no need to fight. Their allies controlled both houses of parliament and Home Rule seemed light years away. But the Conservative monopoly was finally broken in 1906 when the Liberals won a landslide victory. In control of the Commons, they now found that the House of Lords was beginning to consistently frustrate their proposals and resolved to move against it. After a bitter struggle, the Parliament Act of 1911 was passed. According to its terms, the powers of the archaic upper house were finally limited. In future the Lords could not veto legislation which had passed the Commons; in effect, all they could do was to delay passage of such laws for two years.

Few British constitutional developments ever had as much impact upon Irish affairs. A chasm had opened at the feet of the Unionists, for the permanent majority of their Conservative allies in the upper house was now relatively powerless. Home Rule bills were no longer exercises in futility.

The Parliament Act had been passed with the support of the Irish Parliamentary Party, who had demanded a new Home Rule Bill from the government as the price of its support. This was duly presented and passed the Commons in 1912. Predictably, the Lords rejected it, but this only meant a delay of two years before its eventual enactment. It seemed certain that Home Rule would become a reality at last in the autumn of 1914.

Parnell's dream had been realised, it seemed, under John Redmond. But what was a triumph for Irish nationalism was a calamity for the Ulster Unionists. Faced with the certainty of Irish autonomy by 1914, they resolved to act on Lord Randolph Churchill's dictum: they enlisted the aid of Edward Carson.

Carson was a Dublin Protestant with a distinguished legal career in London to his credit. A blunt and powerful orator, he was a good organiser, with a talent for choosing able lieutenants. He galvanised Protestant support in Ulster in opposition to Home Rule, aided by the leadership of the British Conservative Party, who went to the brink of treason in their defiance of an Act of Parliament. In September 1912, over 400,000 Ulstermen signed a document entitled the 'Ulster Solemn League and Covenant'. In this they pledged to

The end of the working day at Harland and Wolff's Belfast yards.

At a Belfast public rally in 1912, Edward Carson (1854–1935), the Unionist leader, makes his point forcefully from a platform bedecked with Union Jacks.

THE BELFAST INFERNO.

"Wot? Fire on the Union Jack! Whatyer like me for?"

The pro-Unionist sentiments of much of the British Army made the desperate situation in Ulster even more precarious during the summer of 1914.

use 'all means which may be found necessary' to prevent the establishment of an Irish parliament in Dublin.

This was no idle boast. Over 100,000 loyalists joined the Ulster Volunteer Force, a paramilitary organisation formed by the Unionist leadership for the 'defence' of the province. Weapons and ammunition were smuggled in from Germany and by the summer of 1914 the Ulster Volunteers were a well-armed and disciplined force. While the Home Rule Bill was due to pass into law in September, it was clear that its enactment would meet stern resistance in Ulster. In the south, nationalists had formed their own paramilitary group, the Irish Volunteers, less in opposition to the Ulstermen than as a warning to the British government lest they weaken in the face of the Ulster threat.

After centuries of religious tension, the explosion appeared to be at hand; Ulster, if not all Ireland, seemed on the brink of civil war. The Liberal government under H. H. Asquith contemplated the coercion of the loyalists only to find that the army – the only body capable of this task – was, for the first time in British history since 1688, unwilling to support the civil power. Sympathising with the seditious activities of their Conservative friends, many officers resigned their commissions rather than march against Ulster. Suddenly, the government seemed naked and powerless. Asquith spoke for his whole cabinet in July 1914, when he said 'I have rarely felt more hopeless in any practical affair'.[4]

A motorised unit of the Ulster Volunteers, 1913, determined to resist the implementation of Home Rule at all costs.

Women unloading guns on the Asgard, *the ship which smuggled arms into Howth for the Irish Volunteers in July 1914.*

11 — Rebellion, Partition and Civil War

This war may be just or unjust, but any fair-minded man will admit that it is England's war, not Ireland's.

Most Rev. Edward O'Dwyer, Bishop of Limerick, 1915.

A 1914 Belfast postcard which expresses Unionist opposition to Home Rule in no uncertain terms.

By the summer of 1914 Ireland stood on the verge of civil war. Home Rule was due to become a reality in September and the Ulster Unionists had already announced that they were prepared to use armed force to resist its implementation in the northern province. Irish nationalists, on the other hand, were equally determined to see an autonomous local parliament established in Dublin. Between the two points of view, there seemed to be no common ground. European newspaper editors had already begun to send extra reporters to Ireland, in anticipation of the big story that seemed about to break.

On 28 June, the heir to the throne of the Austro-Hungarian Empire was assassinated in faraway Sarajevo. By the beginning of September all the major European powers were involved in a war which none of them had wanted. In Dublin, the European journalists packed their bags and turned for home once more. Ireland's difficulties were forgotten as war engulfed the continent.

Both Edward Carson, leader of the Ulster Unionists, and John Redmond, chairman of the Home Rule Party, advised their followers to enlist in the British forces. The declaration of war of August 4 had, of course,

The first motor cars made their appearance in Ireland just after the turn of the century, although many decades would pass before prices were low enough for large numbers of them to be purchased by the population at large.

A British Army recruiting poster, c. 1915. Over 200,000 Irishmen served in the Imperial forces during World War I.

involved the United Kingdom of Great Britain *and* Ireland in war. Thousands of Ulster Volunteers joined the British Army: in fact the 36th 'Ulster' Division was manned almost entirely by members of this group. Redmond also felt genuine loyalty to the British Empire, despite his nationalist sentiments:

> I say to the government that they may tomorrow withdraw every one of their troops from Ireland. I say that the coast of Ireland will be defended by her armed sons, and for this purpose armed Nationalist Catholics in the South will be only too glad to join arms with armed Protestant Ulstermen in the North. Is it too much to hope that out of this situation there may spring a result which will be good, not merely for the Empire, but good for the future welfare and integrity of the Irish nation?[1]

Redmond and his parliamentary colleagues readily agreed with the postponement of Home Rule for the duration of the war. Many Irishmen shared this allegiance to the Empire; roughly 200,000 served with British forces during the struggle, including Redmond's brother Willie, who resigned his seat at Westminster to fight and die in Flanders in 1917. A total of 61,329 Irish soldiers and sailors were killed in World War I, a figure that indicates how large a percentage of Irish recruits served in the front lines.

While virtually all Ulster Unionists supported the British war effort, Redmond faced opposition to his own pro-war position from within nationalist ranks. A small section of the membership of the Irish Volunteers refused to follow his lead, and formed a new organisation under the leadership of Eoin MacNeill, the Gaelic League co-founder. Since Redmond's group had taken the name 'National Volunteers' after the outbreak of war, MacNeill's followers continued to call themselves

Members of the 36th (Ulster) Division in the trenches. This division was based almost entirely on members of the pre-war Ulster Volunteers. It was decimated on the first day of the Battle of the Somme, 1916.

Padraig Pearse (1879–1916) with his brother Willie, in a rare photograph taken when the elder Pearse was only sixteen.

the Irish Volunteers. This breakaway organisation retained the eclecticism of the old Irish Volunteers. Most of its 12,000 members gave their first allegiance to other nationalist groups, such as the Irish Republican Brotherhood and the Irish Citizen Army. All were opposed, however, to participation in World War 1, and adhered to the traditional separatist theory that England's difficulty should become Ireland's opportunity, and that Irish nationalists should seek to obtain a measure of independence during the war, not after it.

Among MacNeill's supporters in 1914 were nearly all 4,000 members of the Irish Republican Brotherhood. With its direct links back to the Fenians of the 1860s, this revolutionary group still sought to achieve complete Irish independence, by force if necessary. Although it attracted little support from the general population, the IRB did manage to secure the allegiance of a number of young Dublin intellectuals who created the theoretical basis for the events of 1916 and after.

Outstanding among this group was Patrick Pearse, a thirty-five year old Dublin schoolteacher. Like many of his generation, Pearse's main interest was in cultural nationalism. A Gaelic League activist, Pearse established an Irish-speaking secondary school in suburban Dublin, and attacked the existing educational system, which he labelled the 'Murder Machine' because of its preoccupation with examination results and its narrow pedagogy.

Redmond's support for the Imperial war effort, however, led Pearse to take a more active interest in IRB activities after 1914. An excellent public speaker, he moved rapidly towards a position of influence within the organisation and was chosen in 1915 to deliver the graveside eulogy for Jeremiah O'Donovan Rossa, a leading Fenian of the 1860s:

> This is a place of peace, sacred to the dead, where men should speak with all charity and with all restraint; but I hold it a Christian thing, as O'Donovan Rossa held it, to hate evil, to hate untruth, to hate oppression, and, hating them, to strive to overthrow them. . . . Life springs from death; and from the graves of patriot men and women spring living nations. The Defenders of this Realm . . . think that they have pacified Ireland. They think that they have forseen everything . . . but the fools, the fools, the fools! They have left us our Fenian dead, and while Ireland holds these graves, Ireland unfree shall never be at peace.[2]

Pearse and his militant colleagues, of whom Sean MacDermott was the accepted leader, represented a minority of no more than 10 per cent of the Irish Volunteers (who in turn were less than 10 per cent of the original pre-War Volunteers). Despite their meagre numbers, they began thinking in terms of a republican uprising, convinced that they could achieve success, particularly if they could gain the support of the other members of the Irish Volunteers. World War 1 had weakened the British military presence; only about 16,000 troops were available for the immediate defence

The Irish Citizen Army, the militia of the Dublin trade-unionists, gathered in front of Liberty Hall, the ITGWU headquarters, in 1915. Note the banner above the main doorway.

James Larkin (1876–1947), Irish socialist and founder of the ITGWU, addressing a crowd of Dublin workers. Born in Liverpool of Irish parents, he was the major force behind the Great Strike and Lockout of 1913.

of the country. One of the more exotic republicans, a former British diplomat named Roger Casement, was already trying to purchase guns and ammunition in Germany. With German arms and the financial backing of Clan na Gael, the American republican organisation, the leaders of the IRB felt that their rebellion could succeed where those of earlier separatists had failed.

Within the Irish Volunteers, there was yet another small group thinking in terms of active rebellion. The 200-odd members of the Irish Citizen Army, the paramilitary organisation of the Irish Transport and General Workers' Union, were also anxious to strike against the British government.

Despite the phenomenal success of the British labour movement, socialist ideas made little headway in early twentieth-century Ireland. Unlike Britain, Ireland remained a largely agricultural country, where a majority of the population viewed movements of the urban working-class with suspicion. In the country's largest industrial city, Belfast, religious animosities were so powerful that they prevented the development of solidarity between working-class Protestants and Catholics. Even in Dublin, the opposition of the Catholic Hierarchy helped to restrict the spread of socialist ideas.

Irish labour organisers did enjoy a certain amount of success in Dublin in the years immediately before World War I. An Irish Transport and General Workers' Union was founded by James Larkin in 1908, and claimed 10,000 members by 1913. A quarrel over membership in the ITGWU by Dublin tram workers led to a lockout and general strike in that year.

While it dragged on for six months, this strike was a failure; the tram workers were eventually forced to accept their employers' conditions. The strike was condemned by the Catholic Archbishop of Dublin, and the workers' demands were ignored by Redmond and the Home Rule Party. Larkin became so despondent that he left Ireland altogether, emigrating to the USA, where he became a leading labour activist. In Ireland the failure of the 1913 strike produced only one tangible result: the formation of the Irish Citizen Army, a socialist group which commanded a certain amount of support in Dublin working-class neighbourhoods.

Larkin's place as leader of the Irish labour movement was taken by James Connolly. Born in Edinburgh of Irish parents, Connolly was as much the theorist of Irish socialism as Larkin had been its mouthpiece. He combined interest in the proletariat with his own particular brand of nationalism. Not for Connolly the romanticism of the Gaelic League or the Abbey Theatre:

> Ireland without her people means nothing to me. The man who is bubbling over with love and enthusiasm for 'Ireland', and can yet pass unmoved through our streets and witness all the wrong and suffering, the shame and degradation wrought upon the people of Ireland, aye, wrought by Irishmen upon Irish men and Irish women, without burning to end it, is, in my opinion, a fraud and a liar in his heart.[3]

'*The cause of labour is the cause of Ireland, the cause of Ireland is the cause of labour. They cannot be dissevered.*'

James Connolly (1868–1916)

British troops on the streets of Dublin during the Easter Rising, 1916.

A view of the interior of the GPO, the rebel headquarters, several days after the Rising. Much of central Dublin was destroyed by British bombardment of republican positions.

Despite his contempt for the more blinkered forms of republican idealism, Connolly realised that an alliance with the IRB was necessary if the Citizen Army was to have any success. Whatever their differences, both groups shared a desire to bring an immediate end to British rule. Connolly was convinced that this would be the first stage of an Irish socialist revolution, and agreed to co-ordinate his efforts with those of the republicans, whose militancy he admired.

In January 1916 a seven-man Military Council was formed; as well as Pearse and Connolly, this consisted of five IRB leaders – Thomas Clarke, Eamonn Ceannt, Sean Mac Dermott, Thomas Mac Donagh and Joseph Plunkett. Easter Sunday (23 April) was selected as the date on which this joint rebellion would begin.

Three events occured in the week before the Easter Rising to destroy any real hope of rebel success. On Good Friday, a German munitions ship arrived off the Kerry coast earlier than planned, and was met by the British navy instead of by the local IRB unit. The German captain scuttled her while she was being towed to harbour and the arms went down with her. On the same day, Roger Casement was put ashore off a German submarine farther up the Kerry coast and was promptly arrested. At the same time, the military council in Dublin had failed to convince Eoin Mac Neill, leader of the Volunteers, that a rising was justified. Mac Neill, who had opposed rebellion on the grounds that the separatist cause lacked widespread popular support, now discovered the secret IRB plot within the Volunteers of which he had been kept completely ignorant. Enraged at the manner in which he had been deceived, and convinced that the proposed Rising was a lunatic enterprise, he issued an order cancelling all Volunteer parades for Sunday, knowing that these were to be the signal for the Rising to begin.

Despite these setbacks, the IRB decided to press on and re-scheduled the rebellion for Easter Monday, determined to do battle with as many or as few Volunteers as turned out. They had simply come too far to turn back now.

Many of the republican leaders were well aware of their historic links with past rebels, the men who had not been afraid 'to strike a blow for Ireland'. In addition, they were coming more and more under the spell of Pearse's theory of the blood-sacrifice, which proclaimed the necessity for Ireland's nationhood to be asserted in arms, even if military failure and death were the certain consequences.

Early-rising Dubliners took little notice of the group of several hundred armed men in green uniforms marching down O'Connell Street on Easter Monday morning. After all, the Irish Volunteers had been holding regular parades for several years. More notice was taken, however, when these men broke into the General Post Office, which was closed for the bank holiday. Several minutes later, the slight figure of Patrick Pearse emerged from the GPO, and read this proclamation to a puzzled and slightly amused crowd:

Irishmen and Irishwomen: In the name of God and of the dead generations from which she receives her old tradition of nationhood, Ireland, through us, summons her children to her flag and strikes for her freedom . . .[4]

Acting quickly, rebel units seized six other positions throughout the city. The British were taken completely by surprise; after the capture of Casement in Kerry they had assumed that any threat of rebellion had been removed.

But if the British were surprised, so too were most Irishmen. Most Irish Volunteers had heeded Mac Neill's instructions to stay home over the Easter holidays. Only in Dublin did members of the IRB and Citizen Army answer the call to arms. Even then, less than 2,000 followed Pearse and Connolly into the streets.

The rebels compounded their numerical weakness by committing some serious tactical errors. While they seized several of the largest buildings in the city, they forgot some of the most important ones: Dublin Castle, Trinity College, and the Central Telegraph Office. British communications remained intact, and reinforcements were quickly sent from around the country and across the Irish Sea. By Wednesday of Easter Week there were nearly 25,000 troops in the city.

Within a week the uprising was crushed. In the face of popular apathy and superior British firepower, the rebels had no military options except to hold their positions for as long as possible. A gunboat was brought up the River Liffey, and the GPO was bombarded until the rebel headquarters was no more than a hollow shell. One by one, groups of insurgents surrendered their positions. Finally on Saturday morning, Pearse announced the unconditional surrender of all remaining forces. As the rebel leaders were led off to prison, they were greeted by jeering crowds. Most Dubliners were upset by the events of Easter Week, which had seen over £1,000,000 worth of property destroyed, and left much of the city centre in ruins. As in 1848 and 1867, the 1916 Rising seemed a complete failure.

At this point, however, the British managed to snatch defeat from the jaws of victory. Pearse, Connolly and the other rebel leaders were tried in Dublin by a military court. Each was convicted of treason and executed. By early June fifteen rebels had been killed, including all seven members of the Military Council.

From the British viewpoint, there were good reasons for these executions. The uprising had occurred while the country was involved in the most extensive war in its history; the rebels had solicited and received aid from Germany, the most powerful of England's enemies in this war. In such circumstances, Pearse and Connolly were considered traitors rather than patriots.

By executing these men, however, the British government committed perhaps its greatest blunder in seven centuries of dealing with Ireland. Exile or long prison terms would have denied the rebels the martyrdom they sought. Execution made them the

A THING OF THE PAST.

JOHN REDMOND—"Bad luck to that infernal machine with the foreign name. Ever since it come on the road I have lost any fares I had. I can't afford to give the poor baste a feed of oats. I'm to blame meself. Me ould yoke is a bit slow, and it's out of date. I was wan time in comfortable circumstances."

By 1918 Sinn Féin was an idea and a political party whose time had come, as this cartoon infers.

Irishmen to join the British Army. Now this same British Army had executed over a dozen republicans, and imprisoned thousands more. At this stage their British connections doomed the Redmondites; public opinion labelled them as accomplices to the 'crimes' of 1916. At Westminster, one Home Rule MP lamented the fate of his party: 'You are wiping out our life's work in a sea of blood!'[6]

In 1917 Home Rule candidates were easily defeated in by-elections in Roscommon and Clare; it was clear that the republican star was rising. The new organisation was called Sinn Fein (we ourselves), and gathered to its ranks all nationalists weary of Redmond's moderation. Sinn Fein, in fact, existed as a tiny nationalist group since 1905, but the British authorities had ignorantly labelled all republicans as 'Sinn Feiners' and the name stuck. Indeed, the original Sinn Fein had not been particularly republican in its leanings, but the new party now committed itself to separatism. It chose Eamon de Valera as its chairman.

Eamon de Valera, (1882–1975), the Sinn Féin leader, flanked by advisors and standing before a green, white and orange tricolour, 1922.

heroes of the nation, as this contemporary letter indicates:

> The leaders were such good men. They died like Saints. Oh! the pity of it! and Ireland wanted them much! They were men of such beautiful character – such high literary power and attainments – mystics, who kept the light burning. What madness came over them! They lived such pure lives; as the priests who shrived them before execution said: 'the clean, pure lives – the absolute resignation – may they pray for us not we for them.' . . . As sure as God's sun rises in the East, if England doesn't get things right – if there's not immediately conciliation, and love and mercy poured out on Ireland – all the leaders will be canonised![5]

The British compounded their error by arresting everyone suspected of having some connection with the rebellion. Over 3,000 men were imprisoned by the end of June, including many Volunteers who had not participated in the Rising, and who, in fact, had counselled against it. The arrest of so many innocent men helped create further sympathy for the republicans.

In the face of mounting public pressure, many of these prisoners were released; most were home by the end of the summer. But the die had already been cast. For the first time, republican separatists commanded a wide measure of popular support. In dealing with the Easter Rising, the British government had used a cannon to kill a fly – and missed.

If the government was a big loser in 1916, so too was the Home Rule Party. Since 1914 John Redmond had supported the British war effort, and encouraged young

THE IRISH PEOPLE

The British attempt to introduce conscription in early 1918 was a blunder of the first magnitude. This whimsical cartoon suggests the sort of effort required to make conscription work in Ireland.

THE FIRST IRISH CONSCRIPT.

Born in New York of Spanish-Irish parentage, Eamon de Valera grew up in Co. Limerick. On the eve of the Rising he was a mathematics teacher in Dublin. He was the highest-ranking republican officer to survive the rebellion, a fact which made him the natural spokesman for those imprisoned during the summer of 1916. After his release in December, de Valera quickly consolidated his leadership. Tall and stern, he was a Gaelic League enthusiast, and the personification of Irish opposition to all things British.

During 1917 and 1918 the British government continued to mishandle the Irish situation. Half-hearted correction measures were attempted, but served only to make Sinn Fein more popular. Perhaps the most incredible British mistake came in March 1918, when the Prime Minister, David Lloyd George, announced plans to extend military conscription to Ireland. Although critical manpower shortages on the western front made this proposal seem attractive to the British cabinet, it met with near-unanimous Irish opposition. Home Rule MPs, Sinn Fein leaders and even Catholic bishops joined together in an Irish Anti-Conscription League. In the face of such united opposition, the government soon withdrew the proposal. Once again the British had needlessly alienated large sections of the Irish population, and the tide of public opinion continued to flow in the direction of the militants.

Proof of this swing to Sinn Fein came in the general election of December 1918, the so-called 'Khaki Election', which came only a month after the end of World War I. For the first time, women (over thirty) had a chance to vote. This and other electoral reforms helped to make the Irish electorate nearly three times larger than it had been at the last election in 1910.

The first meeting of Dail Eireann, the de facto Irish parliament, at the Mansion House in Dublin in January 1919.

A 1919 photograph of the North Cork 'flying column', one of the most successful of the IRA's rural guerrilla units.

These men were imprisoned in early 1918. By arresting thousands of Irishmen, the British contributed to growing republican sentiment in the country.

The election results confirmed the revolution which had occurred in Irish politics. Outside of Ulster, where the Unionists took their usual two dozen seats, Sinn Fein candidates swept the country. Seventy-three separatists were elected in 1918, as compared to a mere six Home Rulers. The once-powerful party of Charles Stewart Parnell was effectively destroyed. Redmond at least was spared the humiliation of presiding over this debacle; he had died in March 1918.

As they had promised during the election campaign, the new Sinn Fein MPs refused to take their seats at Westminster. Most had no option, having been imprisoned during the previous summer as the result of an alleged German plot. But those twenty-seven Sinn Feiners not in jail met in Dublin in January 1919 where they drew up an Irish Declaration of Independence, and took the title 'Dail Eireann', claiming to be the real parliament of the country. A ministerial cabinet was selected and de Valera, although again in prison, was named first President of the Irish Republic.

Sinn Fein was not the only organisation to flourish in the years after the Rising. The Irish Volunteers continued in existence, and became increasingly militant after 1916. In time the title 'Irish Republican Army' came to be used to describe this paramilitary group; Sinn Fein remained essentially a political party.

While there was considerable overlap between these two organisations, the IRA naturally preferred action to debate. On the same day that the first Dail met in Dublin in January 1919, a company of republicans ambushed an ammunition lorry in Co. Tipperary, killing two policemen. This incident marked the beginning of the War of Independence.

For the next two and a half years, the IRA and the British army were engaged in one of this century's first guerrilla wars. Although they faced a highly-trained and better-equipped enemy, the republicans possessed two significant advantages: intimate knowledge of the countryside, and the support of a large portion of the population. Organised into 'flying columns' of several

As one might expect, Irish-Americans were vocal in their support for the Rising and their condemnation of British policy. This is a scene from a protest at the British embassy in Washington in December 1920.

Disruption of communications was a major aim of the IRA and one which was often realised.

'Black and Tans' with an IRA suspect, 1920.

dozen men, IRA units struck at isolated police barracks and troop-carrying lorries. After these ambushes, these citizen-soldiers usually scattered and returned to their normal occupations, where they remained indistinguishable from the general population. There was, however, a minority who remained 'on the run' throughout the war.

The execution of eighteen-year-old Kevin Barry in 1920 created a wave of revulsion in Ireland, and further alienated the people from Dublin Castle.

The British army found itself in a position remarkably similar to that of its American counterpart in Vietnam during the 1960s. The IRA campaign of ambush and assassination had a devastating psychological effect upon the morale of soldiers and policemen. Despite their military superiority, definite limits were placed upon British forces, since the London govern-

Dublin Throngs at Executions and Funeral Parad

WOMEN KNEELING IN PRAYER BEFORE MOUNTJOY PRISON DURING THE EXECUTION OF KELVIN BARRY.

ment knew that domestic public opinion would not tolerate an all-out conflict so soon after the end of World War I. Government policy vacillated between coercion and concession. 'We are drifting', wrote one frustrated British general, 'without any settled course or goal.'[7]

In such circumstances the breakdown of military discipline was almost inevitable. The auxiliary forces sent by the government to deal with the Irish 'problem' were mainly veterans of the trenches in France. Nicknamed 'Black and Tans' because of the mixed colours of their uniforms, these men were totally unprepared for guerrilla warfare, and took out their frustrations on the civilian population. Many small towns were burnt to the ground, as was a large part of the city of Cork in 1920. Such actions only made the populace more hostile to British rule, and more willing to shelter IRA activists.

The entire situation was highly favourable to the Volunteers. By 1920 they controlled most of the country; British strength was confined to the cities and towns. In many parts of the south and west, Sinn Fein provided government services, including courts and police. The IRA, however, lacked the means to drive the

British out of their urban strongholds, just as the British were unable to govern the countryside.

Neither side could break this stalemate. By 1921 the strains of guerrilla warfare were begining to affect Irish morale; even staunch republicans grew weary of sheltering IRA units for months at a time. That summer both sides agreed on a truce, and arranged for peace talks to begin in London in October.

The most surprising omission from the Irish delegation that went to England in the autumn of 1921 was that of Sinn Fein leader, Eamon de Valera. But the de facto Irish President had just returned from the USA, where he had spent eighteen months after his dramatic prison escape in 1919, raising funds for the republican cause. He had been back in Ireland (to which he returned disguised as a drunken sailor) less than ten months, and felt that he should remain in Dublin.

In de Valera's absence, the leading figures in the seven-man Irish delegation were Arthur Griffith, the founder of the original Sinn Fein group in 1905, and Michael Collins, a thirty-year old Corkman whose military and organisational brilliance had brought the rebels so much success during the War of Independence. But neither Collins nor the other members of the Irish group were experienced negotiators. In contrast Lloyd George and his colleagues had just returned from Versailles; with him in the British delegation were such able diplomats as Austen Chamberlain and Winston Churchill.

Four of the five Irish delegates who negotiated the Anglo-Irish treaty of 1921. (l. to r.) Charles Gavan Duffy, Michael Collins, Arthur Griffith and Robert Barton. Collins (1890–1922) was the brilliant military organiser whose guerrilla tactics made it possible for the IRA to hold its own against the British during the War of Independence. Griffith (1871–1922), the leader of the group, had founded the original Sinn Féin in 1905, and was second only to de Valera in the new post-1916 organisation.

The British set the tone of the London talks from the start. Lloyd George made a single set of proposals, which his delegation refused to modify. According to these, Ireland would be given Dominion status within the British Empire, a position identical to that of Canada. This 'Irish Free State' would have its own parliament, army, and government departments, but several imperial links would be maintained. The British king would remain head of state and all members of the Irish parliament would be required to take an Oath of Allegiance to the monarch. Britain also insisted upon keeping three naval bases in Ireland.

While these terms did not confer complete independence, the Irish delegation eventually decided to accept them and the Anglo-Irish Treaty was signed in December 1921. Collins and his colleagues were convinced that rejection would lead to a resumption of hostilities, a prospect which they were unwilling to inflict upon the war-weary Irish people. Collins, moreover, did not view the Treaty as a final solution to the Irish Question; rather he considered it a necessary stepping-stone to a fuller measure of independence in the future.

When the delegation returned to Dublin, however, it was soon apparent that not all Sinn Fein leaders agreed with Collins' analysis. Many, including de Valera, felt that the delegates should have rejected any terms that did not provide for complete Irish independence, even if this meant continuing the war.

In January 1922 the Treaty was debated by a rancorous and bitterly divided Dail Eireann. The widow of Thomas Clarke, one of the 1916 martyrs, spoke out against the terms:

> I have heard big, strong military men say they would vote for this Treaty, which necessarily means taking an Oath of Allegiance [to the king], and I tell those men there is not power enough in the whole British Empire to force me into taking that oath. I took an oath to the Irish Republic, solemnly, reverently, meaning every word. I shall never go back from that.[8]

Arthur Griffith, with Collins at the peace conference in London, favoured acceptance:

> I will not sacrifice my country for a form of government ... I do not care whether the king of England or the symbol of the crown be in Ireland, so long as the people of Ireland are free to shape their own destinies.[9]

A vote was taken after twelve days of heated debate, and the controversial Treaty was ratified by the slender margin of sixty-four votes to fifty-seven. But bitterness reigned supreme, as the anti-Treaty TDs withdrew from the assembly, labelling their former comrades as traitors to the republican cause. Having failed to secure the rejection of the Treaty, de Valera resigned as President. Michael Collins, taking office as head of a provisional government of the Irish Free State, was faced with the cheerless task of leading a divided nation into independence.

The division between pro- and anti-treaty republicans was neither the only nor the most serious rift in Irish society. During World War 1 and the Anglo-Irish War of 1919–21, attention had been directed away from the unionists of Ulster. The latter, however, were no less determined to oppose Irish independence; speaking in 1917, Edward Carson put forward this view of the Ulster situation:

> In the north east of Ireland we have a population alien in race, alien in sympathy, alien in religion, alien in tradition, alien in outlook from the rest of Ireland, and it would be an outrage to the principle of self-government to place them under the rule of the remainder of the population.[10]

British forces preparing to depart Ireland after the 1921 treaty ended hostilities between the British Army and the IRA.

As the British troops left, the Free State troops moved in. This photograph shows the first company to take over Beggars Bush Barracks marching down the main road in the Phoenix Park on the way to their new post.

Sir John Lavery's painting of a Twelfth of July march in Portadown,
Co. Armagh, in 1928.

On the promenade at Bray, Co. Wicklow.

King George V opens the first session of the parliament of Northern Ireland in June 1921. Partition was a victory for the Ulster Unionists.

By the end of World War I, most unionists had come to realise that some measure of independence would have to be granted to Irish nationalists. While making this concession, however, loyalists were determined that Ulster would be excluded from any scheme of Irish Home Rule, and would maintain its traditional place in the United Kingdom.

This concept of partition won considerable support in British government circles; it seemed the only possible way to avoid civil war in Ulster at the end of World War I. The exact area to be excluded was the subject of much debate during the war. Carson fought for the exclusion of all nine Ulster counties, but this was never accepted by the government, in view of the large Catholic majorities in the counties of Cavan, Donegal and Monaghan.

Soon after the end of the war, the British government found itself engaged in guerrilla combat with the IRA. That struggle, however, did not prevent enactment of the Government of Ireland Act of 1920. This historic measure called for the establishment of Home Rule parliaments in the two separate states of Northern and Southern Ireland. In 'Southern Ireland' this Act was a dead letter, since Sinn Fein and the IRA were already fighting for more than Home Rule. The Unionists of

A group of Free State soldiers inspect a Dublin bread van during the Civil War, 1922.

177

Ulster, however, accepted its terms. Accordingly, the new state of Northern Ireland was formed, comprising the six most Protestant of Ulster's nine counties: Antrim, Armagh, Derry, Down, Fermanagh and Tyrone.

Ironically, the greatest opponents of Home Rule now found themselves possessed of a parliament with responsibility for domestic affairs. But this was Home Rule with a difference. Within the six counties of the new state of Northern Ireland, Protestants comprised 66 per cent of the total population. As long as they closed ranks, the Unionists were assured control of the Belfast legislature. They could use this position of dominance to maintain the link with Britain which they valued so highly, and to ensure that the nationalist dream of a thirty-two county Irish Republic remained just that. 'What we have, we hold' became a unionist credo; as Sir James Craig, the first Prime Minister of Northern Ireland, would later boast: 'We are a Protestant parliament and a Protestant state'.[11]

Liam Lynch, the chief-of-staff of the anti-Treaty IRA during the Civil War. His death in April 1923 effectively quenched the last hopes of the Republicans.

A crude Republican cartoon which casts aspersions upon the Free State government and the manner in which it has 'seduced' the people of Ireland.

CAREY COLLINS - GO DOWN ON YOUR B----Y KNEES WITHOUT ANY MORE D----D FUSS AND SWEAR ALLEGIANCE TO KING GEORGE AND HIS HEIRS.

FAKER FITZGERALD - DON'T LISTEN TO DEVALERA. I COULD TELL YOU A LOT ABOUT HIS GREAT GREAT GRANDMOTHER AND SPANISH GOLD.

THE BISHOP - TAKE ANY OATH MY CHILD THAT WILL GET YOU OUT OF YOUR PRESENT DIFFICULTIES.

COMIC COSGRAVE - IT WAS AN AWFUL JOKE TALKING ABOUT FREEDOM AND REPUBLICS, YOU KNOW.

It may seem rather puzzling that the establishment of a Northern Ireland statelet was accepted so placidly by Irish nationalists, particularly since popular sentiment had become so extreme by 1920. Apart from the fact that no nationalist group possessed the military means to coerce the loyalists into a united Ireland, other factors were involved. Many republican leaders, including both Collins and de Valera, were convinced that a six-county Ulster state would prove to be economically unviable; furthermore, they felt certain that Britain would eventually withdraw its political support from the unionist enclave. More importantly, the acrimonious Treaty debates, the controversy over the Oath of Allegiance, and the bitter Civil War fought over the constitutional status of the twenty-six counties combined to focus attention in the south during the formative years of the new Ulster state.

Early in 1922, a group of militant Treaty opponents seized the Four Courts, a group of buildings in central Dublin which formed the hub of the Irish judicial system, and remained in occupation for over three months, in public defiance of the government of the Irish Free State. Collins was reluctant to move against his former comrades, who now appropriated the 'republican' label because of their insistence upon complete independence. But when the Four Courts rebels captured a Free State Army general in June 1922, Collins gave the order for government forces to attack the building.

What followed was nearly a repetition of the events of Easter 1916; now, however, Irishman took up arms against Irishman. The republican garrison eventually surrendered, but not before the centre of Dublin was

A Free State unit combs the streets of the Clare town of Killaloe, during the drive to recapture Munster from the Republicans.

'The Big Fella' – a Free State armoured vehicle bearing the same sobriquet as Michael Collins, who was killed in action in August 1922.

again devastated. The intensity of government intervention led many who wavered, including de Valera, to move into open rebellion. Throughout the country, anti-Treaty republicans prepared to fight against the Free State army.

The Civil War which followed was actually a battle between two very unequal adversaries. While they tried to employ the guerrilla tactics that had worked so well during the War of Independence, the republicans simply did not have the public support which the unified Sinn Fein/IRA had then enjoyed. In the first Free State election, held just before the Four Courts attack, anti-Treaty candidates got only 22 per cent of the popular vote. While they could count on more support in Munster than elsewhere, the republicans could never be sure if the hospitality which they received was genuine or merely the prelude to sudden arrest.

In such circumstances, the Treaty opponents faced an uphill struggle. Far better equipped and organised than its republican counterpart, the Free State army quickly drove enemy units out of the major population centres and into isolated rural areas. After nine months of sporadic fighting, most republican units were out of action. In April 1923 Liam Lynch, the rebel commander-in-chief, was killed in an ambush. A month later, Eamon de Valera – who had maintained a curiously low profile throughout the struggle – asked his republican supporters to lay down their guns. As do most civil wars, this one ended without a treaty and without celebration.

By international standards, the Irish Civil War of 1922–3 was not a particularly costly struggle. Apart from Cork and Dublin, property damage was not significant, and altogether less than a thousand men were killed. Included in this total, however, were many of the outstanding leaders on both sides. No loss was more tragic for the future of the country than that of Michael Collins, killed in Co. Cork in August 1922. Although leader of the Free State government, he was respected by both sides as a man of courage and integrity. With his death went the last hope for reconciliation between the two groups.

This senseless slaughter – a war over what was largely a question of semantics – turned many sensitive Irish people away from the politics of nationalism. Among these was Sean O'Casey, a Dublin playwright of working-class origins. A former member of the Irish Citizen Army, O'Casey made constant reference in his plays to his disillusionment with nationalism. In *Juno and the Paycock*, for example, a young shell-shocked republican is murdered by his colleagues when he refuses to participate in any further operations. The lament of his distraught mother seems a fitting epitaph for the nation itself during this tragic period:

> Maybe I didn't feel sorry enough for Mrs Tancred when her poor son was found as Johnny's been found now – because he was a Diehard! Ah, why didn't I remember that then he wasn't a Diehard or a Stater, but only a poor dead son! . . . Sacred Heart o' Jesus, take away our hearts o'stone, and give us hearts o'flesh! Take away this murdherin' hate, and give us Thine own eternal love![12]

'Changing the colour of the Emerald Isle' – a poignant American comment on the Irish Civil War.

12—Ireland in Isolation

When the soul of a man is born in this country, there are nets flung out to hold it back from flight. You talk to me of nationality, language and religion. I shall try to fly by those nets.

James Joyce, *A Portrait of the Artist as a Young Man*, 1916

The country public house remained a major focal point of community activity.

In January 1922 a quiet ceremony took place at Dublin Castle, traditional headquarters of the British government in Ireland. For the last time the Union Jack was lowered down the flagpole and in its place went the tricolour of the new Irish Free State, with vertical bands of green, white and orange. For nationalist Ireland, it was the culmination of a struggle that went back to the 1790s. And yet, the pride felt in the achievement was tinged with tragedy. The new state included only twenty-six of the island's thirty-two counties. The majority in the six counties of Northern Ireland had turned their backs on the rest of the country. At the same time, there were bitter divisions among the nationalist leaders in the south which were to lead to a tragic Civil War in which, as one participant noted, 'Every devilish thing we did against the British went its full circle and smote us tenfold'.[1]

Political groupings in the Free State were determined by the issues of the Civil War. Cumann na nGaedheal attracted the support of most of those who had supported the Treaty, and was the governing party until 1932. Following its defeat in that year, and again in a snap general election in 1933, it re-grouped and changed its name to Fine Gael. The opponents of the Treaty took no part in politics for a few years after the end of the Civil War, but the formation of the Fianna Fail party in 1926 brought them back into the mainstream. While credit should be given to both parties for taking the gun out of Irish politics, their origins and traditional policies ensured that the issues of the Civil War would not be forgotten for decades.

This perennial concern with the nature of the British connection helped to obscure the real character of Irish independence. Despite the transfer of political power,

W. T. Cosgrave (1880–1965), Collins's successor as head of government and leader of the pro-Treaty Cumann na nGaedheal party, presided over the first decade of Irish independence.

Fair day, Dingle, Co. Kerry, c. 1930. Traditional patterns of rural life continued well into the twentieth century.

the new Ireland was little different from the old. It remained a predominantly rural country; as late as 1951 one-third of the population lived on farms. The Catholic Church maintained its dominant social position. Whatever their political differences, most Irish people were content with the structure of their society. National independence was viewed as the capstone for the existing social order rather than as a signal for social revolution.

Members of the Irish Women Workers Union, c. 1914. Socialist ideas won comparatively few adherents in the Irish Free State, however, and most women remained under-employed, under-paid and under their husbands' thumbs.

Nationalism itself proved to be a hallmark of the status quo. Most of its adherents thought in terms of reviving ancient glories rather than creating new ones. The country did not industrialise, and neither liberal nor socialist ideas took root. A small Labour Party did manage to control twenty-odd seats out of a total of 153 in Dail Eireann, but lack of a large urban base and clerical opposition combined to make Ireland one of the few countries in Northern Europe where a powerful socialist movement did not develop during this period.

The fact that most people were content with their traditional cultural baggage led to a general unwillingness to accept new ideas, many of which were branded as godless, foreign or communistic. This narrowness led one critic to describe the Irish Free State as 'a concentration-camp of the mind'.[2] Even allowing for exaggeration in that statement, Ireland during the 1930s and 1940s did become something of a hermit nation setting its face against contemporary European life.

Despite the fact that the Irish Free State was the product of a rebellion against British rule, its political structure was derived directly from the British model. The constitution of 1922 provided for a cabinet of ministers drawn from and directly responsible to the Dail, the lower house of the Irish Oireachtas or parliament. This consisted of 153 members or teachtaí dála (TDs) who were elected by universal adult suffrage. The upper house, or Senate, was a largely ceremonial body with powers similar to those of the House of Lords at Westminster. The civil service machinery was taken over directly from the British. During the decade before independence, the civil service had been largely Irish in personnel and 95 per cent of these stayed on after 1922 in the service of the new government. While this made for a smooth transfer of power and administrative continuity, it also reduced the possibility of innovative or novel ideas coming to fruition.

The political life of the new Ireland was dominated by one personality: Eamon de Valera. Although an austere and somewhat aloof public figure, 'Dev' aroused considerable emotion among the Irish people. He was worshipped by his admirers and vilified by his detractors. The former, however, were considerably more numerous and made it possible for the sole surviving 1916 commandant to serve as Irish Prime Minister for a total of twenty-one years.

As a leader of the anti-Treaty Republicans during the Civil War, de Valera's political career seemed over in 1924. But he regrouped his supporters in a new party, Fianna Fail ('Soldiers of Destiny'), which pledged itself to the use of constitutional methods to achieve complete independence from Britain. Elected Fianna Fail TDs took their seats in the Dail in 1927, and began to gain in popularity as the Free State government under W.T. Cosgrave found itself faced with increasing economic difficulties. In the general election of 1932, Fianna Fail swept to victory, as de Valera capped an amazing political comeback by becoming Prime Minister of the Irish Free State whose establishment he had so vehemently opposed.

De Valera wasted little time in office before declaring economic war upon Britain. Irish farmers still owed the British government large sums of money, as a result of the long-term loans made to their fathers for land purchase before independence. Arguing that the land had been stolen from the people in the first place, the Fianna Fail leader announced that no further payments would be made. The British retaliated by putting punitive tariffs on Irish goods entering that country; de Valera replied by putting equally high levies on British imports.

This economic situation continued for most of the 1930s, and had serious impact upon Irish agriculture and industry. Many Irish farmers had concentrated on the production of cattle for export to Britain; with this market now closed, there was a dramatic shift towards tillage farming. A host of Irish industrial enterprises were developed, protected by the high tariff barriers. While these did produce some employment, they were hampered by lack of raw materials and thus unable to make substantial growth.

The tariff impasse was finally resolved in 1938, when de Valera and Neville Chamberlain, the British Prime Minister, agreed to a £10,000,000 cash settlement for

Ardnacrusha, Co. Limerick, the site of Ireland's first major hydro-electric scheme, constructed during the late 1920s on the River Shannon.

The leading Irish artist of the early twentieth century was a brother of the country's most famous poet. Jack B. Yeats (1871–1957) borrowed from the European impressionists to create a distinctive style which he applied to a host of Irish subjects.

A 1932 Punch *cartoon which reflects upon de Valera's attempts to sever the links between London and the Irish Free State.*

outstanding land-purchase loans. At the same time, Britain agreed to remove all naval personnel from her three remaining Irish bases.

A year before de Valera's meeting with Chamberlain, the Irish people approved a new Constitution formulated by Fianna Fail. This abolished the Irish Free State; 'Eire' now became the official name of the country and 'Taoiseach' became the official title of its Prime Minister. The king's place as symbolic head of the country was taken by a president directly elected by the people. Significantly, the first president of Ireland was Douglas Hyde, one of the founders of the Gaelic League.

De Valera stopped short of declaring Ireland a republic. The Constitution of 1937 did recognise a rather nebulous state of 'external association' between the two British Isles. Having presented the London government with such a *fait accompli*, however, the Taoiseach was pragmatic enough to stop short of a declaration of complete independence which might prove more than British public opinion would tolerate.

For most of the thirties and forties, Eamon de Valera was 'the Chief', leading political figure at home and virtual personification of the Irish nation in the eyes of most foreigners. This photograph shows him at Baldonnel Aerodrome, near Dublin, with Charles Lindbergh (right) when the latter visited Ireland in 1936.

THE BRIDGE-BREAKER.

MR. DE VALERA. "IF I CAN SHIFT THIS KEYSTONE, THAT OUGHT TO CLEAR THE WAY FOR SOMETHING DRAMATIC."

The Spanish Civil War, 1936–39, aroused strong passions in Ireland. Most people, led by the Catholic clergy, were ardent supporters of Franco. There was, however, a small group of Irishmen who formed a unit of the International Brigade, and fought with distinction for the Spanish Republic. A section of the unit are shown here. Frank Ryan, leader of the Irish in Spain, is third from the left at the back.

The comedian Jimmy O'Dea (1899–1965) dominated the Dublin music-hall stage from the 1920s to the 1950s.

This 1940 photograph shows an Irish Army unit on training manoeuvres. Soon afterwards, the German-style helmets were replaced by less distinctive ones.

During the 'Emergency' Bord na Mona was established so that Ireland could make better use of its extensive peat deposits. By the war's end 'turf' was satisfying a major share of the country's power needs.

Members of the Local Defence Force did what they could to keep the country in a state of military readiness during the 1940s.

In fact Britain had far bigger problems than Ireland in 1937. Within two years Nazi aggression would drag that country and most of Europe into the second great war of the century.

Almost immediately after the German invasion of Poland, de Valera declared that Ireland would not become involved in World War II. His decision was supported by virtually all political parties in the country. Although there was little sympathy for the Axis Powers, memories of the War of Independence and the continued existence of Northern Ireland ruled out any alliance with Britain.

De Valera's neutrality policy won the almost unanimous support of the Irish people. While the country was spared most of the horrors which the 1940s brought to much of the continent, the period was one of grim austerity. Like it or not, Ireland was forced to be self-sufficient. The total acreage under crops doubled while there was a massive increase in the use of peat for heating, since coal was nearly impossible to get. Many other products such as fertilisers, tea, rubber and petrol became almost unobtainable.

While the government did maintain a strictly neutral posture during World War II, it was clear that popular sympathies lay with the Allies. After all, there were few cultural links between Ireland and Germany.

Furthermore, Northern Ireland was directly involved in the conflict. Belfast suffered two major air attacks during the spring of 1941, in which over a thousand people were killed and the city's shipyards were severely damaged.

Hundreds of thousands of Irishmen from both north and south found employment in war-time Britain. An estimated 50,000 citizens of Eire served with the British armed forces; seven won Victoria Crosses. One recalls the comment of the Dublin-born navigator of the all-Irish crew of a British bomber dodging anti-aircraft fire over Berlin: 'Thank God Dev's kept us out of all this!'[3]

For sixteen years, from 1932 to 1948, de Valera reigned supreme in Irish politics. His popularity combined with divisions among the opposition parties helped Fianna Fail win six consecutive elections. Despite this secure position, however, his government never really came to grips with the country's serious social and economic problems. There was little real improvement in the area of social welfare; medical and educational standards remained among the lowest in Europe. While there was a certain amount of industrial development, Ireland's greatest export continued to be her people. Thousands emigrated annually, and the population continued to decline.

Some critics have blamed de Valera's obsession with constitutional issues for these failures. Anglo-Irish relations were indeed his primary political concern, but the Taoiseach was not without his vision of an ideal Ireland. Even here, however, he tended towards an anachronistic rural idyll:

The Ireland which we dreamed of would be the home of a people who value material wealth only as a basis of right living, of a people who were satisfied with frugal comfort and devoted their leisure to things of the spirit. . . .

The first of these latter is the national language. It is for us what no other language can be. It is more than a symbol; it is an essential part of our nationhood. As a vehicle for three thousand years of our history, the language is for us precious beyond measure. As the bearer to us of a philosophy, of an outlook on life deeply Christian and rich in practical wisdom, the language is worth far too much to dream of letting it go.[4]

De Valera's devotion to the Irish language was shared by most political leaders of his generation, and was but one example of a tendency to look to the past in the midst of modern difficulties. The actual amount of money spent by governments on the revival of Irish was not vast, as a proportion of overall public spending, although it drew considerable criticism from those who pointed out that such basic twentieth-century amenities as electricity and running water were unavailable in many parts of rural Ireland. The contrary argument was that the sum in question was too small to have any effect on these problems. The novelist Flann O'Brien, writing under the pseudonym Myles na Gopaleen in *The Irish Times*, defended the revival policy thus:

I hold that it is fallacious to offer the Irish people a choice between slums and Gaelic. . . . The horrible charge is made that Mr de Valera is spending half a million a year on reviving Irish. I may be a wild paddy but I take the view that the free expenditure of public money on a cultural pursuit is one of the few boasts this country can make. Whether we get value for all the money spent on Irish . . . is one question but that we spend liberally on these things is to our credit and when the great nations of the earth (whose civilisations we are so often asked to admire) are spending up to £100,000,000 (roughly) per day on destruction, it is surely no shame for our humble community of peasants to spend about £2,000 per day on trying to revive a language. It is the more urbane occupation.[5]

But despite the efforts of successive Irish governments, the policy was a failure. Financial support did prevent Irish from dying out altogether in the western areas where it was still spoken, but these areas were so badly hit by emigration during this period that the number of native speakers continued to decline. While Irish was a compulsory school subject, few children carried the language from the classroom to their homes. Parents were not always sympathetic either, knowing only too well that proficiency in English was the key to a job abroad at a time when jobs at home were so scarce.

CRÉ NA CILLE
MÁIRTÍN Ó CADHAIN

CRÉ NA CILLE
MÁIRTÍN Ó CADHAIN

SÁIRSÉAL AGUS DILL

The formation of the publishing house of Sáirséal agus Dill in 1945 put Irish-language publishing on a professional basis for the first time. It also gave an outlet to creative writers in Irish. The greatest of these, Máirtín Ó Cadhain, published his masterpiece, Cré na Cille, in 1949. It was subsequently chosen by UNESCO for translation into several major languages, as part of a programme devoted to outstanding works in minor languages. This photograph shows the original dust jacket.

While much of historic Dublin was preserved, many old neighbourhoods suffered from neglect.

The Catholic Church continued to wield powerful influence, especially in rural areas. Here the Archbishop of Tuam greets parishioners in the Aran Islands, off the coast of Galway.

The attitudes of many Irish speakers and teachers were another stumbling block. Rightly or wrongly, many saw them as a kind of elite, holding top civil service jobs because of their proficiency in the language, and given to narrow-minded visions of a rural Gaelic Utopia. One journalist described them as exuding 'a palpable aura of self-satisfaction over being able to say very little in two languages'.[6] Their contempt for the non-Irish-speaking majority inevitably won their cause an equal measure of distaste.

During the struggle for Irish independence, one of the great fears of Ulster Protestants was that the Catholic Church would hold an omnipotent position within Irish society if and when the British connection was severed. To some extent their anxieties were justified by developments in the Irish Free State after 1922.

The influence of the Irish Church was more subtle than blatant. Ireland remained a democratic state, and Church leaders did not take the authoritarian positions that they did in Franco's Spain or Salazar's Portugal. Instead, the strength of the institution derived from the incredible religious dedication of the laity. In few Catholic countries were the people as regular in their observance of religious customs and practices. 98 per cent of Irish Catholics attended Mass every Sunday. Among them there was a willingness to accept without question the teachings of the Church leadership of social as well as religious questions. So strong was their devotion that the Catholic Hierarchy rarely had to involve itself directly in Irish political affairs, since the social conservatism of the masses usually ensured that popular attitudes mirrored its own.

Education remained a clerical preserve in the years after independence. Parish priests remained the managers of the local primary schools, while nearly all secondary schools were owned and operated by religious orders. Successive Irish governments willingly ceded most of the educational system to the Church. The educational system which developed was financially supported by the State, but largely administered by Catholic clerics.

Few primary or secondary schools admitted both male and female students; the large majority of Irish schoolchildren never had class mates of the opposite sex. In many ways the schools were a reflection of the society as a whole. In few other European countries were male and female roles so harshly defined. For much of the first half of the twentieth century it was virtually impossible for women to enjoy successful careers in business or politics. Most Irish men, on the other hand, felt that housekeeping and child care were the natural duties of women. Few friendships passed this sexual divide; even relationships between husbands and wives tended to be extremely formal.

Not surprisingly, the general Irish attitude towards sex was puritanical. This tendency was encouraged and re-enforced by the Church. The sixth commandment was elevated to a pre-eminent position by many Irish priests, some of whom used even prowl the streets to separate courting couples found holding hands! Such a stifling of normal human behaviour helped maintain Ireland's amazingly late marriage age. In 1951 the average Irish man married at the age of 35, and the average Irish woman at 29.

De Valera and Thomas Derrig, his Minister for Education, seated amongst the leading members of the Christian Brothers at an annual convocation at Maynooth. This particular order continued to exercise considerable influence over the shape and direction of Irish education.

Since the Dail was an overwhelmingly Catholic legislature, Irish law tended to reflect Catholic teaching on matters of public morality. Divorce was forbidden under the 1937 Constitution, and the sale or distribution of contraceptives by statute. Adoption laws were tailored to suit the demands of the Church, but perhaps the best evidence of the legalisation of the Catholic moral code was provided by the activities of the Censorship Board, a body established in 1929 to suppress those books and films considered obscene or dangerous to public morality.

Nearly every creative Irish writer of any international standing had some work banned in his native country during the 1930s and 1940s. The list of foreign writers who earned the occasional disapproval of the Board included Faulkner, Hemingway, Huxley, Somerset Maugham, Orwell, Sartre, Steinbeck and D.H. Lawrence. The collected papers of Sigmund Freud were banned. Also prohibited was the 1949 Report of the Royal Commission on Population, because it mentioned certain methods of birth control! While sanctions were not usually applied with great rigour, the activities of the Censorship Board did reveal the narrow confines of the Irish Catholic mentality.

Despite this legal endorsement of the Catholic moral code, the Protestant citizens of Eire, about one in twenty of the population, were treated with considerable justice. While it recognised the special position of Catholicism as a religion of a majority of Irish people, the Constitution of 1937 did guarantee the rights of non-Catholics to practise their religion freely. Indeed, the government bent over backwards to be fair to the Protestant minority. Protestant schools received the

ABBEY THEATRE

Proprietors
Directors — THE NATIONAL THEATRE SOCIETY, Ltd.
ERNEST BLYTHE, ROIBEARD O'FARACHAIN, SEAMUS DE BHILMOT, GABRIEL FALLON
Secretary — ERIC GORMAN

Commencing MONDAY, 17th AUGUST, 1959
AND FOLLOWING NIGHTS AT 8 P.M.   DOORS OPEN AT 7.30

MONDAY, WEDNESDAY and FRIDAY, 17th, 19th and 21st AUGUST

FIRST PRODUCTION OF
STRANGER, BEWARE.
By TOMAS COFFEY

TUESDAY, THURSDAY and SATURDAY, 18th, 20th and 22nd AUGUST

THE COUNTRY BOY
By JOHN MURPHY

LATECOMERS NOT ADMITTED UNTIL END OF FIRST ACT

Prices - Dress Circle, 7/- & 5/-; Stalls, 7/- & 6/-; Upper Circle, 3/6; Gallery, 1/6
ALL BOOKING AT QUEEN'S THEATRE
BOX OFFICE OPEN 10.30 TO 6.   'PHONE 44505

The national theatre lost much of its vitality in the years after independence, and produced an endless stream of quaint, inoffensive dramas like The Country Boy. *Controversial subjects were avoided, as were any suggestions that all was not well with Irish society.*

Some of the leading literary figures of the post-independence era gather at Sandymount Strand, Dublin on 16 June, Bloomsday, 1954. From left to right, John Ryan, critic and editor; Anthony Cronin, poet; the novelist and social critic Brian O'Nolan, (also known as Flann O'Brien and Myles na Gopaleen); the poet Patrick Kavanagh, and Tom Joyce, James Joyce's cousin.

For the first half-century after independence, secondary education continued to be dominated by religious orders. Very few schools catered to both boys and girls, a fact that encouraged the puritanical tendencies within Irish society.

same financial support as Catholic ones. Because they suffered no real economic discrimination non-Catholics continued to control about 30 per cent of the national wealth.

But the Irish government could afford to be generous. Such a tiny minority presented no serious threat to the Catholic establishment. There was no question who was in the driver's seat. In 1931, for example, in a gesture of goodwill towards the minority, the Free State government attempted to appoint a well-trained Protestant woman to the post of head librarian at the Mayo County Library at Castlebar. Public and clerical opinion in Mayo, however, would not accept a non-Catholic in this sensitive local position. After parades of protest and a threatened tax strike, the government was forced to withdraw this nomination. Speaking against the appointment, the Catholic Archbishop of Tuam offered remarkable evidence of the continuing strength of sectarianism in Ireland:

> It is gratifying to see how the representatives of our Catholic people are unwilling to subsidise libraries not under Catholic control. Not to speak of those who are alien to our faith it is not every Catholic who is fit to be in charge of a Public Library for Catholic readers. Such an onerous position should be assigned to an educated Catholic who would be as remarkable for his loyalty to his religion as for his literary and intellectual attainments.[7]

Keeping the name which had won so much glory during the war of Independence, ultra-nationalists continued to attract a degree of support from young Catholics in Ulster.

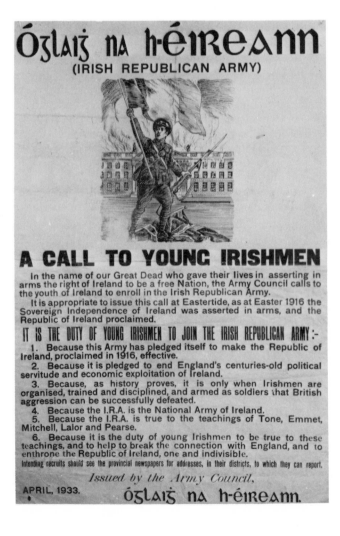

Óglaiġ na h-Éireann
(IRISH REPUBLICAN ARMY)

A CALL TO YOUNG IRISHMEN

In the name of our Great Dead who gave their lives in asserting in arms the right of Ireland to be a free Nation, the Army Council calls to the youth of Ireland to enroll in the Irish Republican Army.

It is appropriate to issue this call at Eastertide, as at Easter 1916 the Sovereign Independence of Ireland was asserted in arms, and the Republic of Ireland proclaimed.

IT IS THE DUTY OF YOUNG IRISHMEN TO JOIN THE IRISH REPUBLICAN ARMY:-

1. Because this Army has pledged itself to make the Republic of Ireland, proclaimed in 1916, effective.

2. Because it is pledged to end England's centuries-old political servitude and economic exploitation of Ireland.

3. Because, as history proves, it is only when Irishmen are organised, trained and disciplined, and armed as soldiers that British aggression can be successfully defeated.

4. Because the I.R.A. is the National Army of Ireland.

5. Because the I.R.A. is true to the teachings of Tone, Emmet, Mitchell, Lalor and Pearse.

6. Because it is the duty of young Irishmen to be true to these teachings, and to help to break the connection with England, and to enthrone the Republic of Ireland, one and indivisible.

Intending recruits should see the provincial newspapers for addresses, in their districts, to which they can report.

Issued by the Army Council.

APRIL, 1933.

Óglaiġ na h-Éireann

Sir James Craig (1871–1940), later Lord Craigavon, first Prime Minister of Northern Ireland and a staunch opponent of Irish unity.

Twelfth of July parades remained an Ulster tradition. Each year, on that date, members of the Orange Lodges throughout the province took to the streets to demonstrate their solidarity with the Unionist cause.

The Protestants of Northern Ireland viewed controversies such as the one described with a certain amount of satisfaction. Such incidents seemed to prove that Home Rule had brought an element of Rome Rule to the South, and that the Unionists had been justified in their refusal to accept a Dublin-based Irish parliament.

Within their own six-county state, however, Ulster Protestants proved anything but ecumenical. Indeed discrimination against the Catholic minority in Northern Ireland was considerably more severe than discrimination against the Protestants in the South.

For fifty years after the creation of the six-county enclave in 1920, the government of Northern Ireland was completely dominated by the Unionist Party. Because about two-thirds of the population was Protestant, and because political divisions corresponded so closely to sectarian ones, this organisation always maintained a comfortable majority in the Northern Ireland parliament, which met at Stormont, outside Belfast. At no time were there less than thirty-five Unionists MPs in a House of Commons whose total membership was fifty-two. United in their determination to preserve the British link, the Unionists never once surrendered political power. In Northern Ireland party and government became synonymous.

Unionist political dominance at the provincial level was perfectly legitimate, and the natural democratic result in a state where party allegiance rarely shifted between elections. But such absolute control made it possible for the Unionists to construct a system of local government that clearly discriminated against the Catholic minority. While everyone could vote in Stormont elections, only householders had the fran-

chise in elections for county and urban councils. Indeed, many prosperous individuals had several votes as a result of their ownership of several pieces of property.

Since the Protestant community was considerably more affluent than the Catholic, this electoral system clearly favoured the former. When combined with judicious gerrymandering, it became possible for Unionists to control local authorities in areas where the Protestant population was a minority. For example, Unionists controlled both Derry Urban Council and Fermanagh County Council, yet in both areas over 60 per cent of the population was Catholic.

Economic discrimination was even more blatant. Most council jobs went to Protestants, while local utility companies usually employed very few Catholics. The Electricity Department of Belfast Corporation, for example, counted less than fifty Catholics among its 1,000 employees in 1949. Many private firms also avoided hiring Catholics whenever possible. Harland & Wolff was one of the many loyalist concerns; there were never more than a few hundred Catholics among the eight to ten thousand employees of the giant shipyard.

While such forms of discrimination may seem mild when compared to places like modern South Africa, they did nothing to reconcile Ulster Catholics to the existence of the Unionist state of Northern Ireland. While a Nationalist Party which spurned the use of force did control ten to fifteen seats at Stormont and formed something of a feeble parliamentary opposition, more violent groups also commanded Catholic support. The foremost of these was the modern Sinn Fein party, which consisted both of Northern extremists and Southern republicans who never accepted the Anglo-

Irish Treaty and considered even de Valera a British traitor for his unwillingness to use armed force to end partition. The military wing of Sinn Fein, which also used a traditional separatist label by calling itself the Irish Republican Army, engaged in spasmodic bombing campaigns both in Ireland and Britain. Lack of wide support from Catholics in the North, however, made the IRA more of a public nuisance than a revolutionary threat.

The Unionists, of course, saw all Catholics as potential traitors. This helps to explain how men with such strong democratic traditions could tolerate such obvious political and economic injustice. The Ulster Catholic was the Enemy Within, far more dangerous than his colleagues in the South. In 1933 Sir Basil Brooke, the Unionist leader who was destined to serve as Prime Minister of Northern Ireland for two decades, gave this famous advice to his Protestant neighbours in Fermanagh:

There are a great number of Protestants and Orangemen who employ Roman Catholics. I feel I can speak freely on this subject as I have not an RC about my own place. Catholics are out to destroy Ulster with all their might and power. . . . I would appeal to loyalists, therefore, whenever possible, to employ good Protestant lads and lassies.[8]

Even at the best of times, economic discrimination had contributed to Ulster's problems. During the first two decades of Northern Ireland's existence, however, the general economic situation was anything but favourable. After World War I the linen industry went into a prolonged slump from which it never really recovered. The depression of the 1930s hit hard at the province's shipbuilding industry, as Workman & Clark went out of business and Harland & Wolff struggled to remain solvent. Few new industrial enterprises were launched, and unemployment reached record levels. In 1931 fully 28 per cent of the adult male population in

Violence also remained an integral part of Ulster life, and few summers passed without incident in Belfast.

One-third of the population of the Republic now lives in the Greater Dublin area. In little more than a generation, Ireland has been transformed into a modern, consumer society. This photograph shows the Dun Laoghaire Shopping Centre.

*The face of modern Dublin. This abstract sculpture by Michael Bulfin
stands in front of the new Bank of Ireland headquarters in Baggot St.*

Basil Brooke (1888–1973), later Lord Brookeborough, served as Northern Ireland's Prime Minister from 1943 to 1963. In 1958, Brooke (right) entertained President and Mrs Dwight D. Eisenhower when they visited Ulster.

Northern Ireland was without work. Not surprisingly, religious tensions ran high in decaying lower-class neighbourhoods in Derry and Belfast. Serious rioting in the latter city claimed eleven lives in 1935.

The power of sectarianism remained undiminished in twentieth-century Ulster. Despite the fact that both religious groups were fairly evenly distributed throughout the province, Catholics and Protestants rarely had more than perfunctory dealings with each other. Each community turned in on itself, practising a form of voluntary apartheid. There were Catholic pubs and Protestant pubs, Catholic dances and Protestant dances. Even on the sporting field, the two communities rarely met. While Protestant youths played soccer and rugby, their Catholic counterparts participated in the traditional Irish games of hurling and Gaelic football.

Perhaps the only way in which this self-imposed separation might have been broken down was through the schools. Lord Londonderry, the first Northern Ireland Minister for Education, recognised as much when he argued in favour of a non-denominational system of education for the province in 1921:

> We must safeguard the educational system from the denominationalism that can only produce division when union is so essential to the well-being of the province.[9]

With rare ecumenical spirit, Anglican, Presbyterian and Catholic religious leaders joined together to oppose Lord Londonderry's proposal. None of the churches would accept a school curriculum in which their own religious views were not reflected; none would tolerate schoolteachers and administrators of faiths different from their own. As a result religious segregation continued in the schools of the six counties, and the great chasm between the Protestant and Catholic communities of Northern Ireland remained unbridged.

"I could have sworn the haystacks were in the other field when we last passed this way."

The establishment of a political border in Ulster gave ample opportunity for the growth of a new industry: smuggling.

13—Exiles in Maturity

*The enemies of Ireland have made it appear that the Irish case is
complicated and delicate. It is not. It is simple. It is that Ireland deserves
liberty and demands it. It may be described in the words of your President
when the United States entered the war, saying that America protested
against the right of the strong to rule by brute force. Shall a people be
dominated by another people solely by might? That is the only question in
Ireland. It is the task of Ireland's enemies to prove their case, not our
task to prove ours.*

Eamon de Valera, reported in the *Boston Post*, 1 July 1919.

*De Valera's American tour of 1919–20 took him to all parts of that
country, and brought him before some rather unusual audiences, as this
poster suggests.*

The paragraph above is taken from a speech which
Eamon de Valera delivered before the Massachusetts
State House of Representatives in June 1919. Seventy
years earlier an Irish rebel would have elicited more
contempt than sympathy in the city of Boston. Now,
however, de Valera received a hero's welcome, even
though he was a fugitive from English justice. In city
after city, banquets and parades were organised in his
honour, as urban America paid homage to the Sinn Fein
leader.

Earlier in the same year, an 'Irish' resolution had
been placed before the national House of
Representatives in Washington. This bill, which called
upon the post–World War I treaty makers at Versailles to
'favourably consider the claims of Ireland to the right of
self-determination', was carried by the extraordinary
margin of 216 votes to 45. While only a handful of the
Congressmen who supported this measure had real
interest in Irish affairs, most of the others realised that
Irish-American voters were both too numerous and too
powerful to ignore.

One who did not was the American President,
Woodrow Wilson, an Anglophile who supported Lloyd
George's contention that the Irish Question was a
British 'domestic' problem. As a result the
Congressional resolution came to nothing, and the issue
of Irish sovereignty was never discussed at Versailles.
But Wilson's pro-British sentiments came back to haunt
his Democratic Party in the 1920 Presidential elections.
His position on the matter not only contributed to the
defeat of James M. Cox, but helped ally Irish-
Americans with isolationist leaders who rejected the

F. Scott Fitzgerald (1896–1940), was the product of an upper-class Irish-American family and became one of the best-respected novelists of his era. The Great Gatsby *remains a fascinating pen-portrait of American society and mores during the Jazz Age.*

Versailles Treaty and kept the USA out of the League of Nations. In the future few Democratic Party leaders would repeat Wilson's mistake. Even the editor of the London *Daily News*, who visited America in 1920, noted the strength of Irish-American opinion:

> They form the most solid and formidable political mass in the country. They are formidable, not so much because of their number, as because they are the one political body moving with a single idea in a compact mass through the life of the nation. They have come across the Atlantic with bitterness in their hearts, and they are revenging themselves upon their oppressor.[1]

The rising position of the Irish was reflected in American business as well as in politics. By 1920 there were several dozen Irish-American millionaires. This group included Thomas E. Murray, whose 1,500 inventions contributed as much to the development of electricity as those of Edison, and James Butler, who pioneered the chain foodstore concept in America. During the early twentieth century these 'lace curtain' Irish carved a niche for themselves in the American social world. Although their religion and the newness of

UNCLE SAM : "Say, this is queer ! John seems to have sent me the wrong picture.'

Their domination of city politics gave Irish-American leaders control of municipal civil service appointments, and helped make the 'Irish cop' a distinct folk-type in urban America.

During 1918 and 1919, Sinn Féin policy was largely influenced by the hypothesis that American influence at the Versailles Peace Conference would work against English involvement in Ireland. Britain's decision to go to war against Germany in 1914 'in defence of small nations' became the subject of sarcastic cartoons like this one.

their wealth combined to exclude them from the highest circles, they could and did live in as much opulence as Yankee aristocrats. They too built magnificent mansions, made Grand Tours of Europe, and summered in plush resort areas. The town of Southampton on Long Island became a favourite watering-hole for these First Irish Families.

While only a handful of Irish-Americans belonged to FIFs, a sizable portion were moving into comfortable middle-class positions. By 1920 there were many Irish building contractors, shop foremen, and business executives. Many held civil service positions, especially in municipal and state governments.

Throughout this period Irish-Americans remained true to their roots and true to each other. A few families moved to the suburbs, but most remained in their old neighbourhoods long after they were financially able to move elsewhere. They took comfort in the local pub, the local Church and friends whose origins were identical.

As the *Irish-American* noted as early as 1853, 'the Irish are a social people, and require great self-denial to forsake the society of their kindred and kind.'[2]

Religion was one element of their tradition which Irish-Americans were loath to abandon. Until the Famine brought millions of Irishmen to the New World in the decades after 1850, the American Catholic Church was of insignificant size and importance. By 1900, however, massive Irish emigration had helped to make the Catholic Church the single largest religious organisation in the United States.

Thanks to their numerical strength, Irish Church leaders were able to build a network of ecclesiastical control which maintained their influence long after the Italians and other Catholic groups began to arrive in large numbers. As late as 1970, when Irish-Americans formed only 17 per cent of the Catholic population, 35 per cent of the clergy and fully 50 per cent of the American Hierarchy was of Irish descent.

Menlo Park near San Francisco was the ostentatious home of James C. Flood, an Irishman who made his fortune in the silver mines of Nevada.

THE AMERICAN RIVER GANGES.

James Cardinal Gibbons (1834–1921) of Baltimore was the leading liberal in the American Catholic Hierarchy. Unlike most of his colleagues, he did not condemn the development of a secular public school system in his diocese (above left).

Leading American nativists, such as cartoonist Thomas Nast (1840–1902), viewed the development of a separate Catholic school system as a serious threat to American democracy (above).

Not suprisingly, the American Catholic Church was thoroughly hibernicised. Bishops in the United States harboured the same fears of non-Catholic dominance as their counterparts in Ireland. Nativist reaction did nothing to lessen these suspicions, which lingered long after the Irish had become fully accepted into American society.

This defensive attitude was reflected in the Church's education policy. Church-State separation was an American tradition; religious instruction was forbidden in most American public schools of the late nineteenth century. While a few American bishops admired this system, most had no time for 'godless' education. As a result the Church developed its own system of 'parochial' schools. Catholic parents were advised, and sometimes compelled under pain of sin, to avoid the public school system.

By 1900 most American cities had their own Catholic primary and secondary schools. Most were run by religious orders, whose members collected modest fees in return for providing Catholic youth with Catholic education. The parochial system extended to university level, and dozens of Catholic colleges were established around the country. The administration of colleges such as Fordham, Holy Cross, Villanova and Notre Dame was dominated by Irish-American priests; to this day, sports teams of the last-named institution carry the nickname 'Fighting Irish'.

Educational segregation did much to keep the Irish separate from the rest of the American population. Growing up in Irish neighbourhoods and attending Catholic schools, Irish-American young people usually married within their own ethnic group. The Church's harsh laws regarding mixed marriages, which persisted down to the 1960s, further turned the Irish community in on itself, discouraging as they did contact with non-Catholics.

Not all Irish-Americans, of course, remained in this ethnic cocoon. The United States was not Ulster; there were strong cultural influences drawing the individual towards the American mainstream. Nevertheless, many preferred to remain 'with their own'. Religious policy reinforced this preference, and helped give Irish-Americans a cultural identity long after their immigrant forbears had been forgotten.

As a pilgrim father that missed th' first boats, I must raise me claryon voice again' th' invasion iv this fair land be th' paupers and arnychists iv effete Europe. Ye bet I must – because I'm here first![3]

So spoke 'Mr Dooley', a bachelor Chicago publican from Roscommon, and the creation of Finley Peter Dunne, the grandson of an Irish immigrant and one of the foremost American satirists of the early twentieth century. Unfortunately, Mr Dooley's sentiments were shared by many members of the Irish-American community. As they rose up the ladder of economic success, the Irish seldom felt compassion for those who took their place on the bottom rungs. With their own positions so recently secured, they resented the social and economic threat presented by new immigrants.

Greatest hostility, however, was reserved for black Americans. Although they were firm supporters of the Union during the American Civil War of the 1860s,

Much of Nast's work was anti-Irish in character. In this 1868 cartoon he portrays the Irishman as a simian brute who, along with Southern white supremacists and big business capitalists, was responsible for the continued suppression of blacks.

most Irish-Americans were opposed to President Abraham Lincoln's anti-slavery campaign. 'One of the oldest established facts of nature', wrote the editor of the *Pilot*, Boston's Catholic newspaper, in 1863, 'is the mental and physical fitness of the Negro for servility.'[4] The New York anti-draft riot of 1863 was accompanied by attacks upon that city's black community, including the burning of a Negro orphanage by a frenzied Irish mob.

Relations between Irish and black Americans continued poor throughout the twentieth century. As large numbers of blacks moved from the South to the cities of the north east, a system of de facto segregation developed. Blacks were rigidly excluded from schools and housing in Irish and other white neighbourhoods.

Latent hostility was brought to the surface during the early 1970s, when the federal government began 'busing' black children into white areas to achieve racial balance in schools. The most virulent opposition to this scheme developed in South Boston, one of the few distinctly Irish-American working-class neighbourhoods to survive into that decade. Children were terrorised and school buses overturned by local residents determined to keep blacks out of South Boston.

Father Charles E. Coughlin (1891–1977) became a dominant political figure during the Depression years. His nationally-syndicated radio programme had millions of listeners who were attracted by his pseudo-fascist formulas for the solution of the nation's economic woes.

Many Irish-Americans combined racial intolerance with super-patriotism. Despite their cultural links with Ireland, most gave complete political allegiance to the United States, and loyally supported the country in both of this century's World Wars. They put increasing emphasis upon 'law and order', and viewed with suspicion those who proposed drastic changes in the structure of American society. Their religious beliefs combined with their patriotism to make them fierce

While opposition to court-ordered school busing was widesprsead throughout the USA during the 1970s, it received its most virulent expression in the streets of South Boston, one of the few remaining American communities with a distinctively Irish character.

James M. Curley (1874–1958) the colourful Boston politico, and four-time Mayor of the city, shown here with silent film star Jane Come in 1920.

opponents of Communism during the several 'Red Scares' of this century. Indeed, the main protagonist of the anti-Communist crusade of the early 1950s was an Irish Catholic senator from Wisconsin, Joseph MacCarthy.

Not all Irish-Americans, of course, were political conservatives. *Commonweal*, a national Catholic magazine, opposed Joe MacCarthy from the outset, as did the young Irish-American senator from Massachusetts, John F. Kennedy. The most important liberal politician of the 1960s was also an Irish Catholic. Senator Eugene MacCarthy of Minnesota was the first major leader to speak out against the Vietnam War, and to reject the view that victory in that war was essential to halt 'Communist aggression'. MacCarthy, however, got little support from older Irish-Americans in his anti-war campaign. Throughout the 1960s and into the 1970s, the Irish-American political consensus remained right of centre.

Urban politics remained an Irish preserve for much of the twentieth century. At one time or another nearly every large American city had a mayor of Irish descent. Among these was the flamboyant James Michael Curley of Boston. Curley was the archetype of the Irish-American politician. A splendid orator and a back-slapping campaigner, he used political office to reward his friends and to harass his enemies. He served four terms as Mayor of Boston, one term as Governor of Massachusetts, and two terms in prison. The first of these came early in his career, after Curley took a civil service examination for a constituent who had little chance of passing. With some justification, Curley's later political posters referred to him as 'the Politician with a Heart'.

Founding father of an American political dynasty, financial wizard Joseph P. Kennedy (1888–1969) stands with his youngest son Teddy in this 1940 photograph.

Al Smith (1873–1944), Governor of New York and 1928 Democratic presidential candidate, reviewing a St Patrick's Day Parade along Fifth Avenue.

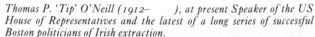

Thomas P. 'Tip' O'Neill (1912–), at present Speaker of the US House of Representatives and the latest of a long series of successful Boston politicians of Irish extraction.

Irish-American leaders continued to dominate city politics long after the Irish had ceased to be the single most important urban population bloc. They learned to bend with the political breeze, to attend Italian festivals and Polish picnics, and to share the spoils of office among all groups. Many tried – and succeeded – in being all things to all men. Perhaps the most remarkable of these durable politicians was Richard Daley, who was Mayor of Chicago from 1955 until his death in 1976. The grandson of Irish immigrants, Daley built up one of America's most powerful political machines, which gave Chicago twenty years of authoritarian but efficient urban government. Dedicated to no ideology except the growth of his city, Daley was immensely popular among Chicagoans; he was regularly re-elected with over 70 per cent of the vote.

Irish success in national politics was more limited. The popular image of the free-wheeling, hard-drinking Irish 'boss' won few votes in rural America. Many Protestants viewed the Catholicism of most Irish politicians with a great deal of suspicion. There remained a lingering fear that an Irish President would respect the pope in Rome more than the wishes of his constituents.

The first Irish-American to attempt to overcome these prejudices was Al Smith, who served as Governor of New York during the 1920s, and who won the Democratic nomination for the Presidency in 1928. A product of New York City's Irish slums, Smith was a

During his visit to Ireland in 1963, John F. Kennedy (1917–1963) took time to visit his cousins in Co. Wexford.

The Depression came as an abrupt jolt to many Irish-Americans who were beginning to climb the socio-economic ladder.

reforming politician who gave his state the most honest and efficient government that it had known for decades. But America was not ready for an Irish President; Smith was easily beaten by his Republican rival.

The Depression helped carry a Democrat to the White House in the next election in 1932. Unlike Woodrow Wilson, the previous Democratic president, Franklin D. Roosevelt was quite willing to work with Irish political leaders. Many held key positions in his administration, including Joseph P. Kennedy, a self-made Boston millionaire who served as American Ambassador to Great Britain. Other Irish-Americans became prominent congressional leaders, including John McCormack and later Thomas P. O'Neill, both of whom were to serve as Speakers of the House of Representatives.

The zenith of Irish success was not reached until 1960. In that year John F. Kennedy was elected as the first Irish Catholic President of the United States. The son of Roosevelt's British ambassador, Kennedy was hardly the typical Irish politician. Educated at Harvard, a Pulitzer Prize winner and the heir to enormous wealth, he was much more at home with the First Irish Families at Southampton than among the working-class residents of South Boston. Nevertheless, his personal magnetism was such that he had enormous appeal among Americans of all ethnic groups. While his brief administration produced few substantial achievements, it did place an emphasis upon youthful idealism which long survived his tragic assassination in 1963.

In the summer of 1963, several months before his death, John F. Kennedy visited Ireland. He was given a tumultuous welcome, but, as one American observed, the first Irish Catholic President was not really 'at home' in the land of his grandparent's birth:

> The overwhelming impression of the visitor, as he watched the great outpouring of public veneration for John Kennedy by the throngs of the Irish who lined the streets to welcome him, was that while they loved the man, gloried in his accomplishment, and shared it with fierce Celtic pride, vast areas of this man's personality eluded their understanding. He was Irish and he was Catholic, but his understanding of these two realities and their own involved differences so momentous that they almost surpassed even token understanding. A typical comment offered by an Irish gentleman standing next to the author that day underlined this confusion: 'It was nice of him to come, you know. It means a lot to our people, but you can't get around the impression that he is much more of you than he is of us.'[4]

This anonymous Irishman had placed his finger on an important development. By 1963 the Irish-Americans had become the American-Irish. Their cultural roots may have been in Ireland, but their present and future belonged to the United States.

Many factors were involved in this gradual transformation. The old Irish neighbourhoods began to break up in the great burst of prosperity that followed World War II. American society became more mobile and more cosmopolitan. Young Irish-Americans had fewer contacts with and less interest in their traditional

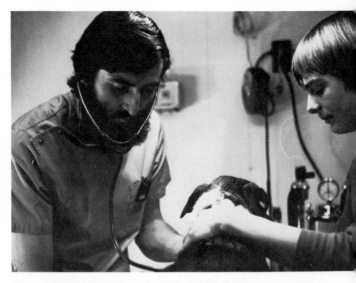

The population drain from Ireland during this century has been especially severe among the professional classes. Doctors, lawyers and engineers have all left the country for more rewarding opportunities elsewhere. One lucky recipient of this talent has been Canada, where this Irish-born veterinarian now practises.

A Belfast native who played down his Irish connections, Van Morrison (1945–), became one of rock music's brightest lights during the 1970s.

culture. They began to marry persons of other ethnic groups and other religious persuasions. By 1975 few young Americans could claim total Irish ancestry.

This transformation may not have occurred so rapidly had regular immigration continued. In Britain, for example, steady migration has helped maintain a flourishing Irish community in the Kilburn section of London. But in America a quota system began to limit the flow of immigration as early as the 1920s. At first the number of Irish allowed to enter the USA annually was quite high; Irish political influence was strong enough to

The interior of an Australian sheepherder's hut during the early years of settlement 'down under'.

Australian gold rushes brought more than miners to the fields. This picture shows the shop of an enterprising Irishman who went into business in the New South Wales boom town of Hill End during the 1870s.

ensure that successive Immigration Acts discriminated in their favour. But this preferential treatment ended in 1965, when a new Immigration Act established a new quota system which allowed only 170,000 immigrants per year from the entire Eastern Hemisphere. Preference was given to the immediate families of United States' citizens; in practice, few others, except political refugees, were admitted. Irish immigration virtually ceased. In 1975, for example, only 906 permanent visas were granted to Irish citizens.

If present trends continue, the American-Irish seem doomed to extinction. By the year 2000 death and intermarriage will have virtually eliminated them as a distinct ethnic group. Those who survive, however, are determined not to give up so quickly. Cities like Boston, New York and San Francisco still maintain strong Irish political and cultural organisations. St Patrick's Day still brings colourful parades to these cities, and 'Irish Hour' programmes can still be heard regularly on the radio.

But the decline is unmistakable. The number of Irish-American newspapers is shrinking, as is the number of hurling and Gaelic football teams in American cities. There are fewer and fewer direct contacts with modern Ireland. The cultural patterns Irish-Americans consider most 'Irish' have often long gone out of fashion in the 'old country'. For better or

worse, we are approaching the end of an era in American history. Just as the Indian was the 'vanishing American' of the last century, it seems the fate of the Irish-American to fill that role in this.

In terms of numbers, the Irish who went to Australia represented a small and seemingly insignificant part of the great nineteenth-century diaspora. Yet even though only one out of every twenty-five emigrants went 'down under', these played a most decisive role in the formation of that new nation.

THE IRISH PEOPLE

The white settlement of Australia began in the 1790s, when the English government decided that the distant island-continent would make an ideal penal colony for United Kingdom convicts. A quarter of these convicts were Irish, making them in a very real sense the 'founding fathers' of Australia. Here they competed on equal terms with other immigrants, in a country where there was no need to worry about a nativist reaction.

Most of these early 'settlers' stayed in Australia after their sentences (usually seven years) were completed. By 1850 the colony had outgrown its penal origins, and the former convicts and their descendants were being joined each year by thousands of free settlers. There were many Irish among these, especially in the years after the Famine. By and large, these were wealthier and more adventurous emigrants than those who went to America; they had to be, in order to afford and to undertake willingly the arduous eight-month journey from the British Isles to Australia.

Ned Kelly's last stand, 1880. The activities of this bushranger of Irish descent, who stole only from wealthy farmers and who burned the mortgage deeds of small land-holders during his bank robberies helped make Kelly something of a folk hero in a country founded as a convict settlement. Note his fantastic headgear.

The crowd restrains Henry James O'Farrell, the former Fenian who attempted to assassinate Prince Alfred in 1868 near Sydney. The wounded Prince lies on the ground on the left.

In sharp contrast to settlement patterns in America, the Irish in Australia did not become an exclusively urban people. While large numbers did settle in working-class districts of cities like Sydney and Melbourne, others made their homes in rural areas of the colony. Some became farmers, but more were miners in the various boom towns that were so much a part of life in nineteenth-century Australia.

From the beginning, the Irish working class was deeply involved in the Australian labour movement. Indeed, a group of Irish miners was responsible for the first Australian strike, during which twenty-two miners and six soldiers were killed in an armed scuffle at the Eureka Stockade in Victoria in 1854.

As the country grew, Irish settlers played an increasingly important part in Australian politics. From the beginning, the Irish were in the forefront of the struggle for increased powers of self-government for the colony. One measure of their political involvement was the fact that all six speakers of the Victorian Legislative Assembly between 1856 and 1891 were Irish-born. One of these was Charles Gavan Duffy, the former Young Irelander, who emigrated in 1855.

In Australia as in America, Irish settlement was closely connected with the growth of Catholicism. Since the Irish were the only significant group of Australian Catholics until after World War I, the Church became their exclusive preserve. For most of the nineteenth century, Ireland provided Australia with nearly all her priests; there was no native seminary until 1885. The first Australian Cardinal, Patrick Moran, a nephew of Cardinal Cullen, was an Irish bishop until his translation to Sydney in 1884.

The religious issue did contribute to a certain amount of tension in Australian society. The Catholic Church leadership insisted upon maintaining its own school system. This retarded the assimilation of the Irish, and was viewed with suspicion by Protestant Australians, especially those whose roots were in Ulster. Fortunately, Catholic-Protestant quarrels usually remained verbal rather than physical, even in 1867, when a deranged Irishman shot young Prince Alfred, Queen Victoria's second son, while he was visiting Sydney. The prince survived the assassination attempt, and Sydney survived without a riot.

The only major controversy involving the Irish and the rest of the Australian community occurred during World War I. Australia supported the British war effort; over 300,000 volunteers served in Anzac units in Europe. But Prime Minister William Hughes decided this was not enough and called for conscription. A referendum was held on this subject in October 1916.

Hughes's proposal was bitterly opposed by many Australians, and was especially unpopular among those 20 per cent who were of Irish descent. While they had great affection for Australia, the Irish did not consider themselves loyal Britons. Government handling of the Easter Rising in Dublin earlier in the same year only reinforced this anti-British sentiment.

Archbishop Daniel Mannix (1864–1963) of Melbourne was the leading figure in the Australian Catholic hierarchy for well over half a century; he gave influential support to the Irish cause during the War of Independence, and his opposition was largely responsible for the government's failure to introduce conscription in Australia during World War I.

The outstanding leader of the anti-conscriptionists was Daniel Mannix, Catholic Archbishop of Melbourne. Mannix won wide support from both the Irish and other Australians who agreed that it was their privilege, not their duty, to fight in the distant European war. In the referendum, conscription was rejected by a narrow majority. Another referendum was conducted in 1917, but it produced an identical result.

The anti-conscription campaign marked something of a turning point for the Irish in Australia. They had taken the lead in a movement to assert Australian independence in a time of crisis. After World War I, they gained complete acceptance as equal citizens whose devotion to the country was unquestionable. One symbol of this acceptance was the election of Joseph Lyons in 1932 as the first Irish Catholic Prime Minister of Australia.

During the twentieth century, the emigration possibilities of the dissatisfied Irish man or woman were gradually limited. The New World was no longer new. First the United States, and later Australia and Canada, put tight controls on the number of foreigners they would allow to reside within their borders. Today it is almost impossible to gain permanent admission into one of these countries unless one has special skills or connections.

One major outlet remains: Great Britain. Thanks to the 'special' relationship between the two British Isles as defined by the Anglo-Irish Treaty of 1921, Irish citizens

John Thomas Toohey (1839–1903) was born in Co. Limerick and came to Melbourne with his parents in 1841. Along with his brother James, he established the brewery which today remains one of Australia's largest.

George Bernard Shaw (1856–1950), one of the most famous of Ireland's literary exiles, photographed on his ninetieth birthday. For over fifty years, he was perhaps the most celebrated dramatist in the world. He won the Nobel Prize for Literature in 1925.

do not need passports to travel to Britain, nor do they need work permits to take employment. Even today, an Irishman can get off the boat, get a job and stay forever in the country if he so desires.

Since 1921 many Irish people have been doing just this. Throughout the depression, through World War II and into the 1950s, a steady stream of emigration flowed at the rate of 50,000 persons per year. While this figure dropped during the 1960s, it has picked up again in recent years, in the wake of the recession that followed the sudden increase in oil prices in 1974.

The modern Irish immigrants continue to have a special place in the British construction industry. The 'Paddy on the buildings' is now as much a part of English folklore as the navvies of the last century. Today, however, opportunities for advancement are much greater. There is little real discrimination and with hard work and luck, even the humblest immigrant can greatly improve his financial position. Many of the country's leading building firms are now owned by Irishmen, and 'Paddies' operate many British public houses. The country has a fair share of Irish lawyers, teachers and businessmen, many of whom are fully integrated into British society.

Most Irish emigrants, however, still arrive in humble circumstances. Most head for the homes of relatives or friends in Irish neighbourhoods such as Kilburn and Camden Town in London. These people often locate jobs for the newcomers, as barmen, waitresses, clerk-typists, or in construction. In familiar surroundings the emigrants go to Mass on Sundays, drink in Irish pubs and go dancing at clubs with names like 'the Shamrock' or 'the Emerald'. Here they bide their time until they get the confidence and financial means to go elsewhere.

Most eventually do. While emigration has remained fairly constant, the Irish districts have not grown. Assimilation drains Kilburn as surely as emigration drains Ireland. The force of British culture is enormous: television, schools, work associates, and girl friends and boy friends. Over two or three generations, the Irish in Britain slowly but surely become Britons of Irish descent.

The vast majority of Irish emigrants of the past two centuries have shared a common grievance against their native land: it offered them few economic opportunities. But other factors have been involved in the movement of Irish people to distant parts of the world.

One motive has been service, the desire to improve the human condition. Throughout the nineteenth and twentieth centuries, thousands of Irish priests, brothers and nuns have devoted their lives to Christian missionary activities in Africa and Asia. Among the many orders involved have been the Holy Ghost Fathers, one of whose Irish members, Joseph Shanahan, became first Catholic bishop of Nigeria in 1905. Today Irish missionaries maintain schools and hospitals throughout the third world.

One layman who left Ireland to serve the world was Sean MacBride, one of the few political figures of international importance which Ireland has produced during this century. MacBride's background was rather special. His mother was Maud Gonne, the famous beauty who rejected a marriage proposal from W.B. Yeats, while his father was one of the sixteen rebel leaders executed after the 1916 Rising. Educated in Paris and Dublin, young MacBride shared his father's republicanism, and became a leading figure in the

The most renowned lyric tenor of his age, Athlone-born John MacCormack (1884–1945) is shown here performing at Latimer Hall, London, in 1930.

extremist IRA during the late 1920s. He soon renounced the use of violent methods, however, abandoning this military organisation and becoming a successful Dublin barrister. He played a major role in the formation of the republican socialist party of the late 1940s, Clann na Poblachta, and served as Minister for External Affairs in the Coalition government which ruled the country from 1948 to 1951. As Clann na Poblachta disintegrated during the next decade, MacBride became more and more involved in the work of the United Nations and other international organisations. Among these was Amnesty International, a group which strove to free political prisoners throughout the world. He served as chairman of this organisation from 1974 to 1976.

In 1972 MacBride was appointed United Nations Commissioner for the Trust Territory of South-West Africa (Namibia). His efforts to mediate in this dispute between black nationalists and the South African government won him the Nobel Peace Prize in 1974 and the Lenin Peace Award in 1975. This dual distinction is a fair measure of the enormous international prestige which he has won.

Unfortunately, not all Irish emigrants had positive reasons for leaving the country. Many were dissatisfied with the stifling intellectual climate of the Irish state after independence. During the 1920s and 1930s many talented Irish artists and writers followed the advice of George Moore, the nineteenth-century novelist who once described Ireland as 'a fatal disease from which it is the plain duty of every Irishman to disassociate himself'.

The son of one of the republican leaders executed in 1916, Sean MacBride (1904–   ), has had a varied and constructive international career, one which has brought him both the Lenin and Nobel Peace prizes.

Limerick-born Richard Harris (1933–   ) went to Hollywood in 1958 and became one of the leading figures of the international cinema. Among his many leading roles was this supremely ironic one: the part of Cromwell in the 1970 film of the same name.

Perhaps the most intriguing of these artistic exiles was Samuel Beckett. Brought up in an old Dublin Protestant family, Beckett studied modern languages at Trinity College, where he took his degree in 1927 and worked as a French instructor during 1931 and 1932. He spent most of the 1930s wandering throughout Europe, contributing poems and articles to avant-garde journals, before finally settling in Paris in 1937.

By this time Beckett was a thorough Francophile. He wrote in French, and only later translated his works into

207

He was placed third to John McCormack's first in an All-Ireland tenor competition in 1903, but today he is better remembered for what he wrote than for what he sang; James Joyce (1882–1941), whose Ulysses *revolutionised the modern novel, photographed in Paris in 1934.*

Samuel Beckett (1906–   ). When his Waiting For Godot *was first produced in 1952, it caused a sensation. The acknowledged master of the theatre of the absurd, he won the Nobel Prize for Literature in 1969.*

English; he was also active in the French Resistance during World War II. Although he wrote several novels during the 1940s, Beckett did not receive widespread attention until his plays, *Waiting for Godot* and *Endgame*, were produced in 1952 and 1958 respectively. Despite the critical acclaim which followed, he continued to live in complete seclusion in France, even refusing to travel to Stockholm in 1969 when he became the third Irishman (after Shaw and Yeats) to win the Nobel Prize for Literature.

Beckett's work is marked by his complete negation of most established literary conventions, and constant reiteration of themes of despair. Most of his works contain no reference to place or scene; his featureless characters simply exist, without meaning or purpose. Witness the closing lines of *Waiting for Godot*:

Vladimir: Well? Shall we go?
Estragon: Yes, let's go.
    They do not move.
    [CURTAIN][7]

James Joyce is usually considered the greatest of the twentieth-century Irish literary emigrés. Yet there is no question that part of his soul always remained in Ireland. After all, many years after leaving Ireland he was still able to write an 800-page novel around the events of a single June day in Dublin in 1904. But Beckett (a personal friend during Joyce's last years in Paris) was the total 'exile', a writer who completely rejected his original environment. With the exception of his early novels and the surnames of some of his later characters,

Beckett never refers to Ireland or to things Irish. It remains for the critics to decide to what extent his nihilist style was the result of his spending the formative years of his life in a Dublin whose dominant cultural influences were self-righteous clericalism and maudlin nationalism.

One did not need to be a literary figure to feel the pressures of the Irish moral climate. Many young people from all classes found the restrictions on personal development simply too much to bear, and fled to the 'bright city lights' of London, Melbourne and New York City. As late as 1970, a twenty-three year old girl from an Irish provincial town offered the following reason for her move to London:

> I had to get out, or burst. I couldn't take the heavy moral respectability. . . . I was afraid that if I stayed I would have ended up marrying some fellow I went out with for a few years, and spend the rest of my life wondering what I might have missed.[8]

14—Modern Ireland

Its shapes and contours make of it a paradise that is unhappy. And so it must forever remain, far away from the stream of life and with the sadness of all things that are a little remote from reality.

Sacheverell Sitwell, 1936

This English traveller's description of Ireland in 1936 could have been written at any time during the first three decades after political independence. Between 1921 and 1950 Europe changed dramatically, but Ireland hardly at all. Cultural parochialism combined with World War II neutrality to keep the country in a state of suspended animation until well after the mid-point of the twentieth century.

There was a certain amount of political turbulence in the years immediately after the Second World War. Between 1948 and 1954 there were three changes of government, but all produced coalition or minority governments that were unable to deal successfully with the massive problems that faced the country. Considerable improvement in medical services was made by Dr Noel Browne during his brief tenure as Minister for Health (1948–51), but otherwise no government leader could point to any achievement of significance. Emigration continued to drain away three out of every five young people; there was desperate need for industrial development of some kind. But Ireland in 1955 seemed little different from what she had been in 1925 – a country locked into its own past without any discernable sense of its future.

> My concern is with national development and with some of the means necessary to attain it in our particular circumstances. . . . Concern has been expressed about the comparatively slow rise in real income per head in Ireland over the past thirty years.[1]

As Secretary of the Department of Finance, Dr T. K. Whitaker was fully aware of just how desperate the Irish economic situation was in the mid-1950s. Things were so dismal that the national GNP (Gross National Product) actually decreased by $3\frac{1}{2}$ per cent in 1955, at a time when the world economy as a whole was enjoying one of its greatest boom periods.

The root of Ireland's problem, Whitaker reasoned, was its decidedly unfavourable trade balance. The value of the country's imports was twice that of its exports,

After Ireland was admitted to the United Nations in 1955, the government was often asked to provide army units for service with UN peacekeeping forces. These soldiers were on duty in Cyprus in the early 1970s.

209

The development of sophisticated farm machinery has hastened the migration from rural to urban Ireland. Since 1950 the agricultural population has declined while the average farm size has increased.

Ireland's break with her isolationist past has brought its share of problems, as this 1977 cartoon graphically illustrates. Political issues are no longer so domestic in character.

almost all of which were agricultural products. This imbalance created a currency drain, and put tremendous strain upon an already enfeebled economy. To escape from this vicious circle, Whitaker proposed a planned course of industrial development, one in which the government was to be actively involved. Unlike the 1930s, the aim would not be self-sufficiency but the establishment of export-oriented enterprises that could produce goods for European and world consumption. Hopefully, this would bring more money into the country, create new jobs, and put the national economy on more solid footing.

Whitaker's ideas got considerable support from Sean Lemass, de Valera's long-time political lieutenant who succeeded 'the Chief' as Fianna Fail leader and Prime Minister when the latter finally retired from active politics in 1959. Lemass had served as Minister for Industry and Commerce for over two decades, and made economic development the first priority of his government. With a comfortable majority in Dail Eireann and the assistance of a new generation of Fianna Fail leaders like Jack Lynch and Charles Haughey, Lemass began to implement the Whitaker Programme.

New scope was given to the Industrial Development Authority, a government-sponsored agency which offered enticements to investors and provided advice and assistance to anyone and everyone interested in new industry. Grants and twenty-year tax exemptions were granted to foreign firms which decided to locate in Ireland. 'Advance factories' were built, offering facilities to newcomers who might otherwise go elsewhere.

Conor Cruise O'Brien (1917–   ), historian, diplomat, journalist and former government minister. His provocative questioning of the traditional republican interpretation of Irish history has made him one of the most controversial figures in the country.

These pump-priming measures produced the desired economic results. By 1964 over 200 new industries had been established and emigration had been cut by half. Between 1959 and 1964 the Irish GNP increased by over 20 per cent. These positive trends continued throughout the decade and into the 1970s.

The encouragement of tourism was another feature of the Whitaker Programme. Thanks largely to the efforts of Bord Failte, the Irish tourist board, and improvements in air travel, the number of foreign visitors increased dramatically over the next decade. By 1970 tens of thousands of continental tourists, and large numbers of Britons and Americans, were visiting the island each summer.

The improving economic situation was accompanied by a dramatic upsurge in consumer demand and spending. The number of motor cars trebled during the 1960s, as for the first time jobs were plentiful enough and wages high enough to allow a majority of the population to own them. The construction industry boomed, especially in the Dublin area, where sprawling new suburbs blossomed on all sides of the city. Modern supermarkets and shopping centres followed. New patterns of consumption gave the revitalised economy a further boost.

Dublin has responded to housing pressures in a similar fashion to many British cities, despite the known social problems which can follow on such solutions. 'Ribbon' development, vast housing estates and poor planning and landscaping are all too common, especially in working-class areas like Finglas, in the north-west of the city.

Interior of a Dutch steel-cord manufacturing complex in Limerick, 1975. Unfortunately, this particular company, Ferenka, terminated its Irish operations in 1977.

Agriculture was not unaffected by the improved economic climate. Cattle remained the country's single most valuable export, and a large portion of the Irish workforce (24 per cent in 1971) continued to be involved in agriculture. Most Irish farmers owned their own holdings, which averaged from thirty to eighty acres in size. While farms were small by international standards, rising meat rices throughout the period brought new levels of prosperity to nearly all rural areas.

By and large, the Whitaker Programme worked wonders for Ireland. But industrial growth was not without its problems. Most of the new enterprises were foreign-based, and as such subject to worldwide economic trends over which Ireland had no control. At the same time development was so rapid that balanced planning was difficult; many factories operated without strict environmental controls, and many suburban housing developments were badly laid out and poorly constructed. Moreover, the pattern of economic growth was very uneven. Dublin grew in leaps and bounds, but often at the expense of already depressed rural areas. In poor Western counties like Mayo and Kerry, the train to Dublin merely replaced the boat to Liverpool in a continuing cycle of migration.

Despite these setbacks, however, it is difficult to imagine where Ireland might have been in 1966 without the Whitaker Programme or something very much like it. Of all the encouraging statistics provided by the census taken in that year, the one which brought the most satisfaction to the Irish government was that of total population. For the first time since the Famine, the number of people in the country did not decline between census dates. Emigration figures were lower than they had been for over a century. The Irish economy was at last showing signs of being able to support all of its citizens.

Since 1962, RTE has been perhaps the single most important influence on Irish society. Here Gay Byrne, Ireland's answer to David Frost and Johnny Carson, interviews Peter Ustinov on his weekly Late Late Show.

The economic development of the 1960s led naturally to a tremendous amount of social change, as thatched cottages gave way to shopping centres and donkey carts were replaced by motor cars. Indeed, the existing social system was subjected to more rigorous stress during this decade than at any other time in Irish history.

As elsewhere, television was perhaps the greatest single factor in this transformation. Radio Telefis Eireann (RTE) began television operations in 1962; within three years over half of Irish homes had television sets. TV personalities like Frank Hall and Gay Byrne became national figures, while foreign programming (most of which was British or American) brought the island into closer contact with trends and customs in other parts of the world. For better or worse, television played a decisive role in shaping the attitudes of the new generation of Irish men and women.

The 1960s also brought considerable educational improvement. In 1966 free secondary education was at last made available to the population as a whole. At the same time government grants made it possible for low-income students to continue their education at university or at the new regional technical colleges which were established to help meet the technological needs of developing industries.

Changes were myriad. Cheap air travel, for example, made it possible for Dublin secretaries to holiday in Spain. Roads were improved, so that one could now drive across the country in several hours. Blue jeans and long hair became fashionable in Ireland at much the same time as they did in other western countries. Censorship laws were relaxed; this contributed to a much livelier cultural scene, as both music and theatre prospered. The regular influx of foreigners and its new international importance helped make Dublin a more cosmopolitan city than it had been at any time since the eighteenth century.

Alcohol still reigns supreme: a staggering 12 per cent of the national income was spent on liquor in 1976.

Garret Fitzgerald (1926–), a leading economist and former Minister for Foreign Affairs, assumed the leadership of Fine Gael, the main opposition party, in 1977.

Dramatic evidence of changing political attitudes came in 1974, when Ireland established full diplomatic relations with the USSR. Here the first Soviet ambassador in Dublin reviews a company of the Irish Army on the occasion of his assumption of office.

Women's Liberation has made little real headway in Ireland. The country remains one of the most male-dominated of western nations.

Not everything changed. Alcohol, unfortunately, remained too integral a part of Irish life; in 1976, for example, the average Irishman spent 12 per cent of his income on beer and spirits. Even in the 1970s Ireland was still a male chauvinist's paradise, where women were under-employed, underpaid, and usually under their husbands' thumbs. The Catholic Church remained a significant force in the lives of most Irish people, although the winds of Vatican II blew away much of the narrow parochialism of earlier decades.

One theme was consistently repeated through the social transformations of the 1960s: Ireland was moving towards a position of fuller participation in the affairs of Europe and the world. Graphic evidence of this new relationship came in 1972 when Ireland (along with Great Britain and Denmark) was admitted to the European Economic Community. The country joined with the other eight members of the EEC to create a single economic unit for western Europe, and helped devise the framework for a degree of political unity in the future. By casting its lot with its western European neighbours, the Irish government put a symbolic end to the geographical and cultural isolation which had been a major feature of the country's history for over two millenia.

> The whole map of Europe has been changed. The mode and thought of men, the whole outlook on affairs, the grouping of parties, all have encountered violent and tremendous changes in the deluge of the world, but as the deluge subsides and the waters fall we see the dreary steeples of Fermanagh and Tyrone emerging once again. The integrity of their quarrel is one of the few institutions that have been left unaltered in the cataclysm which has swept the world.[2]

Although Winston Churchill wrote these words about Ulster in 1929, they could well have been written in the 1970s. Whatever else may have changed in Ireland, the problems of Northern Ireland have not.

Despite a background of considerable social change, the Catholic Church retains much of its power and influence in rural Ireland.

A wedding on Rathlin Island, off the coast of Co. Antrim, 1974.

Today, over half a century after the Home Rule crisis of 1914, the Protestants and Catholics of Ulster are still left with 'the integrity of their quarrel'.

In retrospect, the most remarkable feature of the modern 'troubles' in Northern Ireland is that they did not come sooner. For decades Protestant and Catholic Ulstermen practiced a self-imposed form of apartheid, mingling only with acute consciousness of the differences between them. They drank in different pubs, played different sports, and married within their own groups. The two sections of the community even read different newspapers: a 1971 survey of Ulster's two major papers revealed that 87 per cent of the readers of the *Belfast Newsletter* were Protestant, while 93 per cent of the *Irish News* readership was Catholic.

After World War II the Protestant majority continued to dominate the political and economic structure of Northern Ireland. Since Ulster's economy suffered from many of the same problems as its southern neighbour, continued discrimination against Catholics only aggravated sectarian tensions. For a long period, however, emigration acted as something of a safety valve; even though they represented only one-third of the total population, well over half of the emigrants from Northern Ireland were Catholic.

During the 1960s, legislation in the USA and poorer economic conditions in Britain combined to restrict Ulster emigration. At the same time, a better-educated Catholic minority became more sophisticated in its oposition to unionist domination. Following the example of American blacks, a Northern Ireland Civil Rights Association was founded in 1968. This aimed to use public protests and marches to focus British and international attention upon the problems of Ulster Catholics. Led mainly by young middle-class Catholics like John Hume and Austin Currie, the Civil Rights Association demanded fairer distribution of public housing, a greater share of government jobs, and reform in the system of local elections which gave Unionists control of city and county councils even in those areas where Protestants were in the minority.

While some Unionists were sympathetic to Catholic demands, most of the Unionist Party leadership was against making concessions to the Civil Rights Association. Catholics were viewed as traitors, people whose desire for a united Ireland precluded their being treated as equal citizens. The rank-and-file Protestant population shared the view that 'if you give them an inch, they'll take a mile'. For inspiration they looked to leaders like the Rev. Ian Paisley, a Presbyterian minister cut from the same cloth as earlier zealots like Thomas Drew and 'Roaring Hugh' Hanna. Paisley was a brilliant public speaker whose diatribes against the 'Papists' helped make him champion of those Ulster Protestants who wanted no concessions to Catholic demands.

An historic first: the 1965 meeting between Terence O'Neill (centre), Prime Minister of Northern Ireland, and Sean Lemass (right), Irish Taoiseach. The civil rights marches of the late Sixties provoked a right-wing Protestant reaction which forced O'Neill, a moderate Unionist, from office. The endemic violence which followed prevented fuller relations developing between the two Irish states. Jack Lynch, Lemass's successor, is on the left.

Rev. Ian Paisley (1926–) has taken full advantage of what Geoffrey Bell has called 'the thorough-going reactionary nature of Protestant working-class political consciousness'.

Bernadette Devlin (1947–), civil rights leader and for some years a radical spokeswoman for the Catholic minority at Westminster, where she was MP for Mid-Ulster from 1969 to 1974.

Innocent victims of a 1974 bomb explosion in Belfast. This bomb killed two and injured over a hundred.

215

Members of the Provisional IRA in the Brandywell district of Derry city, 1972. In Belfast and Derry, the IRA is regarded first and foremost as an armed defence force for Catholic areas like this.

After the explosion, Belfast 1972. This was the most violent year in the present Northern Ireland troubles.

By 1969 the two peoples of Ulster were on collision course. In January of that year angry Protestant mobs severely disrupted a Civil Rights march from Belfast to Derry. Several dozen people were injured in scuffles along the route. While the Civil Rights Association did not condone the use of force, this unionist tendency towards violence produced a reaction within the Catholic community. More support was given to extremist groups like Sinn Fein, which advocated the destruction of Northern Ireland by force and the establishment of an Irish state which encompassed the whole island.

Since the 1920s Sinn Fein and its military counterpart, the Irish Republican Army (IRA), had been splinter groups unable to command the active support of even a small segment of the Catholic population. But the events of 1968 and 1969 played into their hands. While the number of IRA activists remained small (never more than a few hundred), the organisation received the passive support of more and more Catholics, especially in the poorer areas of Belfast and Derry. In these neighbourhoods, where unemployment often topped 40 per cent and living conditions were less than adequate, there was a feeling that there was very little to lose.

After 1969, bombings, assassinations and riots became increasingly frequent in Northern Ireland. This IRA campaign produced a natural backlash in the Protestant community, where extremist groups like the Ulster Volunteer Force (UVF) got increased support from unionists afraid of being 'bombed into the Republic'.

Gradually, Northern Ireland drifted towards anarchy. By 1969 it was obvious that the local police could not cope with the growing violence, so the Stormont government asked London to send peace-keeping forces to Ulster, the most troubled part of the United Kingdom. The first British troops arrived in August of that year. Armoured vehicles, troop lorries and army checkpoints soon became accepted features of Ulster life, as the British government maintained a force strength of 12,000 over the next decade.

The British Army, however, could only contain the extremists, not defeat them. In the guerrilla warfare situation which developed, complete control was virtually impossible. As representatives of the Old Enemy, British soldiers became ideal IRA targets; between 1970 and 1977 a total of 275 were killed.

As time passed, the London government became increasingly frustrated by the situation in Northern Ireland. Ulster became Britain's Vietnam, the scene of a 'war' which it could neither win nor lose. Although Northern Ireland was constitutionally bound to remain part of the United Kingdom as long as a majority of the population was in favour of such a connection, London viewed the province as an increasingly burdensome albatross. Most Britons had little sympathy for either side in this sectarian dispute whose roots went back to the seventeenth century.

In British eyes, there was one major obstacle to peace in Northern Ireland; the Unionist-dominated Stormont government. In 1972 Prime Minister Edward Heath abolished Stormont and announed that in future the province would be ruled directly from London. Ironically, this British abolition of an Irish legislature was greeted favourably by the Catholic minority, who for the first time in fifty years were freed from direct domination by their Protestant neighbours.

Over the next few years, the British Secretary of State for Northern Ireland insured that most of the civil rights grievances of Ulster Catholics were resolved.

During the early Seventies, several hundred families were either burned out or intimidated out of their homes by sectarian attacks. This has resulted in the virtual disappearance of mixed Catholic–Protestant housing estates.

Showbands, playing a curious mixture of sentimental Irish ballads and country-and-western music are overwhelmingly popular in the country areas. Even in Dublin, they command a large following in dance halls. Red Hurley, shown here on the stage of the National Ballroom, Dublin, is one of the most popular showband singers.

Belfast women in Catholic neighbourhoods bang dustbin lids to warn IRA guerillas of the approach of British soldiers. Without this kind of civilian support, the IRA campaign could not have flourished.

Irish traditional music enjoyed a tremendous revival during the Sixties and Seventies, spurred by the international success of groups like the Chieftans. This photograph shows two well-known musicians, Jackie Daly and Seamus Creagh.

The unionist population, for its part, was in no more conciliatory a mood. Resenting the loss of 'their' parliament and still motivated by fear and disgust of the Catholic minority, most Protestants refused to have anything to do with a power-sharing proposal drawn up by the British and Irish governments in 1973. Even though the new Northern Ireland Executive was headed by Brian Faulkner, an old-guard Unionist who had served as the last Stormont Prime Minister, the vast majority of his fellow Ulster Protestants would not support a government which included Catholics in cabinet positions. In the midst of a Unionist general strike in 1974, Faulkner was forced to resign, and the power-sharing formula was abandoned.

Since 1974, the Ulster dilemma has remained unresolved, marked only by bombing tragedies and sectarian assassinations. Property damage has run into millions of pounds, and the strains of urban guerrilla warfare have left parts of Belfast and Derry looking like bomb-wrecked leftovers from World War II. Since the first life was taken in 1969, over two thousand people have been killed in this unique religious war between Christians.

Perhaps the greatest tragedy of all is that it is no longer terribly important which flag flies over Ulster, the British Union Jack or the Irish Tricolour. During the 1970s, the most violent decade in the province's turbulent history, Ireland and Britain have drawn closer together than at any time since independence. The economic systems of the two British Isles are closely related; 70 per cent of Irish exports go to Britain, while over half of Irish imports come from there. Furthermore, both countries are now members of the Common Market, partners in the wider economic community of western Europe.

Unfortunately, this was a case of too little too late. Unionist obduracy during the Civil Rights campaign of the late 1960s had put extremist groups in positions of power which they would not otherwise have enjoyed. With financial support from ardent Irish nationalists in Britain and America, and with military control of certain areas of the province (the Falls Road district in Belfast, the Bogside in Derry, and the southern part of Co. Armagh), the IRA was able to continue its fight for the complete destruction of Northern Ireland.

One major casualty of partition has been international sport. Soccer is governed by two competing 'national' organisations in Dublin and Belfast. Rugby is the major exception to the rule. Players from both sides of the border join together to wear the green jersey of the Irish national team.

A former Cork hurling star, Jack Lynch (1917–) has led the Fianna Fail party since 1966. He has served as Taoiseach for all of that period, except for the years 1973–77 when a Fine Gael-Labour coalition ousted him. However, his return to power in 1977 came as a result of the most overwhelming electoral victory in the history of the Republic.

The past is never far away in modern Ireland. Croagh Patrick in Co. Mayo is still regularly climbed by pilgrims intent on emulating St Patrick over a thousand years ago.

In the past decade, increasing attention has been given to scientific and technical subjects in Irish second- and third-level schools.

In terms of culture as well as economics, Ireland is still very much 'John Bull's Other Island'. It is estimated that on any given evening only one out of every five Dublin television sets is tuned to RTE; the rest are tuned to British stations. On weekends during the football season thousands of Irish soccer fans cross the Irish Sea to watch the Saturday afternoon matches of their favourite English teams. Even Cork and Galway have their share of avid Manchester United supporters.

Outside of Catholic Ulster, strident Celtic nationalism of the early twentieth-century variety is dormant, if not actually dead. There is no great surge of popular sentiment in the Republic for the annexation of Northern Ireland; the general feeling is that unification can only come about with the consent of the Protestant population. Most people on both British Isles wish only for an end to the violence, and hope that somehow the people of Ulster will learn to live together in peace.

The problems of the North notwithstanding, Ireland has come a long way since 1960. The nation has emerged from its sociological cocoon, and begun to play a more vital role on the European and world stage. For the first time in modern history, Ireland can no longer be considered an under-developed nation. During the 1970s the economy has continued to expand; GNP increased by a robust 7 per cent in 1977, giving the country one of the most rapid rates of growth in the world.

But present perspectives are no guarantee that the future will be problem-free. Irish society still has more than its share of inequalities. Despite a basic tax rate of around 35 per cent, the level of social services is low when compared to that of countries with similar tax structures like Britain and Sweden. Part of the problem is that large sections of the population are exempt from taxation, including nearly all farmers, who not only pay no income tax but also qualify for free medical services not available to the population as a whole. At the same time, many of the country's most successful entrepreneurs pay low taxes, thanks to exemptions that were used to attract new investment into the country.

Perhaps the single biggest problem which the country must face in the future is presented by its rapidly increasing population. Despite decades of population decline, Ireland has always had one of Europe's highest birth rates. While large-scale emigration was a painful fact of Irish life, this excessive birth rate presented few problems. Now that emigration is no longer as easy as it once was, however, Irish young people have no alternatives but to seek employment at home.

This has been most difficult, despite the expansion which the Irish economy has undergone. Population growth has simply been too rapid for the economic system to keep pace. The result is high unemployment; the official figure has remained around 10 per cent, although, since this does not include school leavers or young people at home on farms, the real number out of work could be much higher. While the birth rate has recently begun to decline, the die is already cast for the next two decades. It is estimated that 200,000 new jobs will be needed by 1990 just to maintain the present dismal level of unemployment. Even in a booming economy such as Ireland's, there seems little potential for growth on the enormous scale that is required.

Whatever problems the future might bring, the fact remains that Ireland is probably better equipped to deal with them than at any other time in her history. Irish society now possesses a degree of technical sophistication and adaptability that was sadly lacking in earlier decades.

Recently an American visitor returned to suburban Los Angeles with these comments: 'I went to Ireland looking for leprechauns and shamrocks; instead I found adolescents who knew more about Kojak than I did.' In a world which daily grows smaller, it is not surprising that this island nation has taken much from the rest of the world. One can only express the wish that the individuality of the Irish people will not die and that Ireland will not simply become a land of second-hand values. It is to be hoped that, in the future, Ireland can contribute to the world as much as she takes from it.

The Irish Sugar Company is a state-run corporation for the production of sugar from sugar-beet. Its activities have expanded, however, into general food processing. Here a farmer harvests a crop of peas destined for one of the company's factories.

The nitric acid plant at Nitrigin Eireann Teoranta (NET). Also a nationalised company, NET has transformed the small fishing port of Arklow, Co. Wicklow. Despite the heavy emphasis on free enterprise in the Republic, many important areas of production and utilities are nationalised, although they are officially called 'semi-state companies'.

Notes

Introduction   (pp. 8–9)
1   J. H. Andrews, 'A Geographer's View of Irish History' in *The Course of Irish History*, ed. T. W. Moody and F. X. Martin, Cork 1967, 17.
2   Quoted by the *New York Times*, 29 June 1963, 2.

Chapter 1   The First Irishmen   (pp. 11–23)
1   Kenneth H. Jackson, *The Oldest Irish Tradition: A Window on the Iron Age*, Cambridge 1964, 55.
2   Quoted by Máire and Liam de Paor, *Early Christian Ireland*, London 1958, 78–9.
3   Quoted by Myles Dillon, *Early Irish Literature*, London 1948, 155.
4   The *Táin Bó Cuailgne*, ed. Thomas Kinsella, Oxford 1970, 191.
5   ibid., 251.
6   ibid., 204–5.
7   ibid., 229–30.

Chapter 2   The Celtic Twilight   (pp. 24–37)
1   M. and L. de Paor, *Early Christian Ireland*, 48.
2   Quoted by Ludwig Bieler in *Ireland: Harbinger of the Middle Ages*, London 1963, 50–54.
3   Translated by David Greene and Frank O'Connor in *A Golden Treasury of Irish Poetry*, London 1967, 64–5.
4   Quoted by Donncha Ó Corráin, *Ireland Before the Normans*, Dublin 1972, 172.

Chapter 3   Medieval and Early Modern Ireland   (pp. 38–52)
1   Quoted by J. F. Lydon, *The Lordship of Ireland in the Middle Ages*, Dublin 1972, 181.
2   Giraldus Cambrensis, *The Conquest of Ireland* (1189), ed. Thomas Wright, London 1963, 223.
3   Quoted by J. F. Lydon, *The Lordship of Ireland ...*, 281.
4   Quoted by John Watt, *The Church in Medieval Ireland*, Dublin 1972, 7.
5   Bernard of Clairvaux, *Life of St Malachy of Armagh* (1151), ed. H. J. Lawlor, London 1920, 13.
6   Quoted by Watt, *The Church ...*, 7.
7   Quoted by Grenfell Morton, *Elizabethan Ireland*, London 1971, 14.

Chapter 4   Conquest and Colonisation   (pp. 53–68)
1   Paul Johnson, *The Offshore Islanders*, New York 1972, 103.
2   Edmund Spenser, *A View of the Present State of Ireland* (1596), ed. W. L. Renwick, London 1934, 55–6.
3   John Derricke, *The Image of Ireland* (1581), ed. John Small, Edinburgh 1883, 14.
4   Quoted by David B. Quinn, *The Elizabethans and the Irish*, Ithaca, N.Y. 1966.
5   Laoiseach mac an Bháird, 'Civil Irish and Wild Irish', translated by Kenneth Jackson, *A Celtic Miscellany*, Cambridge, Mass. 1951, 99.
6   Quoted by Constantia Maxwell, *Irish History from Contemporary Sources, 1509–1610*, London 1923, 169.
7   Quoted by D. M. R. Esson, *The Curse of Cromwell*, London 1971, 113.
8   Translated by Máire MacEntee, *A Heartful of Thought*, Dublin 1959, 11.

Chapter 5   Ireland in the Eighteenth Century   (pp. 69–83)
1   Alexis de Tocqueville, *Journeys to England and Ireland* (1835), ed. J. P. Mayer, London 1958, 172.
2   Le Chevalier de la Tocknaye, *A Frenchman's Walk Through Ireland* (1797), ed. John Stevenson, London 1917, 87.
3   Gustave de Beaumont, *L'Irlande, sociale, politique et religieuse*, Paris 1839, Volume I, 202.
4   Arthur Young, *A Tour of Ireland* (1780), ed. A. W. Hutton, London 1892, Volume II, 29.
5   ibid., Volume II, 57.
6   William McNeill, *The Rise of the West*, Chicago 1963, 664.
7   Jonah Barrington, *Personal Sketches* (1832), ed. Hugh B. Staples, London 1967, 41.
8   Quoted by Peter Somerville-Large, *Irish Eccentrics*, New York 1975, 121.
9   Jonathan Swift, *Prose Works*, ed. H. Williams, London 1951, Volume VIII, 174.
10   Quoted by J. A. Froude, *The English in Ireland in the Eighteenth Century*, London 1873, Volume II, 306.

Chapter 6   The Birth of Nationalism   (pp. 84–102)
1   Theobald Wolfe Tone, *Autobiography*, ed. W. T. Tone, Washington 1826, Volume I, 51–2.
2   ibid.
3   'The Wearing of the Green', in *The Tri-Coloured Ribbon*, Dublin 1966, 33.
4   Quoted by Earl Stanhope, *The Life of William Pitt*, London 1867, Volume III, 173.
5   Quoted by G. C. Bolton, *The Passing of the Irish Act of Union*, Oxford 1966, 172.
6   Herman von Pückler-Muskau, *Tour in England, Ireland and France in 1828 and 1829*, translated by Sarah Austin, London 1832, 101.

Chapter 7   The Famine   (pp. 103–115)
1   William M. Thackeray, *Irish Sketch Book*, London 1843, 207.
2   William Bennett, *Narrative of a Recent Journey of Six Weeks in Ireland*, London 1847, 29.
3   John Mitchel, 'The Distress in the West', in *The Nation*, Dublin, 19 June 1847, 1.
4   Friedrich Engels, letter to Karl Marx, 23 May 1856, in R. Dixon ed., *Ireland and the Irish Question*, New York 1972, 83–5.
5   G. P. Gooch ed., *The Later Correspondence of Lord John Russell, 1848–1878*, London 1935, Volume I, 151.
6   Douglas Hyde, 'The Irish Language Movement: Some Reminiscences', in *The Manchester Guardian*, 10 May 1923, 13.
7   George Petrie, *The Ancient Music of Ireland*, Dublin 1855, xii.

Chapter 8   Tipperary So Far Away   (pp. 116–133)
1   Stephen E. de Vere, letter to T. F. Elliot in *Evidence before the Select Committee of the House of Lords on Colonisation from Ireland*, London 1847, 45–6.
2   Quoted by W. F. Adams, *Ireland and Irish Emigration to the New World from 1815 to the Famine*, New Haven 1932, 342.
3   M. Gore, *On the Dwellings of the Poor*, London 1851, vii.
4   M. J. Whitney, quoted in Poor Inquiry (Ireland): Appendix G, *The State of the Irish Poor in Great Britain*, London 1836, 20.
5   Quoted by Edith Abbott, *Historical Aspects of the Immigration Problem*, Chicago 1926, 530–32.
6   William V. Shannon, *The American Irish*, New York 1963, 142.
7   T. D. Sullivan, 'God Save Ireland', in *The Tri-Coloured Ribbon*, Dublin 1966, 43.

Chapter 9   Wheels Turning Full Circle   (pp. 134–148)
1   Quoted by T. W. Moody and J. C. Beckett, *Ulster Since 1800*, London 1957, Volume II, 37.
2   Thomas Drew, *Sermon Preached in Christ Church, Belfast, on Suday Evening, February 21st, 1858*, Belfast 1858, 4–5.
3   Paul Cardinal Cullen, 'Pastoral Letter' in *The Freeman's Journal*, Dublin, 10 November 1859, 2.
4   Quoted in *The Connaught Telegraph*, Castlebar, 18 May 1880, 3.
5   Bernard H. Becker, *Disturbed Ireland*, London 1881, 102.
6   Quoted by Terence de V. White, *The Anglo-Irish*, London 1972, 31.
7   William B. Yeats, 'Parnell's Funeral', in *A Full Moon in March*, London 1935, 72.

Chapter 10   Nationalism and Unionism   (pp. 149–163)
1   Quoted in *The Freeman's Journal*, Dublin, 10 March 1867, 3.
2   *Hansard's Parliamentary Debates*, 3rd series, Volume ccciv, 1081–4.
3   Liam O'Briain in *Irish Literary Portraits*, ed. W. R. Rodgers, London 1972, 205.
4   Quoted by Roy Jenkins, *Asquith*, London 1964, 321.

Chapter 11   Rebellion, Partition and Civil War   (pp. 164–180)
1   Quoted by Denis Gwynn, *The Life of John Redmond*, Dublin 1932, 356.
2   Quoted by Dorothy Macardle, *The Irish Republic*, Dublin 1951, 137.
3   James Connolly, *Selected Writings*, ed. P. Beresford Ellis, London 1973, 38.
4   *Proclamation to the People of Ireland*, 24 April 1916.
5   'Letter from an Irishwoman', in *1916: The Easter Rising*, Dublin 1968, 205.
6   ibid., 69.
7   Quoted by Charles Townshend, *The British Campaign in Ireland, 1919–1921*, London 1975, 61.
8   Dail Eireann, *Debate on the Treaty Between Great Britain and Ireland*, Dublin 1922, 141.
9   ibid., 344.
10 Quoted by H. Montgomery Hyde, *Carson*, London 1953, 430–31.
11 Quoted by H. Boylan, *A Dictionary of Irish Biography*, Dublin 1978, 73.
12 Sean O'Casey, '*Juno and the Paycock*' in *Three Plays*, London 1967, 72.

Chapter 12   Ireland in Isolation   (pp. 181–193)
1   P. S. O'Hegarty, *The Victory of Sinn Fein*, Dublin 1924, 125.
2   Quoted by Donald S. Connery, *The Irish*, London 1968, 99.
3   Quoted by T. P. Coogan, *Ireland Since the Rising*, London 1966, 89.
4   Quoted by *The Irish Press*, 18 March 1943, 1.
5   Kevin O'Nolan ed., *The Best of Myles*, London 1977, 282.
6   John Boland in *Hibernia*, Dublin, 30 September 1977, 21.
7   Quoted by Paul Blanshard, *The Irish and Catholic Power*, Boston 1953, 98.
8   Quoted by *Fermanagh Times*, 13 July 1933, 1.
9   *Northern Ireland Parliamentary Debates*, 1921, Volume II, 114.

Chapter 13   Exiles in Maturity   (pp. 194–208)
1   Quoted by John Duff, *The Irish in the United States*, Belmont 1971, 113.
2   Quoted by Blanshard, *The Irish and Catholic Power*, 250.
3   Quoted by Andrew M. Greeley, *That Most Distressful Nation*, Chicago 1972, xxvi.
4   Quoted by Carl Wittke, *The Irish in America*, Baton Rouge 1956, 128.
5   Quoted by Norman R. Yetman, 'The Irish Experience in America', in Harold Orel ed., *Irish History and Culture*, Lawrence 1976, 372.
6   Quoted by Connery, *The Irish*, 13.
7   Samuel Beckett, *Waiting For Godot*, London 1956, 94.
8   Quoted by Kevin O'Connor, *The Irish in Britain*, Dublin 1974, 145.

Chapter 14   Modern Ireland   (pp. 209–221)
1   T. K. Whitaker, *Capital Formation, Saving and Economic Progress*, Dublin 1956, 1.
2   Winston S. Churchill, *The World Crisis: The Aftermath*, London 1929, 176.

Bibliography

As a chess player of only moderate ability, I have often lamented the fact that there seem to be only two kinds of chess books: those made for beginners, and those designed for experts. Something much the same is true in the field of historical literature. Nothing is more frustrating for someone beginning to explore a particular subject than trying to read a book which presumes more knowledge than he has yet amassed.

In the following bibliography, therefore, emphasis is placed upon those works which fall into the 'intermediate' category. This book has tried to present a general survey of Irish history, but like all introductions, it has left out far more than it has included. If the reader is interested in digging deeper, he is advised to turn to the list below:

No reference is made here to articles in periodicals. The reader should be aware, however, that *Irish Historical Studies*, a semi-annual journal which is now thirty years old, publishes much valuable material. Other articles appear in *Historical Studies*, the biennial publication of the Irish Committee of Historical Sciences.

I General Works

While many general Irish histories have been produced in the last decade, most concentrate on the events of the past two centuries. The eleven volumes of the Gill History of Ireland represent one praiseworthy attempt to cover the entire chronology, but they do not link together very well.

Therefore, the best books of this set are mentioned under the appropriate headings below.

One book which does cover Irish history from Celtic to modern times is *The Course of Irish History* (Cork 1967) edited by T. W. Moody and F. X. Martin; like most collections of essays, the quality of this work is somewhat uneven. Two entertaining brief surveys are presented in *Ireland* (London 1968) by Terence de V. White, and *A Concise History of Ireland* (London 1972) by Máire and Conor Cruise O'Brien. A more detailed introduction written from an American perspective is *Fractured Emerald: Ireland* (New York 1971) by Emily Hahn.

Of those surveys which confine themselves to the modern period, two volumes stand head and shoulders above the others. *The Making of Modern Ireland: 1603–1923* (London 1966) by J. C. Beckett is essential to serious study, while *Ireland Since the Famine* (London 1971) by F. S. L. Lyons is one of the masterpieces of twentieth-century historical scholarship. Also valuable are *A History of Modern Ireland* (London 1971) by E. R. Norman, and *Ireland* (New Jersey 1968) by Oliver MacDonagh. Those looking for a more general survey might turn to one of these illustrated volumes: *Two Centuries of Irish History* (London 1966) by James Hawthorne, *Ireland: Some Episodes from Her Past* (London 1974) by Howard Smith, and *An Outline of Modern Irish History: 1850–1951* (Dublin 1974) by M. E. Collins.

Ireland (London, 4th edition 1969) by T. W. Freeman remains the standard work on the physical and economic geography of the country. *An Atlas of Irish History* (London 1973) by Ruth Dudley Edwards is indispensable for readers unfamiliar with Irish place names.

Ireland has yet to produce its Trevelyan; the island's social history has never been given the comprehensive treatment which it deserves. A brief general survey is provided by *Life in Ireland* (London 1968) by L. M. Cullen. The same author also produced the very useful *An Economic History of Ireland since 1660* (London 1972).

The beautifully-illustrated volume edited by Brian de Breffny, *The Irish World: the Art and Culture of the Irish People* (London 1977), is already the standard cultural history. Other general works in this area are *A Concise History of Irish Art* (London 1968) by Bruce Arnold, and *A Short History of Irish Literature* (New York 1967) by Frank O'Connor. Excellent introductions to Irish architecture are provided by *Irish Houses and Castles* (London 1971) by Desmond Guinness and William Ryan, and *Irish Castles* (London n.d.) by H. G. Leask. Two more recent volumes, which are extremely useful, are *Irish Art and Architecture* (London 1978) by Peter Harbison, Homan Potterton and Jeanne Sheehy, and *The Painters of Ireland* (London 1978) by Anne Crookshank and the Knight of Glin.

There are some good documentary collections available to help bring the casual reader into direct contact with primary sources. The three volumes of *Ireland: A Documentary Record* (Dublin 1949) edited by James Carty are still valuable, as is Constantia Maxwell's superbly-written *The Stranger in Ireland* (London 1954). Also valuable are documentary collections in the Educational Facsimile Series produced since 1970 by the Public Record Office of Northern Ireland. Over a dozen such collections have been published, including *The Great Famine*, *Plantation in Ulster* and *Steps to Partition*. Recently the National Library of Ireland (Dublin) has begun to publish a similar series.

Historical novels can also help to give the reader a 'feel' for Irish situations. Three of the best are *Castle Rackrent* (Dublin 1800) by Maria Edgeworth, *The Silent People* (London 1962) by Walter Macken, and *Strumpet City* (London 1969) by James Plunkett.

Finally, the reader should be warned against studying Irish history without at least an outline knowledge of developments in Great Britain; the histories of the two British Isles are considerably intertwined. Good general surveys are presented in *A Concise History of England* (London 1966) by F. E. Halliday, and *The Offshore Islanders* (New York 1972) by Paul Johnson.

2 Prehistoric, Celtic and Early Christian Ireland

Ireland in Prehistory (Dublin 1977) by Michael Herity and George Eogan is a very detailed summary of the archaeological evidence regarding early Irish society. A brief, well-illustrated introduction is provided by *The Archaeology of Ireland* (London 1976) by Peter Harbison. Also valuable are Kenneth H. Jackson's *The Oldest Irish Tradition: A Window on the Iron Age* (Cambridge 1964), and the fascinating aerial photosurvey compiled by E. R. Norman and J. K. S. St Joseph, *The Early Development of Irish Society* (Cambridge 1969).

Everyday Life of the Pagan Celts (London 1970) by Anne Ross, while not confined to Ireland, is a useful general survey, as is *Celtic Art: An Introduction* (New Jersey 1973) by Ian Finlay. A. T. Lucas's lavishly-illustrated *Treasures of Ireland* (Dublin 1973) deals primarily with Celtic artefacts. Both *The Táin* (Oxford 1970) edited by Thomas Kinsella, and *The High Deeds of Finn MacCool* (London 1967) edited by Rosemary Sutcliff deal with central figures in Irish Celtic mythology, while Jan de Vries' *Heroic Song and Heroic Legend* (Oxford 1963) relates Irish legends to European saga literature.

Early Christian Ireland (London 1958) by Máire and Liam de Paor is by now the classic survey of this period, while Charles Thomas's *Britain and Ireland in Early Christian Times* (London 1971) is a useful comparative volume. Kathleen Hughes's *The Church in Early Irish Society* (London 1966) is the definitive religious history, and her *The Modern Traveller to the Early Irish Church* (London 1977), co-authored with Ann Hamlin, is an extremely well-written introduction. Also valuable are the following biographies of the three most famous personalities of the period: *Saint Patrick: His Origins and Career* (Oxford 1968) by R. P. C. Hanson; *Saint Columban* (New York 1962) by Frank MacManus; and *The Historical Saint Columba* (Edinburgh 1927) by W. Douglas Simpson.

The art of the Early Christian period is examined in the beautifully-illustrated *Harbinger of the Middle Ages* (London, 1963) by Ludwig Bieler. The period after A.D. 700 is given very comprehensive treatment in Francoise Henry's two-volume study, *Irish Art* (London 1967 and 1970).

The reader interested in literary developments should consult any of these four books: *Early Irish Literature* (Chicago 1948) by Myles Dillon, *The Irish Tradition* (London 1947) edited by Robin Flower, *A Celtic Miscellany* (London 1951) edited by Kenneth H. Jackson, and *Early Irish Literature* (New York 1966) by Eleanor Knott and Gerald Murphy.

The period immediately before the Norman invasion in 1169 has been long neglected, but Donncha Ó Corráin's pioneer study, *Ireland before the Normans* (Dublin 1972) is an important contribution. Also worth consulting are *Dermot, King of Leinster* (Tralee 1973) by Nicholas Furlong and *Celts and Normans* (Dublin 1969), an illustrated survey of the entire period up to 1513 by Gearoid Mac Gearailt.

3 Medieval, Tudor and Stuart Ireland

The medieval period remains the most neglected in Irish historiography; until recently, nearly all material in this area was written by specialists for specialists. Happily, there are now a few exceptions. J. F. Lydon's *The Lordship of Ireland in the Middle Ages* (Dublin 1972) is a surprisingly sprightly account of the rise and decline of the Anglo-Norman community. Kenneth Nicholls gives equally effective treatment to *Gaelic and Gaelicised Ireland in the Middle Ages* (Dublin 1972), while John Watt's *The Church in Medieval Ireland* (Dublin 1972) is well worth reading.

The age of the Tudor conquest has been much better covered. There are several good surveys, including *Ireland in the Age of the Tudors* (London 1977) by R. Dudley Edwards and *Elizabethan Ireland* (London 1971) by Grenfell Morton. *Conquest and Colonisation* (Dublin 1971) by M. E. Collins is an illustrated school text which covers the entire period from 1500 to 1800.

The Elizabethans and the Irish (Ithaca 1967) by David B. Quinn is a first-rate study of English attitudes during this period, while *Elizabeth's Irish Wars* (London 1950) by Cyril Falls offers detailed treatment of the particulars of the conquest. Lighter but equally effective treatment of the same subject is provided by Richard Berleth's *The Twilight Lords* (New York 1978). Also useful if somewhat fanciful is Sean O'Faolain's biography of the last independent Irish chieftain, *The Great O'Neill* (London 1942).

The seventeenth century has never been a favourite of general historians; no single volume gives a completely adequate survey of this tumultuous era in Irish history. *Irish Life in the Seventeenth Century* (Cork 1939) by Edward MacLysaght remains an outstanding social history, however, and there are a few useful studies of specific topics. *The Curse of Cromwell* (London 1971) by D. M. R. Esson looks closely at Cromwell's Irish campaign, while E. McCracken's *The Irish Woods since Tudor Times* (London 1971) is also interesting.

Perhaps the most crucial event of the seventeenth century was the Plantation of Ulster, and this subject is thoroughly explored in two volumes, *The Birth of Ulster* (London 1936) by Cyril Falls, and *Red Hand: The Ulster Colony* (London 1972) by Constantine Fitzgibbon. Pride of place, however, must go to *The Narrow Ground: Aspects of Ulster, 1609–1969* (London 1977) by A. T. Q. Stewart, a brilliant examination of the development of Ulster society since the Plantation.

4 Eighteenth-century Ireland

The Georgian period has always been a fascinating one; one happy result is that there is a wealth of excellent material available to the general reader interested in this century of peace and prosperity. Much of the literature deals with the activities of the Ascendancy, the 'English' aristocracy in Ireland which during this era developed its own peculiar national character. *The Anglo-Irish* (London 1972) by Terence de V. White and *The Anglo-Irish Tradition* (London 1976) by J.C. Beckett are two superb books which approach this subject from very different but equally stimulating angles. *The Houses of Ireland* (London 1975) by Brian de Breffny and Rosemary ffolliott is a lavishly-illustrated architectural history which focuses primarily upon Georgian edifices. Difficult to find but well worth the effort is *The Black Book of Edgeworthstown* (London 1927) edited by H. J. and H. E. Butler. This history of a prominent landlord family during the seventeenth and eighteenth centuries reveals much about how Anglo-Irish society operated. *The Ireland of Sir Jonah Barrington (1832)* (London 1967) edited by Hugh B. Staples is another useful Ascendancy memoir.

The best general history of the period is provided by Francis Godwin James's *Ireland in the Empire, 1688–1770* (Cambridge USA 1973). Also useful is *Ireland in the Eighteenth Century* (Dublin 1974) by Edith M. Johnston. More detailed information is offered by *Irish Public Opinion 1750–1800* (London 1944) by R. B. McDowell, and *The Passing of the Irish Act of Union* (Oxford 1966) by G. C. Bolton.

In the field of social history, Constantia Maxwell's two general surveys, *Dublin Under the Georges, 1714–1830* (London 1936) and *Country and Town in Ireland Under the Georges* (Dublin 1940) are still eminently readable. A more recent general history, *Dublin* (London 1977) by Desmond Clarke, devotes a great deal of attention to the eighteenth century. Two illustrated economic studies *Merchants, Ships and Trade* (Dublin 1971) by L. M. Cullen and *Travel and Transport in Ireland* (Dublin 1973) by Kevin B. Nowlan focus on the same period, although the latter gives equal attention to nineteenth-century developments.

The Hidden Ireland (Dublin 1924) by Daniel Corkery remains the classic study of Gaelic culture during this period. The best insight into the contemporary religious situation is provided by Maureen Wall in *The Penal Laws, 1691–1760* (Dundalk 1961). K. H. Connell's demographic study, *The Population of Ireland, 1750–1845* (Oxford 1950), examines the causes of the extraordinary population explosion which began during this period. Finally, one should not overlook *Irish Eccentrics* (New York 1975) by Peter Somerville-Large, a book which offers fascinating pen-portraits of Georgian Ireland's more exotic personalities.

5 Green and Orange Banners, 1790–1870

Nationalism has always been a very popular subject among Irish historians. The reading public seems to have an insatiable appetite for material about Ireland's national identity. Over half the books produced in the field every year deal with some aspect of Anglo-Irish relations.

Although it often treats its subject in too dramatic a fashion, *The Green Flag* (London 1972) by Robert Kee is the most comprehensive survey of the development of Irish nationalism during the nineteenth and twentieth centuries. *The Irish Question: 1800–1922* (Lexington USA 1968) by Lawrence J. McCaffrey is another solid introduction. *The Irish Question, 1840–1921* (London 1965) by Nicholas Mansergh is a collection of thought-provoking essays on various aspects of Anglo-Irish relations during this period.

The origins of Irish nationalism are perhaps best explored through the writings of its spiritual father. *The Autobiography of Wolfe Tone* (London 1937) is edited by Sean O Faolain. *The Year of Liberty* (London 1969) by Thomas Pakenham is the classic study of the 1798 rebellion, while *Secret Societies in Ireland* (Dublin 1973), edited by T. Desmond Williams, examines some of the more prominent local groups out of which nationalist sentiment eventually blossomed.

There are two standard biographies of Daniel O'Connell, *King of the Beggars* (Dublin 1938) by Sean O Faolain and *Daniel O'Connell* (Cork 1947) by Denis Gwynn; while both have their defects, each provides a useful introduction to the character and personality of the Liberator. *Daniel O'Connell and His World* (London 1975) by R. Dudley Edwards is useful for the illustrations it contains.

The development of Ulster unionist sentiment during the first half of the nineteenth century has not been so well documented. The reader is advised to consult the relevant sections of Fitzgibbon and Stewart (see Section 3). *Orangeism in Ireland and Britain, 1795–1836* (London 1966) by Hereward Senior is a more detailed study.

6 Ireland in the Nineteenth Century

Thanks largely to the wealth of source material available, it has been possible for historians to study nineteenth-century Irish society in considerable detail. Among the best general works available are the two relevant volumes of the Gill History series, *Ireland Before the Famine, 1798–1848* (Dublin 1974) by Gearoid Ó Túathaigh and *The Modernisation of Irish Society, 1848–1918* (Dublin 1973) by Joseph Lee. Both of these books also deal with political developments during the period.

There are several excellent studies of rural life. *The Land and People of Nineteenth-Century Cork* (London 1975) by James Donnelly is a comprehensive study of life in Ireland's largest county, one which was in many ways a microcosm of the country as a whole. Other useful works include *Views of the Irish Peasantry, 1800–1916* (Hamden USA 1977) edited by Daniel J. Casey and Robert E. Rhodes, and K. H. Connell's *Irish Peasant Society* (Oxford 1968), a collection of fascinating essays dealing with such esoteric topics as illegitimacy and ether-drinking. *Humanity Dick* (London 1975) by Shevawn Lynam looks at the other end of the social spectrum, being the biography of Richard Martin, one of the country's wealthiest landlords.

The cataclysm of the 1840s is admirably treated in two books, *The Great Famine* (Dublin 1956) by T. D. Williams and R. Dudley Edwards, and *The Great Hunger* (London 1962) by Cecil Woodham-Smith; the latter is especially well written. *The Land Question and the Irish Economy, 1870–1903* (Cambridge 1971) by Barbara Solow offers insight into rural life at the end of the century, while *Guinness's Brewery in the Irish Economy* (London 1960) by P. Lynch and J. Vaizey is an interesting study of one particular enterprise during this period.

The Irish Administration, 1801–1914 (London 1964) by R. B. McDowell is a detailed examination of governmental structure in nineteenth-century Ireland. D. H. Akenson's *The Irish Education Experiment* (London 1969) is a lively chronicle of the British attempt to develop a progressive education system in Ireland during this period.

There have been numerous studies of artistic and literary developments in nineteenth-century Ireland, and virtually all of the individuals who played important roles have been the subjects of at least one biography. Competent surveys are provided by Richard Fallis's *The Irish Renaissance* (Dublin 1978) and *Literary Dublin* (Dublin 1974) by Herbert A. Kenny. *Infinite Variety* (Dublin 1975) by Eugene Watters and Mathew Murtagh looks at the growth of Dublin music halls in the late nineteenth century, an often overlooked aspect of urban cultural development.

The refinement of photographic techniques during the middle years of the century meant that thousands of images of contemporary Irish life could be preserved. There are numerous photographic collections now available; among the best are *The Light of Other Days* (London 1973) edited by Kieran Hickey, and the two volumes edited by Maurice Gorham, *Ireland from Old Photographs* (London 1971) and *Dublin from Old Photographs* (London 1972). While on the subject of illustrations, it is worth mentioning *Ireland Three*

(Dublin 1972) by M. E. Collins, a well-written school text which contains hundreds of excellent nineteenth-century photographs and prints. Also valuable is *A Seat Behind the Coachman* (Dublin 1972) edited by Diarmuid O Muirithe, a documentary collection which is also lavishly illustrated.

Many if not most of the works cited in this section deal with developments in Ulster as well as the rest of the country. For excellent treatment of social developments in the northern province, however, the reader should try to find the two volumes of *Ulster Since 1800* (London 1955 and 1957) edited by T. W. Moody and J. C. Beckett. These contain essays which deal specifically with themes in Ulster social history.

7 Green and Orange Banners, 1850–1921

The general works cited in Section 5 carry over, of course, into this later period. However, literally hundreds of other works deal with specific topics in this crucial period in nationalist (and unionist) development.

One should begin with *Isaac Butt and Home Rule* (London 1964) by David Thornley, which traces the origins of the Home Rule Party. *Parnell and His Party* (London 1957) by Conor Cruise O'Brien deals with his rise to political power during the early 1880s, while F. S. L. Lyons's awesome *Charles Stewart Parnell* (London 1977) is the definitive biography.

The growth of the separatist tradition is well documented by Leon Ó Broin in two books, *Fenian Fever* (Dublin 1971) and *Revolutionary Underground: The Story of the IRB* (Dublin 1976). *Patrick Pearse: the Triumph of Failure* (London 1977) by Ruth Dudley Edwards is an intriguing biography of the republican leader, while William I. Thompson's *The Imagination of an Insurrection* (Oxford 1967) is essential for understanding the roots of 1916.

The events of Easter Week are well described in James Stephens's contemporary account, *The Insurrection in Dublin* (London 1916) and in a documentary collection edited by O. Dudley Edwards and Fergus Pyle, *1916: The Easter Rising* (Dublin 1968). *Protest in Arms* (London, 1960) by E. Holt remains an excellent survey of the tumultuous decade which followed the Easter Rising, while the essays in *The Irish Struggle: 1916–1926* (London 1966) edited by T. Desmond Williams are also valuable. Charles Townshend looks at the period from another perspective in his *The British Campaign in Ireland* (London 1975), while *The Irish Uprising 1916–1922* (New York 1966) edited by Goddard Lieberson is a volume whose striking illustrations more than compensate for textual weaknesses.

On the unionist side, *Queen's Rebels* (Dublin 1978) by David W. Miller is a perceptive study of the roots of modern Ulster separatism. Patrick Buckland's *Ulster Unionism and the Origins of Northern Ireland, 1886–1922* (Dublin 1973) is perhaps the most comprehensive survey. *The Ulster Crisis* (London, 1969) by A. T. Q. Stewart focuses upon the events of 1912–1914, and sheds considerable light upon that tangled period.

8 The Irish Abroad

While the last decade has seen the publication of dozens of books dealing with the influence of the Irish upon American society, *The Irish in America* (Baton Rouge USA 1956) by Carl Wittke remains the best general survey, despite the fact that it traces developments only as far as the end of World War I. Several other books carry the story down to modern times, including an excellent brief study by John B. Duff, *The Irish in the United States* (Belmont USA 1971) and Lawrence McCaffrey, *The Irish Diaspora in America*

(Bloomington USA 1976). *The American Irish* (New York 1963) by William V. Shannon looks at a score of prominent Irish-American personalities, while *That Most Distressful Nation* (Chicago 1972) by Andrew M. Greeley is a study of the attitudes and perceptions of modern Irish-Americans.

The Great Migration (London 1937) by Edwin C. Gullet is the fascinating story of transatlantic travel during the nineteenth century, and focuses primarily upon the experiences of Irish emigrants. *Boston's Immigrants* (Cambridge USA 1941) by Oscar Handlin is another excellent book with a strong Irish flavour, while James G. Leyburn's *The Scotch-Irish: A Social History* (Chapel Hill USA 1962) is the definitive study of this often-overlooked group of Irish emigrants. *Enter the Irish-American* (New York 1976) by Edward Wakin is also useful.

The Irish and Irish Politicians (Notre Dame USA 1966) by Edward M. Levine examines the role played by the Irish in domestic politics, while *Irish-American Nationalism, 1870–1890* (Philadelphia 1966) by Thomas N. Brown and *Ireland and Anglo-American Relations, 1899–1931* (London 1969) by Alan J. Ward focus more upon the influence of Irish America on political developments in the British Isles. *Real Lace: America's Irish Rich* (New York 1973) by Stephen Birmingham concentrates upon families like Buckleys and Kennedys, while *The Molly Maguires* (Cambridge USA 1965) by Wayne G. Broehl looks at life at the other end of the social scale in the Pennsylvania coalfields during the late nineteenth century.

Considering the wealth of material available on Irish-America, the development of Irish communities in other countries has been rather neglected. John Archer Jackson's *The Irish in Britain* (London 1963) remains the only good survey of Irish settlement in that country, although *Apes and Angels: The Irishman in Victorian Caricature* (London 1971) by Lewis P. Curtis Jr. is a useful illustrated study of nativism in both Britain and America.

The role of the Irish in the development of Australia has never been comprehensively studied, although *The Wearing of the Green* (London 1966) edited by Bill Wanman is a useful documentary collection. Also helpful is *The Australian Colonists* (Melbourne 1974) by K. S. Inglis, a well-written book which contains several chapters on the Irish settlement.

For other countries the reader should consult biographies of specific individuals, such as *Bernardo O'Higgins* (London 1972) by Stephen Clisswold, and *Madame Lynch and Friend* (New York 1975), Alyn Brodsky's fascinating study of the Irish paramour of Francisco Solano Lopez, the nineteenth-century Paraguayan dictator. Another book well worth reading is *The Wild Geese* (London 1973) by Maurice Hennessy, a study of Irish soldiery in European armies during the eighteenth and nineteenth centuries.

9 Modern Ireland

Two good surveys of the post-1921 period are provided by *Ireland in the Twentieth Century* (Dublin 1976) by John A. Murphy and *Nationalism and Socialism in Twentieth-Century Ireland* (London 1977) by E. Rumpf and A. C. Hephurn. Each of these works, however, emphasises political developments; the best general survey may be that provided by D. H. Akenson's deceptively-titled *The United States and Ireland* (Cambridge USA 1973), a lively and very perceptive analysis of modern Irish society.

Detailed study of political developments during this period should begin with two works: *Peace by Ordeal* (London 1962), Frank Pakenham's study of the 1921 Treaty negotiations, and *Ireland's Civil War* (London 1968), Calton Younger's definitive chronicle of this traumatic conflict. *The Restless Dominion* (Dublin 1969) by D. W. Harkness examines Anglo-Irish relations during the first decade of independence, while *Ireland in the War Years* (London 1975) by Joseph T. Carroll looks at Ireland's peculiar neutrality during World War II.

The definitive biography of Eamon de Valera, the most important political figure during this period, has yet to be written; *De Valera and the March of a Nation* (New York 1956) by Mary C. Bromage remains the best of a mediocre lot. *Irish Political Parties* (Dublin 1972) by Maurice Manning is indispensable for the reader not familiar with the structure of modern Irish politics, while *The Blueshirts* (Dublin 1970) by the same author is an intriguing study of the Irish pseudo-fascist movement of the Thirties.

The Irish Economy since 1922 (Liverpool 1970) by James Meenan is the definitive work in that field. There are several excellent social studies. *Family and Community in Ireland* (Cambridge USA 1968) by C. Arensberg and S. T. Kimball is somewhat dated but still invaluable, as is Timothy P. O'Neill's *Life and Tradition in Rural Ireland* (London 1977). *The Irish and Catholic Power* (Boston 1953) by Paul Blanshard, and *Is Ireland dying? Culture and the Church in Modern Ireland* (London 1968) by Michael Sheehy are two enlightening studies of the place of the Catholic Church in modern Irish society. *New Dubliners* (London 1966) by Alexander J. Humphreys looks at internal migration and suburban development. *The Emergency* (Dublin 1978) by Bernard Share is a somewhat nostalgic view of life in Ireland during the 1940s.

Of books dealing with the arts, two of the best focus upon the theatre, *The Irish Drama from Yeats to Beckett* (Athlone 1978) by Katherine Worth and the illuminating *Theatre and Nationalism in Twentieth-Century Ireland* (London 1971) edited by Robert O'Driscoll. Also useful are Richard Ellmann's biographies of the twin pillars of modern Irish literature, *Yeats: The Man and the Mask* (New York 1948) and *James Joyce* (New York 1959). An often-overlooked gem is *Irish Literary Portraits* (London 1972) edited by W. R. Rodgers. *The Matter with Ireland* (London 1962), a collection of George Bernard Shaw's writings about his native country, edited by David H. Greene and Daniel Laurence, is interesting because of Shaw's unique perspective of Irish affairs.

Unfortunately, the events of the past decade have thrust Ulster and its traditional problems into a prominent place on the international stage. In addition to the works previously cited, *The Irish Border as a Cultural Divide* (Amsterdam 1963) by M. W. Heslinga provides an excellent foundation for understanding the tragedy of Northern Ireland. *The Ulster Question, 1603–1973* (Cork 1974) by T. W. Moody is another valuable primer, as is *Belfast: Approach to Crisis* (London 1973) by Ian Budge and Cornelius O'Leary. *Divided We Stand: A Study of Partition* (London 1955) by Michael Sheehy is an analysis of the first thirty years of Ulster Home Rule which has well stood the test of time, as has the more recent *Divided Ulster* (London 1970) by Liam de Paor.

The 'troubles' of the past several years have been the subject of literally hundreds of reports and investigations. Not all have been objective; not all have contributed significantly to our understanding of the Ulster situation. Among the best are two studies of the unionist community, *Northern Ireland: The Orange State* (London 1976) by Michael Farrell, and *The Protestants of Ulster* (London 1976) by Geoffrey Bell. Also valuable is *Conflict in Northern Ireland: the Development of a Polarised Community* (Dublin 1976) by John Darby.

SOURCES OF ILLUSTRATIONS

Sources of Illustrations

The following abbreviations have been used in listing these sources:
(b)   bottom of page
(c)   centre of page
f.   facing page
(l)   left-hand side of page
(r)   right-hand side of page
(t)   top of page.

The jacket photograph is reproduced by kind permission of the Crawford Art Gallery, Cork, and the frontispiece by kind permission of the National Library of Ireland.
The endpapers show John Speed's map of Ireland, 1616, and are reproduced by kind permission of the National Library of Ireland.

AIDAN HICKEY, DUBLIN 7, 113(b)
ALISON STUDIO, ARMAGH 91
ANN HAMLIN 21(t)
ANTIKVARISK-TOPOGRAFISKA ARKIVET, STOCKHOLM 33(b)
ARTHUR GUINNESS SON & CO. 139(t)

BELFAST TELEGRAPH 191(r)
BILL DOYLE, DUBLIN 181, 188(l), 218(b)
BIRMINGHAM REFERENCE LIBRARY (Sir Benjamin Stone Collection) 155(tl)
BORD FAILTE f. 32(b), 39(tr), 47(tr), 55(t), 57(bl), 80
BORD NA MONA 186(b)
BRID BEAN NI hEIGEARTEAGH, DUBLIN 187
BRITISH LIBRARY 40(b), 43
BULLOZ, PARIS 84

CAMBRIDGE UNIVERSITY COLLECTION (Director in Aerial Photography) 10, 16(l), 17(r), 18(b), 30(tl)
CAMERA PRESS, LONDON 218(tr); Don McCullin 215(c), Michael Charity 215(bl), Newlands Hamilton 216(t), Harry O'Brien 217
CENTRAL BANK OF IRELAND 37(t)
CHICAGO HISTORICAL SOCIETY 123(t)
CITY OF MANCHESTER LIBRARY DEPT 132(b)
CIVIC MUSEUM, DUBLIN f. 81(b)
COMMISSIONERS OF PUBLIC WORKS IN IRELAND 12(t), 12(b), 13, f. 17, f. 32(tr), 35(lr), 36(b), 54(b), 68(b)
COUNTRY LIFE, LONDON 89(l)
CRAWFORD ART GALLERY, CORK f. 128(b)
CULVER PICTURES INC., NEW YORK 109(t), 118, 119(t), 119(b),

INDEX

Index

THE KINGDOME OF IRLAND

Devided into severall Provinces, and the
againe devided into Counties.
Newly described.

The Gentleman of Ireland   *The Gentlewoman of Ireland*

The Civill Irish Woman   *The Civill Irish man*

The Wilde Irish man   *The Wilde Irish Woman*

Iodocus Hondius cælavit

THE WEST OCEAN